C000179592

THE

Royal Ocean Racing Club

MANUAL OF

SAFETY & SURVIVAL AT SEA

HM COASTGUARD
BRISTOW
G-BIMU

THE

Royal Ocean Racing Club

MANUAL OF

SAFETY & SURVIVAL AT SEA

DAG PIKE

David & Charles

Acknowledgments

My sincere thanks to many safety organisations and equipment manufacturers who helped with information and advice. In particular I should mention the RYA and the RORC. I would also like to thank the RNLI for giving me the chance to experience rescue work at first hand and to Virgin Atlantic and others for giving me the experience of abandoning ship and being rescued.

My thanks also to Jess Bennett for tackling the difficult job of the diagrams for the book, and to my secretary Gia Haines who typed the manuscript, did the index and helped in a thousand other ways.

A DAVID & CHARLES BOOK

First Published 1993

A catalogue record for this book is available from the British Library.

ISBN 0 7153 0063 6

Typeset by Creative Publicity Consultants, Newton Abbot Devon and printed in England by Butler & Tanner Ltd, Frome for David & Charles, Brunel House, Newton Abbot, Devon

The Royal Ocean Racing Club

The Royal Ocean Racing Club was formed by the participants of the first Fastnet Race held in 1925. After the race the entrants formed the Ocean Racing Club, later to become the Royal Ocean Racing Club. Since 1925, the Fastnet and other races in the English Channel, North Sea, Irish Sea, (and also in the Mediterranean and the Far East) have been run on a regular basis, interrupted only by the Second World War.

The Fastnet is held biannually (there have been 34 Fastnet Races since 1925), and forms part of the Champagne Mumm Admiral's Cup series, first held as a team event to challenge the United States of America in 1957.

In addition to organising races and events, the RORC co-ordinates British participation in team events such as the Southern Cross, Sardinia Cup and IOR 'Ton Cup' world championships.

A handicap rule known as the RORC Rule was devised in 1925, giving each yacht a Time Allowance based on Rating; this was the forerunner of the International Offshore Rule (IOR). The RORC through the rating Office, is the National Authority for measurement and rating of offshore racing yachts and administers the IOR and International Measurement System (IMS) in the UK.

Jointly with its French counterpart UNCL, the RORC devised and supervises worldwide the increasingly popular Tesco Channel Handicap System (CHS). RORC races cater for all three rating rules.

In 1990 the RORC was invited by the organisers of the Whitbread Round the World race to oversee the development and administration of the new Whitbread Rule.

The RORC is not a governmental agency but is a private members club organising offshore racing for members and non-members alike and is closely involved in the development and management of yacht racing as a worldwide sport. Club membership is strictly limited to competent offshore yachtsmen and yachtswomen who qualify by completing a minimum mileage of offshore racing. There are currently 3,450 members.

The RORC has taken a keen interest in ensuring that yachts taking part in the races it organises are adequately equipped for the task and has produced a comprehensive list of safety items that must be carried. Yachts that do not meet the RORC safety standards are not eligible to enter any of the RORC organised races.

Dag Pike

Dag Pike is a seaman by profession. Now well established as a marine journalist and author, Dag built his first boat at the age of twelve and went to sea as an apprentice in the Merchant Navy at the age of sixteen, going round the world three times. Qualifying as a ship's officer in 1954, Dag was employed on ships servicing lighthouses and buoys around the English coastline. After ten years, in which time he rose to captain, he left to become an Inspector of Lifeboats with the Royal National Lifeboat Institution. It was experience gained in this position, testing new designs of lifeboats and developing the world's first rigid inflatables, that led Dag in to writing.

His first book, *Powerboats in Rough Seas*, which is based largely on personal experience, was the definitive book on advanced powerboat handling. He has since written a sequel *Fast Boats and Rough Seas* which looks at the subject in greater depth. In all, Dag has written twenty books including: *Motor Sailing*; *Electronic Navigation for Small Craft*; *Fishing Boats and their Equipment*; *Electronics Afloat*; *Practical Motor Cruising*; *Boat Electrical Systems*; and *Fast Boat Navigation*.

Dag started offshore powerboat racing in 1969, competing in the first Round Britain Powerboat Race. Now a top navigator in this demanding sport, Dag has navigated for the World Champion Carlo Bonomi and in 1984 was navigator aboard the winning boat in the Round Britain Race. In 1988 has was navigator for Fabio Buzzi, winning the World Championships. He was selected as navigator on both the Virgin Atlantic Challenger Transatlantic record attempts and as navigator and project director for the Italian Azimut Atlantic Challenger Trans Atlantic record attempts. In 1990 Dag was navigator aboard the boat which won eight out of the nine legs in the Venice to Monte Carlo Race, and in 1992 he was navigator on the successful attempt at the London-Monte Carlo record. Other recent successes include being skipper/navigator aboard *Drambuie Tantalus* on its successful Round Britain record attempt, and weather consultant to the Italian *Destriero* on their record-breaking Atlantic crossing.

His successes include being runner-up in the 1989 Yachtsman of the Year Award and he was marine safety consultant for TV AM in Britain. He currently writes for yachting and shipping magazines in many parts of the world; works as a marine surveyor and consultant and is a Fellow of the Royal Institute for Navigation.

He is particularly suited to the task of writing about rescue at sea having been rescued himself ten times and having rescued others eight times – 'I hope to get the balance right before I retire', he quips. His was the voice that sent out the distress signal when Virgin Atlantic Challenger sank just 130 miles from the finish line.

Contents

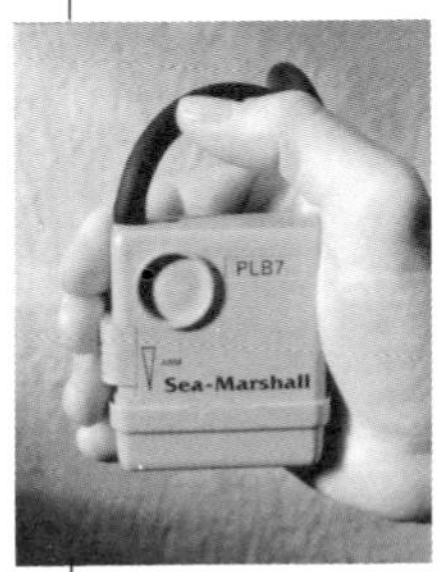

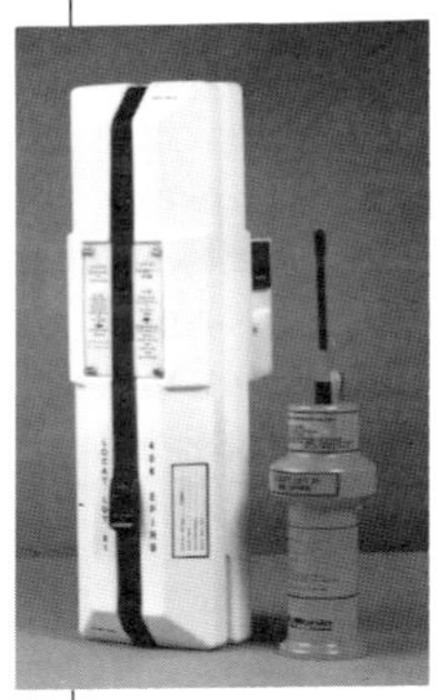

I	Introduction	8
2	Psychology of Survival	16
3	Preparation for Safety	27
4	Calling for Help	41
5	Search and Rescue	61
6	Survival Equipment	80
7	Safety on Board	102
8	Coping with Emergencies	124
9	Seasickness and Survival	147
10	First Aid	155
11	Rules and Regulations	166
Index		190

From the top:
Rescue by Helicopter,
Man Overboard Alarm,
EPIRB,
Richard Branson and Chay Blyth awaiting rescue.

1 Introduction

There is no such thing as absolute safety. If you were to cocoon yourself in cotton wool, you would probably suffocate! When it comes to safety at sea, you must decide what level of risk you are prepared to accept, take what seem to be reasonable precautions, and then accept the consequences if things do go wrong.

In many walks of life the level of 'acceptable risk' is decided for us. When you fly in an aeroplane you don't have a lot of control and there is little you can do to improve things. You have to take it for granted that the plane has been serviced and maintained to a reasonable standard. You have to take it for granted that the pilot and crew are well trained and capable and not under the influence of alcohol or drugs. You have to take it for granted that all the services and systems which support the plane, including the air traffic controllers, are working efficiently. All you can do is listen to the safety briefing and pray that everyone else is doing their job. Most of the time it works.

Travelling by train involves a similar act of faith. By buying your ticket and travelling, there is an implicit assumption that you have assessed the risks and are prepared to accept them. You won't be very happy if things do go wrong, but there is not a lot you can do to minimise the impact of an accident.

Travelling by car is a very different story. Here, control of the situation is very much more in your hands. To a considerable degree, your skill and ability can keep you safe. However, you only have a certain amount of control because you are operating close to all the other motorists on the road. If they make mistakes or lose concentration, it can directly affect your safety. On the road you are operating within a framework of rules and regulations which are designed to enhance your safety, and provided you and all the other drivers stick to these rules, there can be an acceptable level of safety.

This 'acceptable level of safety' can only be judged by statistics, but statistics don't really come into the reckoning if you personally become involved in an accident. However, the fact that you drive, or continue to drive after an accident, means that you are prepared to accept the risks inherent in this mode of transport for the convenience it offers. The question of responsibility also comes into the equation: whilst you might drive aggressively when you are alone, you may drive more slowly or more defensively when you have children in the car.

Safety of Yachting

Now let's look at the safety aspects of yachts. At sea there are very few rules and regulations to govern your behaviour and there is very little policing to keep you in line. The assessment and implementation of safety is left almost entirely to you, the skipper. Even your crew will probably not raise their voices about safety, assuming that you know what you are doing and that you have taken the necessary precautions.

Of course, there is plenty of advice and there are recommendations about what you can do to maximise safety at sea. There are lists of equipment you should carry on board in case of various emergencies. You will get advice about whether you should go to sea or not in the light of the prevailing or forecast weather, but by its very nature this has to be general. It can't take into account your particular situation, your experience and the type of craft.

Some countries have tried to take yacht safety a stage further by making certain levels of safety equipment mandatory. This is the situation in France and Italy, where it is enforced along with a yacht licencing system. In the US, strict rules on safety equipment are also enforced, as is both boat licencing and driver licencing. They even take safety to the point where 'small craft advisories' – special warnings – are issued if the coastguard thinks the conditions at sea are too severe for small craft. Such mandatory control and its enforcement brings the force of law to marine safety, but it doesn't necessarily improve safety. Accidents still happen. In fact, there is little evidence to suggest that mandatory controls have much effect, unless they are fully comprehensive and strictly enforced.

Air travel is undoubtedly the most tightly legislated means of travel in the modern world, yet accidents still happen. There is a limit to how much you can legislate for safety, short of banning something altogether, because safety still rests so much in the hands of the person controlling the craft. However, the strict operating environment for aircraft has come about in response to public demand for higher safety standards.

In the yachting arena, too, serious accidents, such as the Fastnet disaster, are inevitably followed by demands for 'something to be done'. The authorities have to be seen to be doing something, and one of the few routes open to them is to introduce regulations of one sort or another. Fortunately, in Britain wise counsel tends to prevail and the situation tends to be dealt with by improved recommendations rather than by legislation.

Safety when Racing

In competition, whether yacht or powerboat racing, the situation is different. Here, the race organisers are given responsibility for the safety of the event, but the safety of the individual boat still rests firmly in the hands of its skipper. However, the grip of the racing rules is continually tightening as the authorities seek to compensate for things that have gone wrong in the past. If race organisers are not seen to be behaving responsibly and showing a strong concern for safety, they can be held liable if things go wrong during the racing.

For example, in the 1991 Cowes Classic Offshore Powerboat Race thick fog came down over part of the course and two boats ran up on to the beach in Torbay. The drivers concerned received minimum reprimands for what seemed to be the unforgivable sin of travelling too fast in fog and endangering other people's lives, whilst the race officials took most of the blame, on the grounds that the race should never have been started in the prevailing conditions.

The message here seems to be that if the race organisers say conditions are suitable for racing, then you have a free hand to behave in any manner you think fit to win the race, regardless of other people's safety. This is plainly not the case: every yachtsman, whether racing or not, has a responsibility for the safety, not only of his own boat, but of any other boat he encounters.

Safety Legislation

You will begin to appreciate, therefore, the dilemma which results when authorities start to legislate for safety. You could argue that if you have the correct safety equipment on board or, in the case of the US, if there is no small craft advisory, then you will be quite safe heading off to sea. The British yachtsman, subject to few rules, restrictions and recommendations, is unlikely to be so naive. But if legislation and licencing do increase, so will people's tendency to assume that, provided they have the necessary equipment and have fulfilled all the other requirements, they can be confident of being safe at sea. Certainly, the odds will be weighted in their favour but, at the end of the day, safety lies firmly in the hands of the people on board the yacht. It will be mainly the skipper's responsibility, but each member of the crew has to contribute to the safety of the craft as a whole. Rules, regulations and recommendations should be considered as the bare minimum: a platform upon which to build a safety umbrella, which will combine assessment of the risks, precautions and experience. This is what happens with car driving. Passing your driving test is only the starting point. You know the basics, but if you are sensible, you proceed with a degree of caution because you still lack that vital factor – experience.

Experience, however, can be both a good and a bad thing. On the positive side, it can help to teach what is safe and what is risky, and you can then appreciate the risks in any particular situation. On the negative side, experience can allow you to cut corners. You have a much better idea of what you can and what you can't get away with, and experience can lead to you pushing your luck, cutting the safety margins to the point where the risks can increase and the fine line between success and failure can become very slender.

First-stage Safety

Most yachtsmen will tend to keep a good 'cushion' of safety between normality and disaster. This can help reduce the risks, but it is only valuable when you become aware that the margins are being eroded. We will look at this aspect in more detail in the next chapter, but, for example, most competitors will realise that in racing safety margins can be considerably reduced. The attitude is that you push things as far as you dare. If something breaks, you won't succeed because you will be out of the race. You take the risks as they come, whereas in normal yachting you keep a margin of safety because you know that if something breaks, you and your crew could be at risk and disaster one step closer.

However, we shall leave the racing people to their risk-taking and concentrate on what might be termed 'normal' boating where the emphasis tends to be on pleasure and comfort. Whilst you are aware that there can be risks involved, you want to minimise this aspect yet have something in hand if things go wrong. On a powerboat with twin engines, for example, you know that if one engine fails, you can still get home on the other. It is the same with sailing boats: if the rig fails, there is always the engine to get you home.

This is what is called 'first-stage safety' and it covers some of the more obvious aspects. As far as possible, nothing on a boat should be so critical that if it fails you will be immobilised and at risk. For instance, if the navigation electronics fail, you can go back to manual navigation. The only thing which can't easily be duplicated is the hull, but even here, to a certain extent, you have a back-up because there should always be the tender or a liferaft on board.

Even so, you have to appreciate that when one item fails, it can start to put pressure on both you, as the skipper, and on the boat itself. After a single failure, some aspects of the boat will have lost their back-up and you will have run out of redundancy. This is where the situation starts to become more critical and where you can start down the slippery slope to disaster. For instance, you may suffer an engine failure on a twin-engined boat. Fine, you say, I can still get home on the other one, but, of course, the second engine is now working under less than ideal conditions. The propeller will be the wrong size for single-engine operation, which may impose higher loadings on the engine and increase the risk of it also failing.

Certainly, your safety margin will have been reduced. You might therefore want to look for ways to try and restore it. You may drive the boat more cautiously, or give a wider berth to dangers. Safety margins are probably not something you think about consciously when you are at sea, or even before you set out. You have probably made some sort of subconscious assessment of your safety, vaguely thinking, 'If it is blowing force 5, perhaps I had better not go.' Or, if you are already at sea, 'Perhaps I'd better start looking for shelter.' You think of safety in vague terms, without any real conscious effort to make a critical assessment of what you are doing and what the risks are.

Assessing the Danger

But such an assessment can be made quite simply. You weigh up each of the more critical aspects of a proposed voyage and work out what might happen if something were to fail at that point. It would be nice to think that your boat is perfectly maintained and that nothing might fail, but you are probably aware of jobs that need doing, of weaknesses that need sorting out. It happens on most boats and is a fact of yachting life. There is no real reason why it should put you more at risk, provided that you acknowledge that the weakness is there and allow adequate safety margins to cope with it. The weakness could be a frayed halyard which could let you down at sea. You may have other sails left, or the engine to get you home, but if the halyard fails when you are close to rocks or a sandbank, then you could be in serious trouble before you get a chance to sort out the problem.

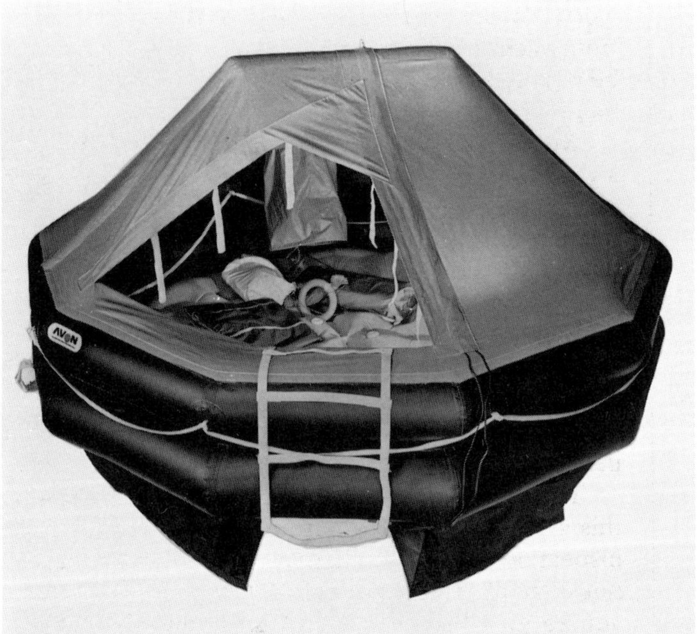

Liferaft

An Avon double-tube liferaft which meets RORC and DTp liferaft requirements . The water ballast pockets can be under the raft. Flexible boarding ladders of the type shown are difficult to climb and it is much better to board the liferaft direct from the yacht rather than enter the water first.

So, what is being suggested here is that you be much more conscious of safety margins, that you assess and be aware of the risks you might be taking. Unlike an aircraft, in the event of a failure, a boat can stop at sea while work is carried out, provided there is sea room. Because an aircraft can't stop and do repairs when it is in the air, the whole structure and its stresses are analysed to ensure that failure cannot occur and, where feasible, back-up systems are provided. Yachts are not generally built and maintained to the same critical level, so you will have to expect a higher incidence of failure and be prepared to cope when such failure does occur.

It is interesting to note that the recommended safety equipment for yachts is geared not so much to coping with disasters, but towards ensuring that if they do occur, you will be able to call for help in your hour of need and to survive until that help arrives. In other words, it tends to focus on liferafts, lifejackets, flares etc, rather than on some of the more practical things, such as engine tools, spares and other equipment which might enable you to find your own way out of a disaster. You must be aware that the recommended safety equipment may help to ensure your survival when all else has failed, but disasters tend to occur in stages, and if you have the practical equipment on board, you may be able to redeem the situation before having to resort to desperate measures.

Being Self-sufficient

It boils down to being as self-sufficient as possible when you are at sea. Engine tools and spares, for example, are just as important as lifejackets and flares, and could go a long way to preventing a bad situation getting worse. What needs to be carried in the way of tools and spares will vary from yacht to yacht, but an assessment of what might break and what can be repaired away from port will help ensure that the right equipment is on hand when something does go wrong.

We have already mentioned the hull as being one of the critical parts of a yacht, but equally critical, and more subject to wear and tear, is the stern gear. The propeller and rudder, the latter in particular, are vital to the operation of the yacht, yet they are hidden away underwater and it is very easy to forget about them and their significance. The chances of effecting a repair at sea are remote, yet if something breaks here, then it may be difficult to make port under your own steam. The only solution is to give this area a thorough examination every time the boat comes out of the water, and do something about even the slightest sign of wear and tear. Wear and tear can only get worse and it may be some time before you have the chance to examine these underwater areas again.

There are quite a few critical areas in a boat which should be subject to this sort of scrutiny. If you take safety seriously, you will set up a regular inspection routine so that you can anticipate trouble. This procedure will not only allow you to get to know your boat much better, but will permit you to go to sea secure in the knowledge that you have a sound boat underneath you which, in turn, will make your yachting more relaxed.

There is no doubt that safety at sea begins in harbour, and this type of safety inspection is the prelude to a safe voyage. Analysis of accidents at sea tends to indicate that they often occur as a result of cumulative problems, the accident developing in stages to the disastrous climax. Fortunately, the vast majority of potential disasters are averted at an early stage: the problem is uncovered and corrective action taken long before it has become serious. The preliminary check in harbour can help to identify the risks long before they get anywhere near the critical stage.

The sort of incident which could lead to trouble might be something as simple as a compass light going out at night. Without a torch handy to keep you on course, you could quickly find yourself in difficulties in a strong blow. Loss of concentration on other aspects as you attempt to sort out your heading could lead to a gybe or a broach. Suddenly, what had been a comfortable sail becomes a major struggle. A bulb blowing seems a relatively trivial occurrence. In many cases it would be, but when you are trying to assess the safety of your boat, you can't look at things in isolation. Every potential failure has to be considered in terms of what effect it might have on other parts of the boat, or on the operation of the boat itself.

KISS – Keep it Simple

Since the early days of yachting, it has been the rule to keep things as simple as possible. If you look at yachts built as recently as thirty years ago, you will see a refreshingly simple approach to design and construction. Few parts of the boat were highly stressed, which reduced the chances of failure, and the relatively simple technology used put repair well within the capability of the skills and equipment on board.

In the quest for increased efficiency – for greater speed under power or sail, for more space below and greater comfort – the technology employed in yachts has become increasingly sophisticated. Modern yachts make use of every inch of space; every item of the rig or machinery has a more critical role to play. The design is much more integrated than in the past. Consequently, the failure of one item can lead to further failures because of the interdependence of the individual fittings and structures.

The increasing application of sophisticated technology is at its most marked in the area of electronics. Electronic systems are now used for navigation, communication and entertainment. By making navigation much more reliable, they have done a great deal in recent years to add to the safety of yachts. Accurate positions are readily available at the touch of a button, which can take much of the risk out of making a landfall or operating in poor visibility. Modern radios provide a much more efficient means of communicating the need for assistance than any of the traditional methods. When all else has failed, an EPIRB (emergency position-indicating radio beacon) can send a continuous distress signal.

Electronics can offer so much to improve safety, by way of both prevention and cure, yet there is still a strong reluctance to embrace them and to use them to their full. This attitude probably stems from their early days, when reliability was questionable and any information provided was a bonus. However, reliability has improved dramatically, so that today there is much greater reliance on electronics for navigation and communication. Indeed, the worry now is that yachtsmen will rely so heavily on them that they will be unable to cope if the system should fail. Electronic systems are now the primary source of information for navigation purposes, yet the authorities and the navigation schools still persist in calling them 'aids' to navigation, with the inference that they are not to be trusted.

Faced with a choice between an electronic and a dead-reckoning position, the electronic position will always be first choice. The now-vital role that electronics can play in safety should be recognised and full advantage taken of their capabilities. Electronics can greatly reduce the chance of error in navigation but, if you should get into difficulties, you can give an accurate position to hasten rescue. The ability to use the radio to call for help has revolutionised distress situations and EPIRBs are designed to cope with the most dire emergencies.

There can, however, be a negative side to electronics. Position accuracy is now so good that it encourages yachtsmen to cut corners. Because navigation can be much more precise, the tendency is to sail closer to rocks and sandbanks and the coastline in general, and this can reduce safety margins if something should go wrong. You will have less time to sort out what may be a comparatively minor problem before you are in serious difficulties.

Safety Margins

'Safety margins' is what safety is really all about. Despite the tendency to concentrate on the hardware – the flares, the liferaft and suchlike – everything you do at sea has safety implications. Because you, as a yachtsman, have so much freedom to do as you please, to operate largely free from restriction, you have a much greater responsibility for the safety of the operation. You have to decide what safety margins are appropriate to any particular situation and try to keep something in hand so that you can cope if things go wrong.

There are no hard-and-fast rules about safety margins. There are so many variables involved – wind and sea conditions, visibility, reliability, navigation accuracy, etc – that it is up to you to establish what seem to be margins appropriate to any particular situation. Most of the time you will probably do this almost subconsciously, in the light of your experience, but it will pay to think a bit more deeply about the more critical aspects of a passage, so that you have a positive idea about the safety margins you are considering. It is very difficult to quantify safety in any meaningful way, but one aspect you might, for example, consider is how long you can drift if you have to stop at sea. With onshore winds, you might want to keep further off, to give yourself more time than you would need if the wind was blowing off the land.

Safety is a complex subject. It involves both prevention and cure. It involves your ability to cope with emergencies, as well as the hardware. In the following chapters we shall look at many of the factors involved so that you will have a deeper understanding of safety at sea and its wide implications. Everything you do at sea involves or affects safety, but here we have to concentrate on the more limited aspects of emergencies and how to cope with them. There are already many books available on navigation and seamanship. We shall therefore touch on these topics only where they directly affect safety; we shall look at the sort of advanced techniques that will enable you to cope in emergencies; we shall examine how to operate and use the safety equipment that you carry on board – in the hope that you will never have to use it.

2 Psychology of Survival

When we look at safety and survival, our tendency is to focus on the hardware. The emphasis tends to be put on items such as liferafts, lifejackets and flares. However, even if you know how to use the equipment, there is still much to learn about safety at sea. Just as the computer you buy won't produce the information you want without the right software, so, at sea, safety and survival are as much, if not more, a matter of your attitude of mind as of special equipment. This is the vital ingredient which will decide whether you – perhaps literally – sink or swim. Like the software in the computer, it is the right state of mind that produces the right results.

One of the reasons why this key factor is rarely covered in the literature on the subject is because it is the unquantifiable element in safety. Certainly, the legislators concentrate on the equipment side because that is comparatively easy to quantify and can be legislated for. But attitude of mind, or the psychology of safety and survival, is a much more complex area. It can be quantified to a certain extent in that training will help improve a person's attitude and the degree of improvement after training can be measured. In this chapter we shall be looking at the value and importance of training, but the right attitude of mind is a much wider element which should permeate every aspect of yachting.

Attitude of mind encompasses equally vague concepts such as 'seamanship', because it is seamanship that helps you to develop the correct attitude of mind. This, in turn, will help to promote safe practice at sea. However, even that is oversimplifying. The right attitude of mind is the one that ensures that you think through every aspect of what is going on, assess the risks involved in a particular course of action, and instinctively build in safety margins to reduce the risks to an acceptable level.

Positive Mental Attitude

But that is still only part of the story. If you get into a dire situation, where perhaps you are in a liferaft or about to abandon ship, then adopting the right attitude becomes even more important. The positive frame of mind which is necessary to survive the situation becomes *absolutely vital.* It's probably safe to say that more people have lost their lives at sea through having a negative attitude towards survival than have done so through ignorance of what to do with the available survival equipment.

The psychology of yachting is a very interesting and intriguing area. On a racing sailing or powerboat, you see a very positive approach: one where there is a strong intent to make the boat go fast and to beat the opposition. The crew are in a very positive frame of mind, willing and eager to get things right, to avoid mistakes and, probably most important of all, concentrating on the job they have to do to the exclusion of everything else. This question of concentration is important. Even if you don't have anything particular to do at any given moment, your mind is still able to analyse what is going on. You are trying to anticipate what might occur and exploring possible scenarios whilst all the time concentrating on the job in hand. When the unexpected does occur, the solution probably springs rapidly to mind and reactions become more or less instinctive.

Cruising Mentality

However, the very nature of cruising makes this level of concentration unlikely to be maintained. You are out there sailing with family or friends, enjoying the relaxation which is such an essential ingredient of the exercise. Without the restrictions and regulations that abound on shore, the sea promises unlimited freedom. Immediately, you enter an environment where relaxation is the order of the day. You will need to concentrate as you leave harbour, but after that the wide open sea beckons and you settle into a routine which in itself will tend to be relaxing, with the demands on your concentration much lower. This is what yachting for pleasure should be all about. But bear in mind that when you reduce your level of concentration, you are also lowering your guard, and this is when disaster could strike.

This is not to say that relaxation should not be part of the yachting scene. The important thing is to know when you can afford to relax, and when you should start increasing your levels of concentration. You will do this almost instinctively, matching your level of concentration to the conditions in which you find yourself. We have already mentioned how concentration will be fairly high when you are leaving harbour, partly because you take time to adjust to the boat's surroundings after leaving land, but also because the navigation can be fairly demanding. Once out at sea, if there is clear, open water, you will start to relax, but when you are making the next landfall you will find your level of concentration rising again. Similarly, if you encounter bad weather, you will find a great deal more of your mind occupied with how to handle the boat in the prevailing conditions.

While these adjustments will be made to a large degree automatically by an experienced seafarer, the novice may be much less aware of the increased risks involved in particular situations. Consequently, the concentration level may not be raised, as required by the deteriorating conditions, until something goes wrong. In these situations, at sea on a cruising yacht, the responsibilities tend to fall firmly on the shoulders of the skipper, which is as it should be. He is the person who has to make the relevant decisions and his is the overall responsibility. But there is no reason why some of these responsibilities should not be devolved upon the crew. Indeed, it can be highly beneficial in an emergency if the crew have been involved in the operation of the boat before that time. It is much more difficult to maintain concentration if they have nothing to do.

For some of the crew, going on a cruise will simply involve sitting around watching the scenery, with very little to occupy their minds. They are therefore less likely to respond rapidly to any change in circumstances because they must first 'put their minds into gear' in order to get the thought processes going. Even as skipper you can get lulled into this state of lethargy. As the boat sails or motors peacefully over the waters, you can find yourself slipping into an almost hypnotic state. Fortunately, in conditions where you can unwind to this point of relaxation, the prospect of a situation occurring is slight. You are much more likely to be brought back to reality and increase your concentration gradually as you approach land, or as weather conditions deteriorate.

Concentration

The contrast between cruising and racing crews can be seen quite clearly in fine conditions. Even in these conditions, the racing crew have to maintain concentration. In a sailing racer this concentration is necessary to get the best possible performance from the yacht in light wind conditions. In a powerboat, the speed rises in these conditions, creating a need for maximum concentration.

In the short term, there is no problem in maintaining the right level of concentration to ensure that you are operating the yacht safely, but in the longer term, this can be more difficult. Concentration can fall off quite markedly after an hour or so if there is nothing specific to occupy the mind. You can see this when a boat is being steered on a compass course. For the first half-hour the helmsman will concentrate quite hard, but then gradually the accuracy of the steering deteriorates as his concentration lapses. The same applies to keeping a lookout: there is nothing more tedious or boring than scanning the open sea. Unless there are other boats around to focus on, you will find the lookout tending to concentrate on what is going on on board the yacht rather than what is going on around the horizon. So a skipper should seriously consider constantly rotating the crew around the limited duties available. Switching the helm every half-hour, for example, can be a good way of maximising concentration without imposing too much on the relaxing atmosphere of cruising. People like to have something to do, but at sea there are generally only a limited number of jobs available, so changing over at frequent intervals can enhance both enjoyment and concentration.

Similarly, if you are on a longer passage, perhaps overnight, then establishing a proper watch-keeping routine can be important for maintaining levels of concentration and safety. With a proper routine, every member of the crew has a better idea of their particular role and their involvement. At any particular time, there can be no doubt as to whose is any particular job and the crew will concentrate on the routine of running the yacht: keeping the lookout or steering the required course, and thinking 'safety'. If the crew members are permitted to drift on and off watch with no set pattern, while there may be two or three people in the cockpit, no one is ostensibly in charge and making decisions and, in consequence, concentration levels will be considerably lower.

Effects of Bad Weather

In the event of bad weather, there will be considerably more to occupy your mind. Even the sea conditions will provide something upon which to concentrate. You may have to nurse the boat over waves, particularly if it is a fast powerboat, and the noise and general excitement will help to keep you alert to changing conditions. At the same time, however, the very conditions will create circumstances in which your concentration may be deflected into other areas, such as personal discomfort. It is human nature to tend to concentrate more on the physical discomfort you are suffering than on the job you have to do. In a rough sea, there will be spray flying about, making you wet and uncomfortable, and it may be cold. The motion of the boat will obviously become more violent, with the result that you will need to concentrate more on holding on which, again, will deflect your concentration from the job in hand. In these conditions, too, producing food and drink will be much more difficult, if not impossible, and once again this feeling of deprivation will affect your ability to concentrate. None of these factors is, in itself, particularly serious, and an experienced seafarer will quite easily be able to compensate for them all. However, it is important that you should be aware of what is going on: of the fact that, because of the conditions, your level of concentration has deteriorated to a certain extent at a time when you need to be particularly aware of what is going on, both with regard to the yacht and to its environment.

It is in such situations that things can start to become critical. If you are aware of what is going on, you will see that your safety margins are diminishing and will be able to do something about it. For example, if on a powerboat, you might want to ease the throttle back or change course to find a more comfortable ride, to seek an environment where both boat and crew are under less stress. On a sailing boat, the deteriorating conditions should be a warning, a sign that you need to reduce sail and keep the situation well in hand, particularly if you are sailing with a small crew.

Mental Stress

It is also in these deteriorating conditions that your mental reserves come under strain. This tends to happen at the same time as the boat itself is coming under more stress. The more violent movement of the boat and the higher stresses imposed by wind and sea will all increase the prospect of a failure in the boat, its equipment or its crew. This is the time when you need a high level of concentration so that you are more aware of these stresses and strains and try to minimise them in order to keep reserves in hand. Not only do you need to keep reserves for the boat itself, so that it is working well within its operating limits, thus reducing the risk of any failure, but you also need some reserves of mental energy to cope with any emergency that might arise.

This aspect of mental reserves is vital to safety and survival: indeed, is probably the key factor. In good conditions you have plenty of reserves to cope with anything the sea might throw at you. In deteriorating conditions you will find that your mental reserves are drained quite rapidly. But experienced seafarers will have learned to pace themselves and to endeavour always to keep something in hand for emergencies.

The Comfort Factor

There are many factors which affect your ability to cope with emergencies. Each of these needs to be considered carefully and its effects minimised as far as possible. Time is certainly one of the most important factors when you are out at sea in deteriorating conditions. If you know that you have, say, another twelve hours to go before there is any possibility of reaching harbour, the very prospect of this long period at sea in difficult, and perhaps dangerous, conditions can be quite challenging mentally. If you are cold and wet into the bargain, then the situation can be even worse because, as mentioned earlier, you will find yourself concentrating on your discomfort rather than the job in hand. One of the important lessons that becomes obvious here is that you put your foul weather gear on at a very early stage in the proceedings – before you get cold and wet! Comfort and mental ability go hand in hand, so keeping warm and dry will help to reduce the drain on your mental resources.

You should therefore try and put yourself in a position where you get as much protection as possible from the elements. This could mean putting up a spray dodger on a sailing boat, or moving to an inside steering position on a powerboat. It may seem the tough, rugged thing to do: to stand up there exposed to the full force of the elements whilst you steer the boat before a gale. Indeed, it can be positively exhilarating, but after an hour or so, you will start to find yourself becoming mentally drained. If there are still many hours to go, then this is the time when you start on the slippery slope of increasing risk.

Early preparation can be an important factor in maintaining mental alertness throughout a long night in deteriorating conditions. Preparing food and hot drinks when the conditions still allow this to be a practical proposition can be a great stimulus and can help considerably to boost morale. Hot food and drink can be a sign of normality in an increasingly chaotic world. Checking and planning the navigation so that, right at the onset of adverse conditions, you have in mind a good grasp of all the possibilities and alternatives, can be a tremendous help in making the right decisions at a later stage. The other thing that should be done is a general check round the boat to make sure that all stowages are secure, that there are no signs of any deterioration in equipment or fittings and that there is adequate fuel for the proposed course of action. Doing this at an early stage of the proceedings will pay off handsomely later, when many of these tasks would be much more difficult, if not impossible.

If you can be confident that all is well down below, that everything is taking the strain, that you are reasonably warm and comfortable, and that you have the navigation situation well in hand, then your mind will be unfettered and free to concentrate on the task of driving the boat. The mental stress will be reduced and you will maintain reserves.

Seasickness

One factor that can have a significant impact on your mental processes is seasickness. We will look at the means of reducing or avoiding this affliction later on in the book, but it is probably safe to say that seasickness has been responsible for more accidents at sea than any other single cause. It is not generally a direct cause of accidents, but one of its effects is a marked reduction in mental capability which can have a significant impact on your attitude to safety and survival. On the one hand, it can reduce your ability to make a critical assessment of the situation; on the other hand, it can make you take risks which in other circumstances you would not contemplate.

In severe cases, seasickness sufferers 'just want to curl up and die'. It generates a strong 'couldn't care less' attitude, which is obviously not conducive to safety. Any seasick member of the crew should be a cause for concern because the ability to respond to safety requirements will be greatly reduced. Those afflicted run a much higher risk of injury which, in turn, will put pressure on the rest of the crew and on the safety of the boat itself. Many sufferers like to be out in the open air. A favourite place is by the lee rails or on the lee side of a cockpit where they can relieve themselves without interfering with the rest of the crew. However, here they are at considerable risk of injury or even of being washed overboard, because they will not hold on or locate themselves with the same level of concentration as an unaffected crew member. The enormous feeling of lethargy which accompanies seasickness makes it very difficult to react or respond to a changing situation. So, any member of the crew who is seasick must be regarded as bringing increased risk to the situation while you, as a skipper, may have your attention diverted from the safety of the boat by concern about a seasick member of the crew.

Seasickness in the skipper can have even more serious consequences because it can adversely affect judgement. Faced with alternative courses of action, the seasick skipper is much more likely to plump for the option which would appear to get the boat into harbour or calmer water at the earliest possible moment and thus relieve the affliction. However, the chosen course of action may not always be the best one in the circumstances. Let us take the example of a boat out at sea in deteriorating conditions, with the nearest harbour downwind. It might seem the sensible solution to head for harbour, and safety, as quickly as possible. But, because the harbour is downwind, its entrance will be open to the full force of the wind, and if there is a bar, then negotiating that entrance could be a very risky and dangerous business. To a seasick skipper, however, the alternative – of heading upwind, of tacking a sailing boat or driving a powerboat into head seas – may be unthinkable because of the time involved, which will prolong the agony. If seasickness were not a consideration, heading upwind could be the right course to take in these conditions, yet the more risky alternative is likely to be seen as the better option, because it promises an end to the seasickness.

Fortunately, seasickness affects different people in different ways. There are many people who suffer from seasickness but who are still able to raise themselves above the affliction and concentrate on the job in hand. These people have probably learned from experience to pace themselves in difficult conditions, to be aware of the limitations which seasickness can impose, and have the right sort of mental ability to cope with difficult conditions. An emergency takes their minds off the seasickness and allows them to concentrate on the job in hand.

Current cures for seasickness do not necessarily help the situation. Although the different proprietory tablets affect people in different ways, one of the most common side effects is a feeling of drowsiness. This may be preferable to the seasickness in itself, but at times this drowsiness can become an almost overwhelming urge to sleep, which is certainly not conducive to the sort of concentration needed to operate a yacht in deteriorating conditions. The problem can usually be resolved by half an hour's sleep, but it does need to be recognised because tiredness can significantly reduce your mental alertness at a potentially crucial time.

Tiredness

Physical tiredness can be equally detrimental to concentration, and it is interesting to observe how it usually reaches its peak in the hour or two before dawn. Once daylight arrives, people tend to get a new lease of life, to be able to concentrate better and cope with the coming day. There is no doubt that at night levels of concentration do become lower. This is not just caused by tiredness but is exacerbated by the fact that it is not possible to see what is going on in the sea around the yacht: there is less of the outside world visible to provide a picture of the operating environment.

Prepared, Just in Case

We can see, then, that the correct mental attitude and concentration make a significant contribution to safe and sound yacht operation, by reducing the chance of mistakes and errors. But the psychology of an emergency situation is equally important to survival. Most emergencies develop quite suddenly, and when one happens, every member of the crew will feel a desperate need to do something. Any emergency brings about a rapid release of adrenalin. This release of adrenalin demands action, but the question is 'what action?' Everyone wants to do something to help, and in the mere act of rushing around they may feel they are helping. Confusion and panic are never very far away. It is now that the skipper must take firm control, and issue orders. Telling each member of the crew exactly what to do can go a long way to reducing panic and to bringing the situation quickly under control.

Prior training can have a vital influence here. A safety briefing in harbour before heading off to sea will give the crew specific responsibilities should an emergency arise, and will help them to react much more instinctively to the situation and keep panic at bay. Such a briefing would allocate such duties as: preparing the liferaft for deployment; getting the emergency flares ready; attending to the radio and such like. If every member of the crew has a specific job to do there is far less need for orders and everyone can react in a much more positive and purposeful way.

Of course, this still leaves the problem of dealing with the emergency itself, which might, for example, be the mast coming down or a total engine failure, or fouled propellers. There are so many possibilities that any individual event is difficult to anticipate and plan for. However, part of the mental training of any skipper should be an attempt to make an assessment of likely emergencies and to have some plan of action in mind. Thus, when an emergency occurs, you will already have formulated some basic ideas about how to cope. It is this mental planning which is important to survival, and we shall examine this is some detail in the next chapter. Here we are dealing rather with the psychology of the situation. Skippers who have a quick response to problems and who give the crew immediate orders will not only feel more in control of the situation themselves, but will also keep the crew occupied and reduce the onset of panic.

If the Worst Happens

The need for the right mental approach becomes even more critical if the emergency gets out of hand and you are obliged to take to the liferaft. The liferaft is an apparently fragile habitat compared with that of a yacht and now you are alone in a small craft in the middle of a vast expanse of sea. The situation can be compounded if you did not manage to get a distress signal out over the radio before you abandoned ship. Being adrift in a liferaft can be a lonely and frightening experience which can put the occupants under severe mental stress. This may take some time to develop, however. Initially, there is likely to be a considerable feeling of relief.

Consider the situation. Perhaps there has been a fire on board. Attempts to extinguish it have been unsuccessful and you have to abandon ship. You rush to get the liferaft overboard and get the crew on board, then cast off. On board the yacht it was all noise, rush and panic. Then, suddenly, you are adrift in the liferaft where relative peace and quiet prevail. The initial feeling is one of immense relief that you have escaped from the chaos of the yacht into the quiet haven of the liferaft. Then the reality of the situation starts to sink in. Now you are alone at sea in a small inflatable craft. The rush of panic that you felt when you were first aware of the emergency on board the yacht will be followed by a second wave of panic, as you realise that you may have merely exchanged one problem for another. The liferaft is keeping you afloat and providing a safe haven of sorts, but it is not so much a safe haven that you need, but rescue. It dawns on you that, in fact, you are no closer to rescue than you were in the pandemonium on the yacht, and that you are now running out of resources to cope with the emergency. You, or members of your crew, are likely to experience considerable stress. The remedy, as always, lies in action.

Liferaft

A posed scene.The liferaft is Avon's single-tube design which reduces stowage space requirements but does not give the reassurance of a double-tube liferaft. This photograph demonstrates that even in calm conditions, it would be very difficult to make any progress with the paddle, particularly as the ballast water pockets under the liferaft would create enormous drag.

In a liferaft there is limited scope for action. Whilst there is a certain amount to do in the initial stages, such as deploying the drogue, pumping up the floor and trying to settle down into some sort of routine, this will occupy no more than half an hour. After that, you can be faced with a long, lonely vigil until you are found. Apart from the feelings of panic which will hit different members of the crew at different times, being enclosed within the fabric of a liferaft is not a particularly pleasant experience, particularly if there is any sort of a sea running. You may not have been seasick on board the yacht, but unless you managed to take a seasickness tablet before you boarded the liferaft, the chances are that you will quickly succumb to seasickness which, within the confines of a liferaft, is not something which helps the situation. The lucky person is the one allocated the job of lookout. He will have his head outside and in contact with the outside world, such as it is. This can help to maintain a degree of sanity, and the lookout should be changed at frequent intervals so that all those capable take a turn. Not only will this help to maintain the right level of concentration, but it will give to give each of the survivors a chance to restore some sort of mental equilibrium.

So, the mental stress of life in a liferaft is high, and it is made worse by the fact that there is now very little you can do to help yourself. This is where a strong will is required: to maintain a good level of discipline, to keep the environment inside as dry and as supportive as possible, and to prevent fear and panic spreading amongst the crew. After the violent activity of abandoning ship, the inactivity on board the liferaft can rapidly reduce mental activity, and the effect of this on the prospects for survival can be considerable. Problems are exacerbated by the lack of space and the consequent close physical proximity of everyone.

It requires great mental effort to maintain some sort of normality in a liferaft, although it is surprising how quickly you can adapt to the changed circumstances. What might, at first glance, have seemed a very fragile and hostile environment, can quite rapidly become the norm. You might also see character changes in the people involved. For example, the strong crew member who was a tower of strength on board may become worse than useless within the confines of the liferaft. Confinement in a liferaft, where there is virtually no scope for physical activity, can have a very debilitating effect on those who are active by nature.

The Importance of Willpower

It is mental, rather than physical, strength that will aid survival in this situation, and it will not be easy to predict how crew members will perform. It is necessary to maintain this sort of willpower throughout, and it is absolutely vital to remember that you are not rescued until you are actually standing on the deck of the rescue vessel, or seated inside the rescue helicopter, or standing on dry land. There is a great temptation, when you see a rescue vessel or helicopter approaching, to imagine that from that moment you are, in fact, rescued and to ignore the risks involved in the rescue itself. This can often be a dangerous and delicate business, even more risky than abandoning ship in the first place. The help of the survivors is usually essential for efficient rescue. It is therefore vital that you maintain your mental alertness right up to, and beyond, the rescue: that you do not give up at the sight of a rescue boat and assume that everything will be fine from then on.

Such an example occurred off the Welsh coast. A dinghy sailor left his capsized dinghy and tried to swim ashore. Fortunately, the dinghy was sighted and the coastguard alerted. When the lifeboat found no one at the dinghy, it headed for the nearest point of land, on the assumption that the survivor would have gone that way. The survivor was sighted swimming for the shore, which happened to be sheer cliffs where landing would have been virtually impossible. When the survivor saw the lifeboat approaching, he made the assumption that he was rescued – and promptly passed out with exhaustion! He was finally rescued only after one of the lifeboat crew went into the water to assist, and he was only revived with difficulty. If he had only managed to keep his willpower going for a bit longer, he could have swum to the lifeboat and been able to co-operate with the crew in getting aboard, at which point he would have been free to relax.

Any rescue service will give similar examples, and will confirm that rescue is a great deal simpler, more efficient and reliable if the survivors can help in the operation. The moral, then, is that you must not give in until you are rescued.

The Unquantifiable Factor

From this chapter you can see that the unquantifiable factor – the psychology of safety and survival – can have a decisive impact on your ability to cope. Physical strength and technical ability are certainly important factors, but by far the most important factor is your mental ability to cope with situations as they develop and change. The ability to think situations through and find solutions is the key to employing appropriate physical activities and techniques which will ensure your safety and survival.

3 Preparation for Safety

When an emergency happens at sea, it is liable to happen very quickly. Your immediate response to that emergency – what you do in the first few minutes – is likely to have a significant influence on the final outcome of the situation. If you respond in the right way in those early moments, the chances are that you will nip the emergency in the bud. Hesitate at this point and you could well find that you have lost the initiative. An emergency situation can deteriorate rapidly, but it can just as often be resolved by quick action. Most yachtsmen will have to cope with a crisis at sea at some time or another, and most will manage. The ability to cope in a crisis is largely a result of careful and adequate preparation beforehand.

We have already looked at the psychological aspects of safety and survival, and there is no doubt that having the right attitude when an emergency occurs, and having the mental resources to cope with it, will go a long way to providing a solution. However, there is also a practical aspect to this preparation, and it is this practical aspect that we shall look at in this chapter.

Prevention

The first rule of preparing for emergencies is to try to prevent them happening in the first place. This should be your number one priority. Prevention is always better than cure and the recipe for prevention lies mainly in your hands. Prevention is largely a matter of careful planning, of working with the weather rather than against it, of having a safe, sound and seaworthy boat and a competent crew to sail it. These are the essential ingredients for safety and it will pay to look at them in more detail because they will form the basis of any preventive measures you can take.

Weather

The weather has a vital influence on everything you do at sea, and to a large degree it will dictate both your pleasure and your pain. When planning a voyage, you will naturally keep a watchful eye on the weather and heed what the forecasts are saying, and you will obviously try to work well within the limits of your particular boat. This is straightforward common sense and applies equally to sailing as to powerboat operation. If you work with the weather, there is obviously less likelihood of an emergency arising. However, there is always the risk of getting caught out, of the weather changing unexpectedly, resulting in difficult and dangerous conditions.

In almost any emergency, you will have to plan a course of action to get you out of trouble. If the boat's performance is impaired in some way, this course of action will be much more sensitive to the weather. For instance, you may be sailing along a lee shore and decide to use your engine to get you a bit further offshore because the tide is setting you in. You find that the engine won't start. Now the wind becomes a much more critical factor in your reckoning. You need to know whether it is likely to back or to veer, to increase or decrease in strength, so that you can plan a strategy to extricate yourself from the situation.

When you are faced with the unexpected like this, it helps to have a picture of the prevailing weather conditions already in mind. You must keep up to date with the weather situation and take note of the forecasts, not just before you go to sea, but also all the while you are at sea. In this way you will remain in control and be aware of what the weather is likely to do for at least the next twelve hours. This applies to powerboats and sailing boats equally. Whereas sailing boats tend to be more sensitive to wind direction than strength, powerboats can be very sensitive to wind strength variations. The sea conditions thus generated can greatly influence the speed at which powerboats can travel and, in some circumstances, on the direction in which they can go.

The Boat

The weather may have a strong influence on the environment in which the boat operates, but preparation is also needed on the boat itself. Here, it should take the form of making sure, as far as possible, that nothing on the boat will fail. Emergencies at sea occur far more frequently as a result of the failure of one or more parts of the boat, than because the boat itself is not up to the prevailing conditions. The latter situation should have been avoided anyway by keeping a watchful eye on the weather forecasts. Most boats being operated within reasonable limits could probably withstand worse conditions, should they get caught out, provided that nothing on the boat were to fail. Life might be uncomfortable and difficult, but with most modern boats there is no real reason why you shouldn't make harbour safely, even though there has been a gale of wind and difficult sea conditions, provided the boat is seaworthy and is handled competently.

Keeping a boat in a sound and seaworthy condition involves regularly checking a multitude of things. There are the obvious things, like checking that ropes are not worn and frayed on a sailing boat, and carrying out regular engine maintenance on a powerboat, but there are also some much more subtle checks that you need to make. It is a fact of life that the obvious things tend to get checked at regular intervals and therefore present no problems, but it is the more subtle and less easily accessible things that tend to get neglected and then cause problems when the boat is put under stress. And an unexpected failure can get you into difficulties quite quickly at sea.

The sort of checking we are talking about here usually requires the trained eye of a surveyor,. who will know from experience what to look for and which areas are likely to give trouble. However, these same problems should be obvious to any owner or skipper who takes the trouble to look. Identifying problems doesn't require any particular skills, except the ability to look at every aspect of the boat with a critical eye.

The Hull

Let us take the hull first. This should not pose problems, provided it has stood the test of time, although there are certain areas where weaknesses could become apparent. On a sailing boat the ballast keel is obviously one of these. If you see signs of weeping or movement, or simply a crack in the paintwork around where the keel is attached to the hull, it is time to have a thorough look at the keel bolts and their condition. The other likely points of weakness in the hull are the skin fittings, particularly those below the waterline. You should remember that it is not just the skin fittings themselves which could be vulnerable, but also the pipes attached to them. Any break in these will let water into the hull as surely as a hole in the hull itself. Probably one of the main reasons for boats taking on water and sinking in unexplained circumstances is a failure of one or more of these pipes.

Security for Seacocks

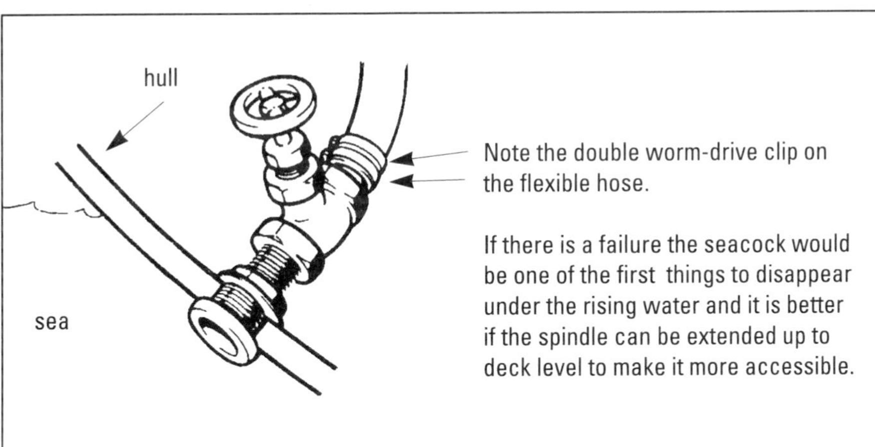

The main underwater connections are likely to be those to the toilet and the engine. Since these are where water is drawn in, the inlets have to be underwater. The piping in these systems should be checked, and double-checked, to make sure that it is sound and secure. Plastic piping should not be used because it can harden and crack, although some types of reinforced plastic piping are adequate for the purpose. However, heavy-duty reinforced rubber piping is a better proposition, particularly in the engine compartment where it can be subject to considerable vibration and movement if the engine is flexibly mounted. All these pipes should be secured at each end with double worm-drive clips. They should be checked to make sure that they are not rubbing against fixed parts of the boat which could chafe. In the engine compartment itself, the whole salt water cooling circuit is effectively open to the sea and needs to be maintained to the highest standards, and this includes the inlet filter system.

Cockpit Drains

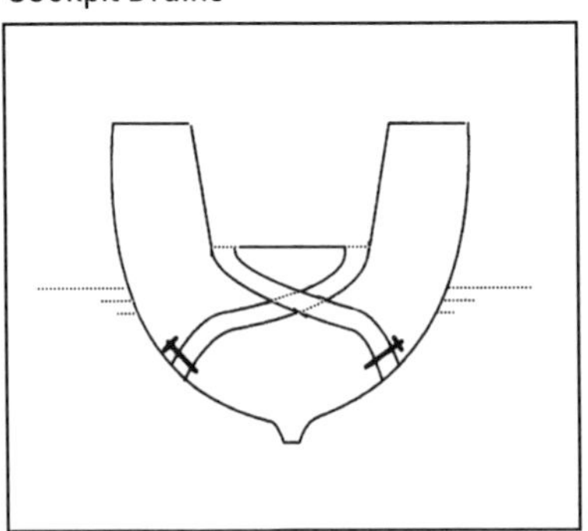

Cockpit drains are taken to the opposite side of the hull so that when the yacht heels, water does not run back up the drain on the lower side

Dorade Ventilator

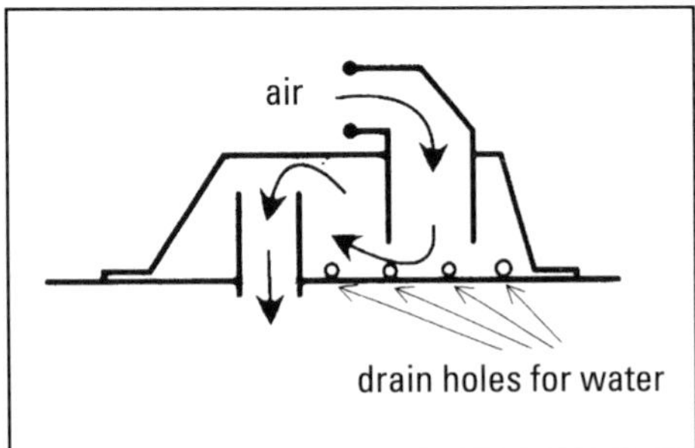

A Dorade type ventilator which should allow fresh air into the cabin but which should prevent water entering. The drain holes need to be checked to make sure they are clear of any obstruction

Although your main concern when inspecting the skin fittings and connecting pipework will be to prevent water getting into the boat, any failure in the pipes could lead to a fire. Now, you may wonder how a leaking inlet water pipe could start a fire when the rising water would seem much more likely to put one out, but remember that the engine cooling water finally ends up being injected into the exhaust system where it is used as the cooling medium. If the sea water inlet fails, this injection of water into the exhaust system will also fail, and it will take only a few seconds for the very hot exhaust gases to raise the temperature of the flexible rubber exhaust pipe to the point where it will burn through. Now you can have quite a serious problem on your hands: water coming in, the engine exhaust on fire! With a bit of luck, one might put out the other, but it does demonstrate how emergencies can rapidly compound themselves. In this example, the first indication you may have of trouble is when the water rises to a level high enough to stop the engine. Then you can end up with a triple problem: the boat filling with water, the engine exhaust on fire, and no power. You are quite close to the point where the lifeboat may be your only salvation – and all because a water pipe failed!

If a pipe connected to a skin fitting should give way, one of the first items to be submerged as the water rises inside the boat is the skin fitting valve itself. This presents you with the problem of trying to find the skin fitting valve by fumbling about under the rising water. One solution is to mark its position, so that, even if you can't see it, you know roughly where to find it. A much better solution, however, is to raise the operating position of the valve so that it can be switched off higher up in the hull. This means extending the spindle of the valve, if it is a screw type, or, if it is of the lever type, fitting a secondary lever. You will want to get to these valves in a hurry if something does go wrong. In the case of the exhaust piping catching fire, which could rapidly fill the engine compartment with smoke, there is a lot to be said for placing the operating position of these valves outside the engine compartment. You can see, then, that when you examine your boat with a critical eye, you are not just looking to see that things are in good condition, you are also trying to work out the implications of any failure.

The Electrics

The electrical system should come in for equally careful scrutiny because this is the primary cause of fires in boats. Moreover, any failure in the electrical system could lead to the failure of some of the most vital equipment on board, such as the engine itself, or the radios or navigation equipment. We saw earlier how the failure of a compass light bulb could develop into a major crisis; the failure of one of the navigation lights could be just as serious, should this occur when you are in crowded waters. The electrical system could also be responsible for powering the bilge pump, which could be a vital in the event of a water pipe failure. More and more these days, a boat's safety is dependent upon its electrical system. If you want the convenience and safety aspects of the electrical system, then you must also accept responsibility for maintaining it properly. This means checking it at frequent intervals to ensure that no problems are developing and that the risk of failures and fires is therefore minimised.

Battery Installation

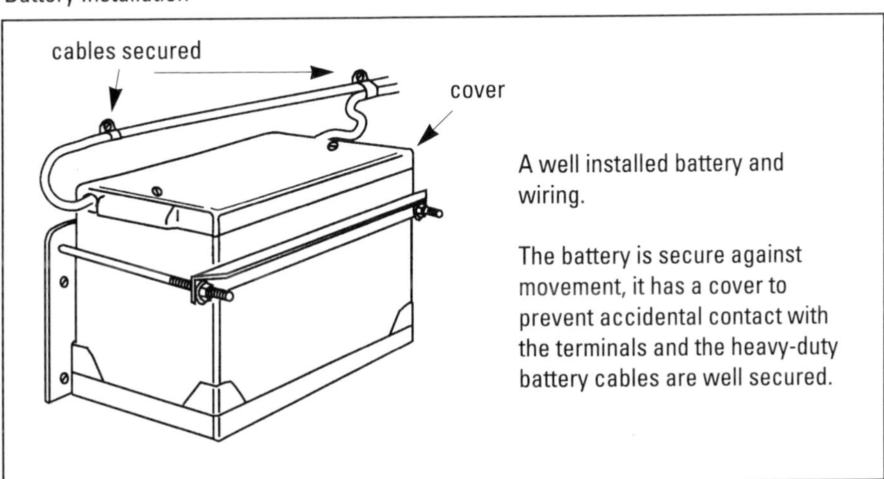

A well installed battery and wiring.

The battery is secure against movement, it has a cover to prevent accidental contact with the terminals and the heavy-duty battery cables are well secured.

The place to start with the electrical system is the battery. It is surprising on how many boats the battery is not secured against movement. Try and picture the situation if that battery shifts slightly every time the boat rolls or pitches: the connecting wires, which include the heavy-duty starter wires, will move with the battery – which is the last thing you want. This constant movement over time could lead to failure. Remember that the main battery cable is not protected by fuses. If the wire does fail, the bare end could fall across some metal object and create a major short circuit, which would not only put the electrical circuit out of action, but could well start a fire into the bargain!

Electrical Circuits

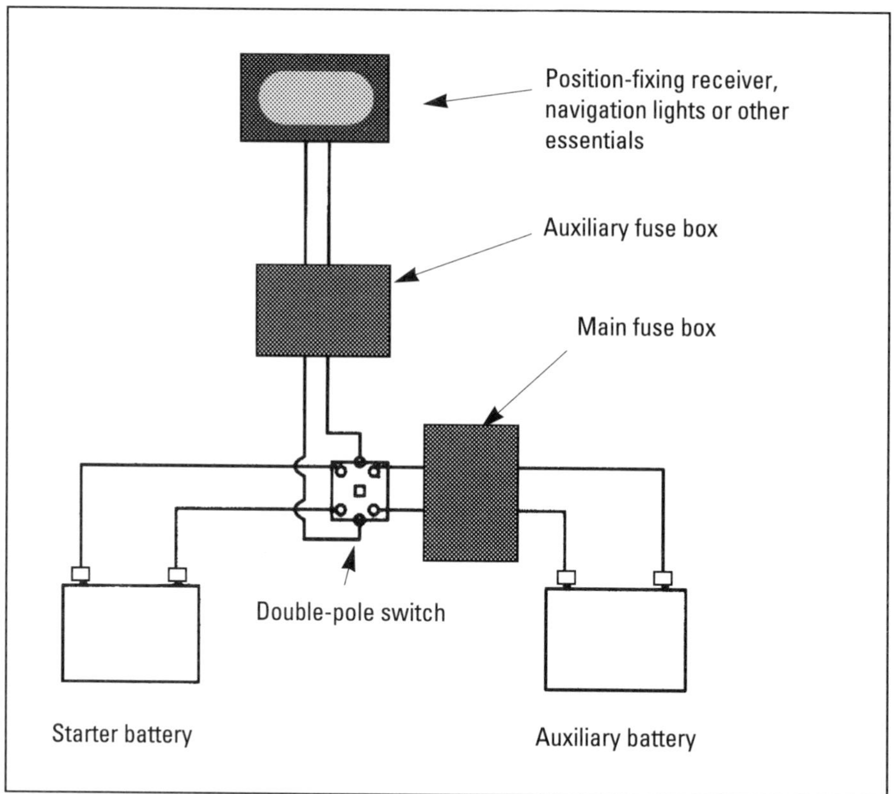

Electrical circuits which can allow electrical supplies to essential equipment to be obtained from either battery in the event of a supply failure.

Those circuits protected by fuses are slightly less vulnerable in this respect, but even here a fuse blowing can put the piece of equipment it protects out of commission, possibly when you most need it. If this is, say, a position-finding receiver, this could put you under considerable pressure in adverse conditions. All electrical wiring needs to be checked for any signs of chafe, movement or corrosion, so that you can rely on it not to let you down in a crisis.

When you are checking the electrical system, a cursory glance is not enough. Rather you have to explore thoroughly all the corners where wires pass through bulkheads or across other fittings, and look carefully at the installation of the wire where it actually touches the fitting, because this is where the chafe will occur. One of the main culprits is those wires which are normally out of sight. On many boats you will find that wiring that is concealed behind panelling has just been laid loose, without any means of fixing, and it is in such spots that trouble can brew, unseen and undetected until a major problem flares up.

One way to safeguard vital electrical supplies is to have a switching system which allows the essential requirements to be supplied from an alternative battery in the event of a failure. These essential supplies will include items such as the compass light, the navigation lights, the position-fixing electronics and the VHF radio. If these are wired up with secondary circuits fed into a changeover switch supplied from the engine starting battery, rather than the auxiliary battery, then, if a failure does occur, there is every chance that you will be able to bring the circuits back into action very quickly.

Fuel Systems

Fuel systems present another potential area where careful checking is required. Once again, chafe or wear on the fuel pipes needs to be detected at an early stage and corrective measures taken. The fuel filter needs to be checked at frequent intervals because no engine will run without clean fuel, although this should, of course, be one of your routine tasks when checking the engine before each passage. Similarly, the fuel tank should regularly be drained of water and sediment, if this is feasible. If there is a gas system on board, this should obviously be checked in a similar way. As far as is practicable, shut-off valves for fuel and gas should be readily accessible, so that they can be turned off quickly in the event of a fire.

Fuel Pipes

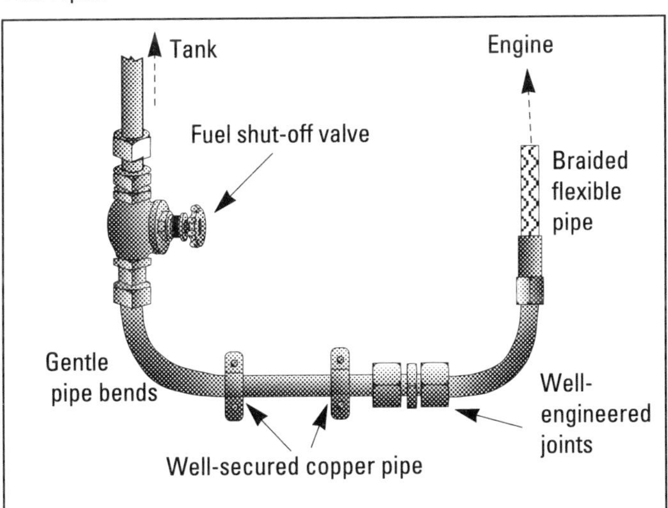

Note the use of braided flexible pipe to prevent vibration failure and no sharp bends in the pipework.

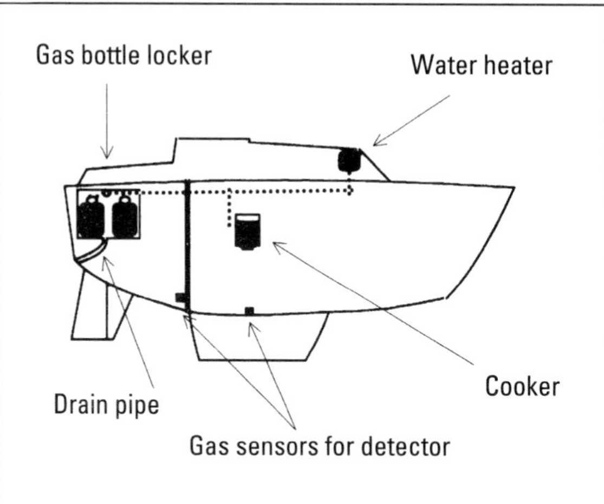

Gas Installation

A gas system needs careful attention to detail. Pipes should be well secured and the cylinders fixed to prevent movement. Turn off the gas when it is not in use.

Mast and Rigging

On a sailing boat the mast and rigging are subject to a very high degree of wear and tear. While most owners will check halyards and sheets for chafe and wear at frequent intervals, the standing rigging rarely gets the same attention. Wear here can go largely unnoticed – until a failure occurs. There will be constant vibration in the standing rigging, and wear tends to occur in the nip, perhaps where a shackle is fixed to a turn screw. The wear can occur largely unseen here because it is in the area where the two metal surfaces rub and it will only be detected by slackening off the rigging and opening up the links. Such checking only needs to be carried out annually. At the same time the wires of the standing rigging should be checked for broken strands. Particular attention should be paid to any point where a wire enters a terminal or passes over a spreader. Blocks should be given the same scrutiny, and should be dismantled occasionally to permit checking for wear in the bearings. The halyards inside the mast are usually hidden from sight but should be

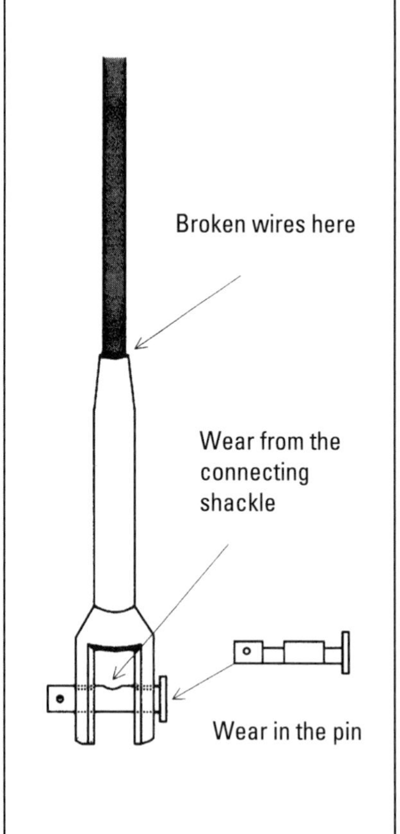

The places to look for wear and tear when checking the standing rigging.

inspected carefully when an opportunity arises. Modern rigging systems are so carefully designed and integrated that the failure of any one part could lead to the whole system becoming unbalanced and, ultimately, the loss of the mast!

Stern Gear

Finally, the stern gear should be given the same sort of careful scrutiny at least once a year. You won't be able to get ready access to the underwater parts except on the occasions when the boat is slipped, but you should then take full advantage of the opportunity to carry out a thorough check. Any signs of movement in the bearings should be taken as a message that repair or replacement is necessary. Wear in the stern gear bearings can only get worse, and will eventually lead to the type of failure that will be very difficult to correct at sea. The checks on the operating systems for the steering will depend on the type of steering involved. With hydraulic systems, leaks should be tackled as soon as they are discovered; wire and pulley systems should be checked in much the same way as advocated for the rigging; mechanical systems should be checked for slack.

As an example of cumulative failure, let us look at the experience of a small powerboat which had wire and pulley steering to the outboard motor. The wires on such a system are obviously prone to considerable movement and wear and tear. In this instance, one of the steering wires finally parted. This alone would not have been too serious and could have been mended without too much difficulty, even at sea, but, in breaking, the loose ends of one of the steering wires fell across the battery terminals. The resulting short circuit started a fire, and the two occupants were lucky to be rescued before the boat burned down to the waterline!

Check Properly

When checking all the systems on board, the critical eye is absolutely vital to your safety. Ask yourself what would happen if such and such a component were to fail, and go round the whole boat considering the

Octahedral Radar Reflector

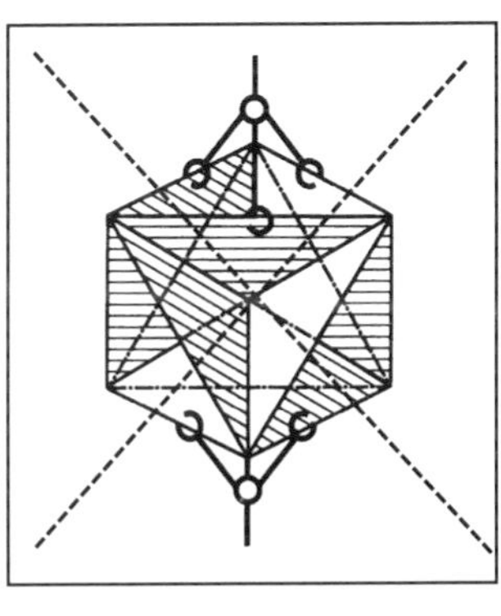

wrong way

It seems logical to hang an octahedral radar reflector this way up, but it will be less effective when the boat is upright as one plate is horizontal.

The correct way. This provides the maximum reflection of the radar beam over a range of heeling and pitching angles

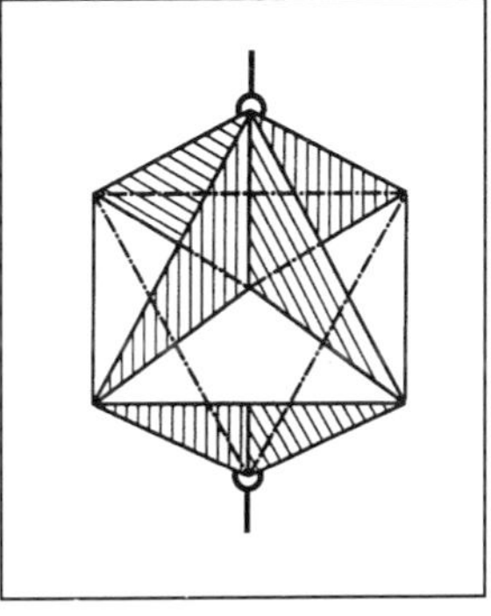

correct way

consequences of failure. Access to many of the parts may be difficult: for instance, on many modern sailing boats the engine is tucked away in such a small compartment that it is not easy to see what is going on inside. The toilet is an area which tends to be neglected. The pipes may pass out of sight, but should not pass out of mind. Admittedly, it is not always easy to summon up the motivation for such detailed checking, and it is obvious from the number of failures at sea that many yachtsmen turn a blind eye to what is going on, either through ignorance or neglect. However, at the end of the day, if you don't carry out the necessary careful inspection, you will have to be prepared to suffer the consequences of any failure.

Spares and Tools

Your preparations for safety should also include ensuring that you have the right equipment on board to cope with emergency situations. In addition to the prescribed liferafts and lifejackets, flares etc, which we will look at in more detail later on, emergency equipment should include the wherewithal to effect repairs at sea. Engine spares and tools are, of course, important, but you should also have equipment for, and know how to deal with, electrical failures. This should include spare fuses and bulbs, spare wire etc. You don't need to be a trained mechanic or electrician: there are books on the market explaining fault-finding procedures, which should at least help you identify problems and give you some ideal of how to deal with them.

Apart from the engine and electrical system, where specialised spares and fittings may be required, your emergency kit should include a variety of general-purpose items which may enable you to make jury repairs if something does fail. It should perhaps include pieces of canvas, pieces of wood and tubing, clips and fastening brackets, spare shackles and rope, and the like, all of which could be of use in effecting emergency repairs and get you to port where more permanent repairs can be carried out. A toolkit which covers wood and metal working tools as well as the normal outfit for engine repairs is useful. If you have such bits and pieces on board, you should be able to improvise and cope with most of the breakages or failures which might occur. There is nothing worse than being out at sea with a problem which you have been able to identify, but which you don't have the means with you to fix, at least temporarily, and having to summon help to solve the problem. When you go to sea you should aim to be as self-sufficient as possible.

Personal Equipment and Training

Personal equipment can play a key role in survival. In the last chapter we looked at the need to keep warm and dry as far as possible, so good protective clothing is an important element in preparing for emergencies. With the right clothing you will be in a much better frame of mind to cope when something goes wrong. Exactly what you use, and when, will depend to some extent on personal preference. A safety harness is another item of personal equipment which can be absolutely vital on a sailing boat, while a knife and seasickness tablets can be very useful, too. It is just as important to prepare yourself properly as it is to prepare the boat.

Training can also be an important part of personal preparation, although the usual emphasis of training tends to be much more on the positive side: teaching navigation and teaching seamanship skills, rather than how to cope with emergencies. However, the best training is undoubtedly practical experience, preferably gained by going to sea with more experienced people. There is a tendency these days for people with only limited experience to buy boats, and for them a training course of some sort on a charter yacht could provide a useful prelude to going it alone. Where experience is limited, larger safety margins need to be built into early ventures at sea to offset the inexperience.

In preparing for safety, one of the most valuable types of training is practice in using the emergency equipment. The liferaft is shut up in its valise or container, and in many cases will only see the light of day when it is inflated for use in an emergency. Any emergency is traumatic enough, without you also having to learn what a liferaft looks like, what equipment it carries and what it feels like to be inside. If you, the skipper, don't have experience of a liferaft and how it performs and behaves, it is going to be much more difficult to make a sound judgement about when is right to abandon ship, and to take effective command of the liferaft. The problem with advance practice in liferafts is that they tend to be one-off shots: once inflated they have to be returned to the manufacturers or service agents to be repacked. This makes it difficult to use your own for training purposes and, indeed, some service agents actively discourage using the liferaft in this way, even if it is done just before it is packed off for servicing. If you can get their co-operation to allow you to inflate it at, say, the end of the season when the boat is being taken out of commission, this could be invaluable experience, because there is nothing quite like knowing your own liferaft and its equipment. You will have a lot more confidence in using the liferaft if you have seen it inflated in this way, and you should be able to use it much more effectively.

An alternative is to go to one of the demonstrations held by yacht clubs or by the manufacturers themselves. The liferaft is inflated, often in a swimming pool, so that you can practise climbing into it from the water, get some idea of just what it is like to be inside, and what equipment you can expect it to contain. These artificial conditions may be far removed from the grim reality of having to abandon ship, but such a demonstration and exercise is better than nothing.

The same problems arise with the firing of distress flares. To someone who has never done this before it can be quite a frightening experience, yet the difficulties of practising can be even greater, because it is illegal to fire a distress flare when you are not in distress. Away from the water you are unlikely to incur anybody's wrath (although there is always the risk that the police may investigate what is going on because these flares are extremely bright). Firing parachute distress flares is to be actively discouraged, simply because they will attract unwelcome attention. Again, the best chance you are likely to get to see flares fired is at demonstrations organised by yacht clubs in conjunction with the manufacturers. It is worth attending one of these demonstrations because if you know what to expect when a flare is fired, it will at least reduce your apprehension if you are obliged to do it for real. If nothing else, you will learn that a hand-held flare must be held out to leeward and not to windward, and held away from you, because flares of both types can be lethal if used incorrectly.

Lifejackets and Safety Harnesses

Fortunately, practice in the use of lifejackets and safety harnesses is easier to arrange. And practise you should: you may think that putting on a strange lifejacket is quite a straightforward operation, but wait until you try it. The number of people who get tied up in knots trying to get the apparatus on correctly demonstrates the need for practice and familiarity, so that if an emergency occurs you will know exactly how it is done. In a true emergency your hands may be cold and it may be dark, so if you can get your lifejacket on in a few seconds rather than having to fumble for perhaps several minutes, this could significantly improve your prospects for survival. The same goes for safety harnesses, although these tend to be worn more as a matter of routine on sailing boats. However, you want to make sure it is adjusted properly and fully ready for use before you need to to use it. There may be times when lifejacket and safety harness are worn in combination, and this is something you should try out in the calm of harbour, rather than out at sea on the pitching deck of a yacht, ensuring in advance that they will work together effectively.

A modern safety harness made from 2,000kg breaking strain webbing. Note the special hook which prevents accidental disconnection through the hook 'capsizing'.

Training the Crew

One of the most obvious yet most valuable ways of preparing for emergencies is for everyone to know where things are and what they must do. In the last chapter we looked at the psychology of this and the need for a positive approach. A briefing session on safety is essential before you put to sea. The whole crew should be present and it needn't take more than five minutes. But the very act of calling such a briefing will make the crew aware of the requirements for safety, of the need for them to work together as a team, and will give them some idea of their individual roles in an emergency. The briefing needs to be fairly comprehensive, perhaps starting off by making sure that everybody knows how to operate the bilge pumps and where to find the fire extinguishers. If there are different types of extinguisher for different types of fire, this should be pointed out, and the fire blanket – which may be by the galley stove – should also be demonstrated. The briefing should take in the positions of seacocks and how to gain access to them, and where to find the taps to switch off the fuel and gas systems. The location of the liferafts and flares should be pointed out, and if an EPIRB is carried, this should also be demonstrated and its storage place noted. Each item of safety equipment should be covered, briefly but thoroughly, one by one. You could set out a checklist, to make sure that nothing is missed.

If you follow this procedure, the crew will be in a much better position to cope. The safety briefing, combined with giving each crew member a specific emergency role, as discussed in the last chapter, will go a long way to reducing panic and ensuring an efficient approach to emergencies. This will take the pressure off you, the skipper, so that you can concentrate on the immediate effects of the emergency, knowing that all the routine tasks are being coped with. If you sail regularly with the same crew, then you probably only need a safety briefing once or twice in a season. If the crew changes frequently, it is no bad thing to have one every time you go to sea. There is certainly a lot to commend this latter approach, anyway, because it does concentrate the crew's minds briefly on safety requirements and procedures.

The same briefing session can also be used to check that you have all the necessary equipment on board for the particular passage, including adequate fuel and water supplies, sufficient and appropriate charts, and probably for many people most important of all, plentiful food and drink. You may think that this approach is far too structured and that the atmosphere should be more relaxed, but this type of informal discipline will pay dividends in an emergency.

Pre-empting Problems

Finally, in your role as skipper, your preparation to cope with emergencies should include going through a 'what if' exercise. You don't necessarily have to do this before you go to sea; it can be something of an on-going game that you play, perhaps to while away long, lonely hours at the helm. Think about all the possible situations which could arise on your particular boat when you are at sea and try to work out what sort of action you might take. In relative safety, you can let your mind run riot and come up with a whole host of emergencies – 99% of which you will, with luck, never experience. But the fact that you have thought about the 1% you may be faced with could mean the difference between coping adequately and getting into even more serious trouble. As you never quite know what you are going to have to face up to as the skipper of a yacht, if you have tried to anticipate all likely problems, there is a good chance that you will be in a much better position to come up with the right answers should an emergency occur.

We will look at some possible scenarios in greater detail later on, in Chapter 8 Coping with Emergencies, but you might, for example, think about how you would cope with a fire on board and what the effects might be of a fire in different parts of the boat. Could people escape from compartments in which they might be asleep when the fire broke out? What facilities have you on board to put out the fire? Or, if the yacht went aground, what steps could you take to get it off again? Could you launch the dinghy and lay out an anchor? Are the propellers protected so that they could still be used? Is the rudder likely to be damaged? Or, if the steering failed, could you rig emergency steering to get you home? With a twin-screw boat, could you use the engines for steering? If the boat had to be towed back to harbour, where on board could you make a towing rope fast, or, if you had to tow somebody else, how would you go about it?

There are literally hundreds of such questions that you might like to ask yourself. When it comes to towing, for instance, you could even set up an exercise with another boat, to see how effectively you could tow someone else, or what it is like to be towed. Such an exercise would give a degree of fun and purpose to your pleasure yachting, and would certainly add to the fund of experience which is such a necessary part of being a competent yachtsman. That fund of experience is one of the most valuable attributes you can have, and will probably do more than anything else to enable you to cope with any emergency which might develop at sea.

4 Calling for Help

Despite all your preparation and care, the time may come when things go wrong. This is the time when you will need not only all your personal resources, but also help from others. Before you can get this help, you will have to let people know that you are in trouble. There are many different ways of doing this, some of which have come into existence as a result of improved technology, whilst some of the time-tested methods of indicating distress use very low levels of technology. At the end of the day, it doesn't particularly matter how you communicate that you are in trouble, as long as you get the message across. The method you use will depend a great deal on the circumstances in which you find yourself, and the facilities you have available on board.

Arm Waving

One of the simplest methods of attracting attention is simply to wave to passing vessels. This system obviously has only a limited effective range, and these days you are more likely to get people waving back, assuming that it is a friendly gesture rather than a signal of distress. The official distress signal is to stand on deck and raise and lower your outstretched arms on each side. This is a more positive approach to indicating distress, and you will probably be able to bring some emotion into the signal which will attract attention. Even so, the vast majority of those in the boats within range would assume that you were merely doing physical jerks on deck. However, when all else fails, this is the most basic of distress signals, and it has the merit of not requiring any equipment to get your message across. An alternative to waving your arms is to tie a piece of clothing to an oar or pole and wave that.

Flag Signals

Flags have been an important method of communicating at sea for a long, long time. The distress signal comprises a square flag with a ball, or anything resembling a ball, above or below it. The idea is that it can be made up from virtually anything you have on board. For instance, the flag could be a piece of canvas, and the ball a fender. Obviously, for maximum visibility and impact, the two items should be as large as possible. This signal has the advantage that, once hoisted, it can continue to display your message even though the crew may be down below trying to sort out the problem. However, like arm waving, this is a somewhat limited means of indicating your predicament and, like many of the distress signals which we shall examine, it requires somebody to be actively looking out from another vessel, or from the shore, to notice your plight.

Another flag signal, one of the international code of signals, is the flags N and C hoisted one above the other. These days, however, such a signal, even if you have the correct flags on board, is quite likely to pass unheeded. The vast majority of vessels are unlikely to realise that you are actually trying to send a message, and if they do realise, the chances are that they will not have a book on board which will enable them to interpret the message. So, it is really necessary to find a more forceful and reliable means of indicating your plight. One such means is to have smoke or flames billowing from your yacht.

Smoke and Flame Signals

If a vessel is on fire, it is very visibly in distress, hence the thinking behind this signal. This signal dates from the time when a vessel would have had on board some sort of container which could be filled with oil, tar, or a similar combustible product, and set alight. The crew on a modern yacht are unlikely to have the means, or inclination, to use such a signal. After all, if the fire were to get out of hand, it could worsen the situation considerably rather than bring succour. These days we prefer to use the more effective visual signals created by pyrotechnics.

Pyrotechnic Signals

Officially there are four different types of pyrotechnic distress signals. These are: a red hand flare; a red parachute flare; a rocket or shell which emits a series of single, bright red stars at frequent intervals; a smoke signal which gives off orange-coloured smoke. One or more of these signals should be carried on every yacht, although their effectiveness will be affected both by the conditions and the

A full complement of distress signals and the plastic container in which they are stowed. They should be packed securely inside to prevent being damaged. A couple of parachute flares should be kept close to the helm available for immediate use in the event of collision or grounding on rocks.

time of day. It is worth looking a bit more closely at these alternative signals and the way in which they can be used:

Red Hand Flare

The red hand flare is probably the simplest and oldest of these pyrotechnic signals. It is rather like an overgrown firework with its own built-in ignition system. There are several proprietary brands on the market but they are all similar, with a pyrotechnic unit above a handle. Methods of ignition vary: you may have to pull a striker out from the bottom of the handle and rub it across a friction plate on the top to set off the firing system; alternatively, there can be a release-pin mechanism which fires the flare. Whichever ignition system is used, these flares need to be handled with great care because ignition is pretty well instantaneous. You must also be prepared for the red-hot ash and the smoke which spews out while the flare is burning.

Red Mark 6 Hand-Held Distress Flare from Pains-Wessex Ltd

The flare is held out at arm's length to reduce the risk of hot ash landing on board. It would have been better held out to leeward. Note the angle at which the flare is being held which helps protect the hand.

The first thing to remember is that you must always be on the lee side of the boat when you let off a flare. Stand to windward and the smoke and ash will blow back in your face, with painful consequences which may well make you drop the flare. Equally dangerous would be if the hot ash were to fall onto the boat, where it could start a real fire. This might create a good distress signal, but it would certainly compound your problems! You have to be even more careful if you ignite a flare in a liferaft because the hot ash will quickly burn through the fabric of the raft and you could find it deflating rapidly. So, with hand-held flares, the answer is to let them off on the lee side of the yacht or liferaft with your arm outstretched. And, if you have a petrol-engined boat, keep the flare well away from the engines or fuel.

When you light the flare, hold it at arm's length and then keep it well out over the water where the hot ash can fall harmlessly. The flare will burn for half a minute or more. The higher you can hold it, the more likely it is to be seen but, of course, you have to balance this against the safety aspect. Choose your firing position carefully, particularly if you still have the sails up, because you want the flare to be seen all round the horizon. These flares have an effective range of probably two or three miles (three to five kilometres) in daylight and up to ten miles (sixteen kilometres) at night, depending on the visibility and the weather conditions. For example, strong winds will reduce the flare's visibility because it will tend to burn sideways rather than give a clear corona above the container.

Parachute Flares

Parachute flares are much more effective. The flare is taken up to a height of around one thousand feet (three hundred metres) by a rocket and then released to descend slowly, suspended below a small parachute. The flare will burn for about forty seconds, during which it gives a very brilliant red light. At night, this should be visible for up to fifteen miles (twenty-four kilometres). Even in daylight the flare should be visible for five miles (eight kilometres), although in strong sunlight the effective visual range tends to be considerably reduced. Obviously, a parachute flare will not be very effective if there is low cloud, but in these conditions you should try and fire the rocket downwind at an angle of about forty-five degrees so that it will burn below the cloud base.

As suggested in the previous chapter, firing a parachute flare can be quite traumatic, particularly if you have never done it before. You should follow the printed instructions on the outside of the container very precisely, especially those dealing with of making the trigger mechanism operative. This usually involves taking off the end cap and folding out the trigger, which then fits snugly under the palm of your lower hand whilst your upper hand is used to grip the container. Simply by squeezing the trigger, which also tightens your grip on the container with the lower hand, the rocket is fired. Ignition is instantaneous. The end caps of some rocket types are held on by sticky tape and this must be removed from both ends before firing. In light winds the rocket should be held vertically and, on a sailing boat, you should be as far away from the masts and rigging as possible to avoid the rocket striking anything on its way up. On a ketch or a schooner this might not be easy, and here probably the best place to stand is up in the bow. On most yachts, standing in the cockpit, well over to one side so as to keep clear of the backstay, is probably the best position. In a powerboat the cockpit is also generally the best position. In strong winds, the rocket should pointed downwind, inclined at about fifteen degrees from the vertical, because, once fired, it will tend to turn into the wind and ascend almost vertically.

Rocket and Shell Flares

The use of rockets and shells throwing out red stars harks back to the days when most ships carried guns of some sort which could be used to fire special shells. The system went out of use for many years, but has recently been reintroduced in the form of pocket-sized distress flare kits with a simple type of gun which can be loaded with cartridge-type pyrotechnics.

The forerunner of this modern system was the Very pistol, which simply fired a star shell up into the air, whereupon it dropped to the sea, without any slowing mechanism such as a parachute. The modern versions fire flares which rise to a height of about one hundred feet (thirty metres) and last for no more than ten seconds. Because of their low trajectory and short burning time, there is less chance of such flares being seen than hand or parachute flares, but they do provide a useful and compact distress kit for small boats such as dinghies or sportsboats. Being pocket-sized, you can keep them in your oilskin pocket, and being waterproof, they can also be fired if you are actually in the water. However, they are really a last-resort type of distress signal; you would have to be reasonably close to other craft or to the shore to have some hope of them being seen. At night the maximum range is probably two or three miles (three to five kilometres), but in daylight it is probably little more than a mile (about one and a half kilometres). Some police authorities classify this type of pyrotechnic as a firearm and demand that you have a firearms licence to carry them, so check on this before you purchase them.

Smoke Flares

Finally in this look at pyrotechnics, we come to smoke signals. These come in large canisters and, when triggered, give off copious quantities of dense orange smoke. There are also smaller versions available, which are rather like hand flares and which are fired in a similar manner, but in use these last a very short time and do not compare in effectiveness with the canister-type of smoke flare, which lasts for between one and two minutes. Once triggered, the canisters should be thrown into the water to the leeward of the vessel, otherwise you will be engulfed in the smoke which, whilst it is non-toxic, is not particularly pleasant.

Shown above, the buoyant type of smoke signal is designed for launching overboard after firing.

Holding a hand smoke flare out to windward. The smoke retains its character in light winds but it quickly disperses in stronger winds.

As you might imagine, these smoke flares are a daylight-only signal, and their effectiveness will vary a great deal, depending on the weather conditions. They are much less effective in strong winds, when the smoke will disperse very rapidly. They are at their most effective in calm conditions when the dense cloud of smoke can be visible for up to five miles (eight kilometres). In any sort of fresh wind conditions, the effective range is more likely to be reduced to two or three miles (three to five kilometres).

Sound and Light Signals

Another form of distress signal uses noise to attract attention. A traditional one which is rarely, if ever, used today is a gun, or other explosive signal, fired at intervals of about one minute. Although the signal can be heard over quite a distance, it does require having a comparatively large gun on board – not the type of equipment found on the average yacht. However, your fog signal could be a substitute; continuous sounding of either the vessel's built-in horn or one of the portable fog horns is one of the recognised distress signals. The ranges of such a signal is going to be comparatively low, perhaps only up to half a mile (800 metres), except in calm conditions when it could extend to one mile (one and a half kilometres). This is the sort of signal that could be of more value in congested waters than out in the open sea.

Instead of the continuous sounding of the horn, which will rapidly expend the pressure canister on the portable type of horn, or quickly run down your batteries if it is a built-in electric horn, an alternative is to use the traditional Morse Code SOS signal. This comprises three dots, three dashes, and then three dots, sounded off in sequence on the horn. An intermittent signal is more likely to attract attention than a continuous blast.

The same SOS signal could be made by means of a flashing light, using a torch or signalling lamp. This could be a useful night-time signal, particularly if you don't have any flares available or you have used them all up and you can see significant lights on the shore or other vessels in the vicinity. By using a torch or similar lamp, the signal can be directed towards the intended recipient, and a flashing light is much more likely to attract attention than a fixed light.

Response to Audio-Visual Distress Signals

So much for the audio and visual distress signals. There is a wide variety here, to suit different conditions and to meet different requirements. The problem with any signal of this type is how to ascertain whether it has been seen or heard by other vessels or on shore. You may get some indication from other vessels that your signal has been seen by seeing them turn towards you. If your signals are sighted from the shore and the right equipment is available to acknowledge them, this will take the form either of an orange smoke signal or of white star rockets fired at intervals of about one minute. Such responses will only normally be available at a manned coastguard station, so the chances of getting an acknowledgement to your distress signal are comparatively small. This can be very frustrating and worrying because, until you have confirmation that your distress signal has been seen, you do not know whether help is going to be sent. You will have sent up a distress signal only if life is in imminent danger, so any form of acknowledgement will be very reassuring.

Therefore, if you are out at sea and you see or hear someone else's distress signal, even if you don't have the prescribed signals to hand with which to acknowledge it, at least flash a light or wave a flag, anything to indicate to those on board that their signal has been noticed and that you are coming to the rescue. This will not only give them reassurance, it will also enable them to prepare themselves mentally and physically for a rescue operation.

Radio

Radio has revolutionised the sending of distress signals. The great advantage of radio is that you can not only indicate that you are in trouble, you can also give your position and details of the problem so that the appropriate rescue facilities can be sent. Even more advantageous is the fact that it can extend the range of your call for help beyond the horizon. With certain types of radio, the range can extend for several hundred miles or more. Via radio, the distress signal can also be properly acknowledged, and the continuous link which radio provides enables the rescuers to give reassurance and to let you know how far away they are and when rescue can be expected. It also allows the actual rescue procedure to be discussed so that everyone involved is familiar with what is going to happen. This can greatly expedite the rescue.

VHF Radio

The history of using radio to signal distress goes right back to the Titanic disaster in 1912. But, as far as yachts are concerned, it has only generally been available for the last ten years, since the prolific expansion in the use of VHF (very high frequency) radios. The VHF radio on most yachts will have a range of between sixteen and fifty kilometres (ten and thirty miles), a range which is more than adequate for most coastal regions, where a shore radio station or another vessel can be expected to be within radio range.

We shall look at actual radio distress signalling procedures later in this chapter. At this stage it is vital to know that the radio is your primary lifeline in any emergency. Any response is likely to be much quicker and, because the system enables information to be passed to and fro, the quality of the rescue operation is likely to be much higher.

MF Radio

Radios operating on medium frequencies (MF) are fitted to many yachts which undertake a more adventurous itinerary and which operate further offshore, outside the normal range of VHF coverage. MF radios have their own distress and calling frequency, on 2182kHz, to which every other vessel and shore station should be tuned. The type of MF radio fitted to most yachts will have a range of up to 320 kilometres (200 miles), which is generally adequate for most cruising yachtsmen, except the blue-water sailor. The procedures for indicating distress are the same as those with the VHF radio.

HF Radio

The type of radio which suits the requirements of the ocean-going sailor, but is also being increasingly fitted to many larger yachts operating in coastal waters, is the high-frequency (HF) radio. HF radios can have a trans-ocean range, given the right atmospheric conditions. HF radio has no specific frequency allocated to distress signalling, although a Mayday call on the working frequency of any of the coastal radio stations will usually draw immediate attention to your predicament. If it is available on your radio, the radio telegraphy distress frequency of 500kHz may also produce results – if you can cut through the Morse Code transmissions for which this frequency is specifically allocated.

In the past, most of the problems associated with radio transmissions on the high-frequency waveband have tended to be related to the uncertainty of the communications. This is particularly true for yachts, which have comparatively low-powered transmitters battling for air time with the powerful transmitters of large ships. Anyone with experience of working with these frequencies will know that it can sometimes take half an hour or more to get through. Another problem is that transmitting and receiving functions are on different frequencies, so it is probable that only shore stations will be listening on the frequency you transmit on, not other ships in the vicinity.

Satellite Communications

This uncertainty with HF radios has led to the development of satellite communication, and there seems little doubt that, in time, all blue-water yacht communications will be via satellite. This medium may even eventually take over some of the work being done on medium-frequency transmitters as well. Although currently prohibitively expensive to most yachtsmen, satellite communication is a rapidly developing area. It is anticipated that the cost of the equipment and antenna will reduce considerably over the next few years to the point where it should become an affordable proposition for yachts. Already the Standard C terminals, which handle telex only, use yacht-sized antennae, and the below-decks equipment is comparatively cheap. Available imminently is the Standard M terminal, which will offer voice, fax and telex communication, using a much smaller dome antenna than the current Standard A terminal. This equipment will be suitable for yachts over nine metres (thirty feet) in length, although the cost, both of the equipment and the transmissions, may prove a limiting factor for routine communications. However, with a virtual 100 per cent chance of getting through, they will be ideal for the free distress transmissions.

Quite apart from these advantages of satellite communication, there is also a very positive safety aspect. All equipment is required to have a single- or double-digit code which will automatically transmit a distress signal. This has priority over other traffic and will automatically be routed to the appropriate ground station where, communication established, the necessary search and rescue vehicles will be activated. The signal can also be retransmitted to vessels in the area of the distress to alert them to the situation. If for any reason it is not possible to establish voice communication between the stricken vessel and the shore station, the distress signal will include a special code to indicate the vessel's name.

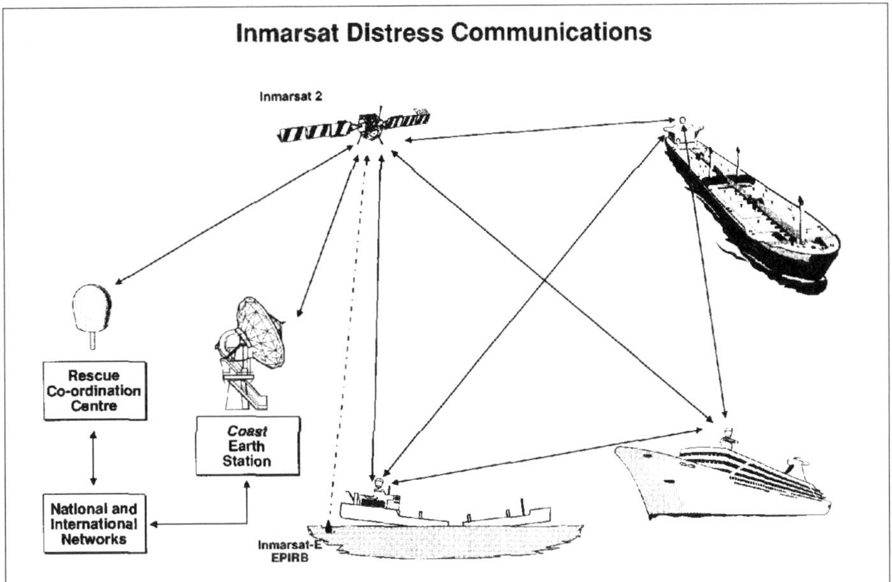

GMDSS

The advent of satellite communication has been largely responsible for the development of the Global Maritime Distress Safety System (GMDSS). This is a system, developed in co-operation with the International Maritime Organisation (IMO), which uses the Inmarsat satellites in conjunction with those operated as part of the Cospas/Sarsat system. These two independent satellite systems between them provide worldwide coverage, although there is reduced coverage in the Arctic and Antarctic regions. Inmarsat satellites pick up distress signals transmitted over satellite communication links as well as EPIRB signals on 406MHz. The Cospas/Sarsat satellites are specifically aimed at picking up EPIRB signals on all the recognised frequencies. The GMDSS system is fully integrated and also involves coastal radio stations operating on HF, MF and VHF radio links. For the first time, there is a fully integrated distress system which, in theory at least, will provide a much better chance of distress signals being received by the appropriate authorities and rescue action being initiated.

As far as yachts are concerned, the GMDSS uses the existing radio services and facilities, and its main function has been to integrate these into a worldwide system. Because of the different requirements, the world is divided up into four different types of region:

Area 1 — The area covered by VHF coastal radio stations which provide Digital Selective Calling (DSC) alerting.

Area 2 — The area covered by MF coastal radio stations providing continuous availability of DSC alerting.

Area 3 — The area covered by the Inmarsat geostationary satellites providing for continuous availability of alerting, but excluding Areas 1 and 2.

Area 4 — The area outside Areas 1, 2 and 3, mainly comprising the extreme polar regions.

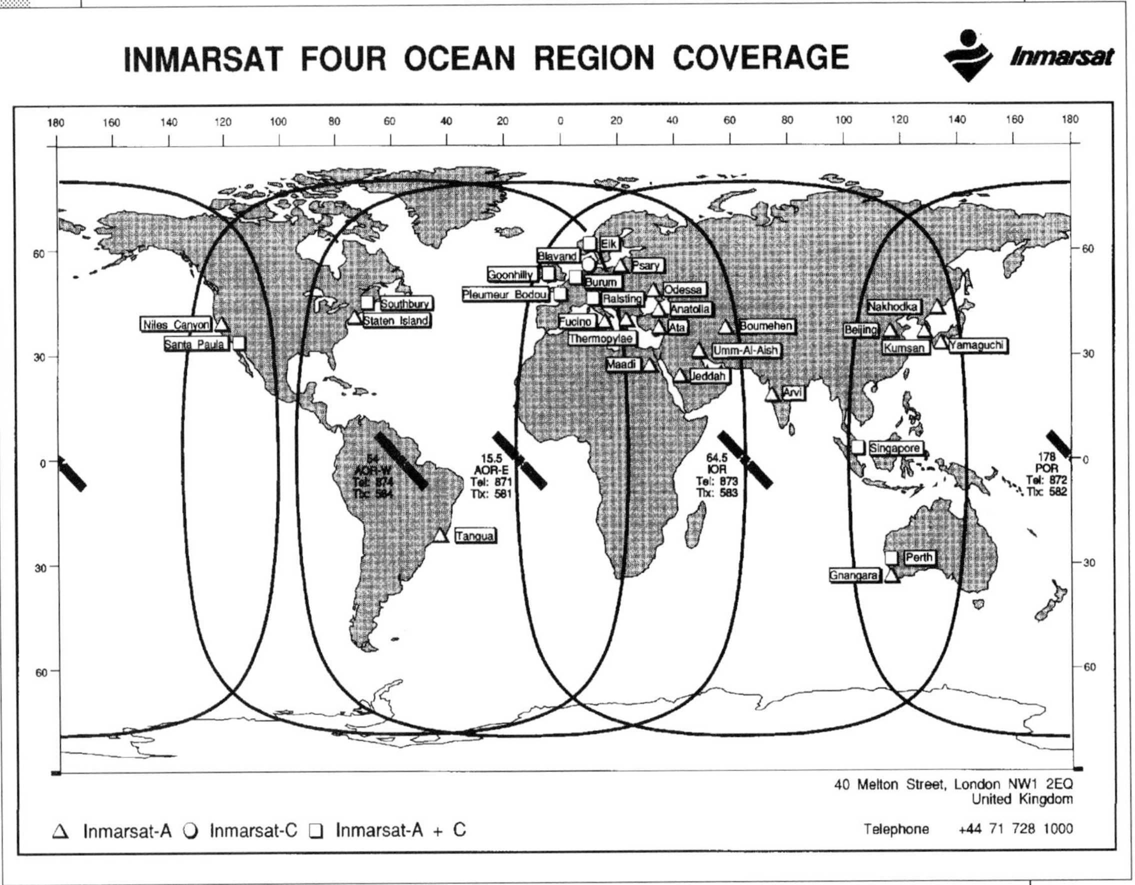

INMARSAT FOUR OCEAN REGION COVERAGE Inmarsat

54 AOR-W Tel: 874 Tlx: 584
15.5 AOR-E Tel: 871 Tlx: 581
64.5 IOR Tel: 873 Tlx: 583
178 POR Tel: 872 Tlx: 582

40 Melton Street, London NW1 2EQ
United Kingdom

△ Inmarsat-A ○ Inmarsat-C □ Inmarsat-A + C

Telephone +44 71 728 1000

The coverage provided by the Inmarsat satellite communications system and the corresponding earth stations which relay distress messages.

GMDSS Standard Requirements

Although GMDSS is primarily aimed at larger ships, and is mandatory for ships over 300 gross tonnage which have to carry a minimum installation of equipment, yachts should be aware of the requirements of this service and, as far as is practicable, should be equipped to the minimum standards for the area in which they operate, as follows:

1 VHF installation capable of transmitting and receiving DSC on Channel 70 and radiotelephony on Channels 6, 13, and 16.

2 Equipment able to maintain continuous DSC watch on VHF Channel 70.

3 Radar transponder operating in the 9GHz band.

4 Receiver capable of receiving international Navtex service broadcasts, if the ship operates in any area where Navtex is provided.

5 Facility for reception of maritime safety information by the Inmarsat enhanced group call system (International SafetyNET TM Service) if on voyages in areas of Inmarsat coverage where Navtex is not provided.

6 Satellite emergency position-indicating radio beacon (EPIRB) capable of being manually activated and of floating free and activating automatically (406MHz Cospas/Sarsat or Inmarsat-E).

Additional Requirements for Sea Area A1

1 The VHF installation shall be capable of general radio communications using telephony.

2 (Optionally) a float-free EPIRB capable of transmitting a distress alert using DSC on VHF Channel 70 in lieu of a satellite EPIRB.

3 Another approved installation capable of initiating the transmission of a distress alert from the navigating position, either by: (1) VHF using DSC. (2) manual activation of an EPIRB. (3) MF using DSC. (4) HF using DSC. (5) an Inmarsat ship earth station.

Additional requirements for Sea Areas A1 and A2

1 An MF installation capable of telephony on 2182kHz and DSC on 2187.5kHz.

2 Equipment capable of maintaining continuous DSC watch of 2187.5kHz.

3 Equipment capable of general radio communications on working frequencies in the MF band 1605–4000kHz, or an Inmarsat ship earth station.

4 Another approved means of initiating the transmission of distress alerts from the navigating position by radio service other than MF either by: (1) manual activation of a satellite EPIRB. (2) HF using DSC. (3) Inmarsat ship earth station.

Additional Requirements for Sea Areas A1, A2 and A3 (within Inmarsat coverage area)

1 MF installation capable of telephony on 2182kHz and DSC on 2187.5kHz.

2 Equipment capable of maintaining continuous DSC watch on 2187.5kHz.

3 Inmarsat-A or Inmarsat-C (Class 2) ship earth station, or an HF radio installation as required for Sea Area A4.

4 Facilities must include at least two of the following radio systems for transmitting the distress alert from the navigating position: (1) Inmarsat ship earth station (Inmarsat-A or Inmarsat-C). (2) Manual activation of a satellite EPIRB. (3) HF radio installation.

Additional Requirements for Sea Area A4 (beyond Inmarsat coverage)

1 MF/HF radio installation capable of transmitting and receiving on all distress and safety frequencies in the band 1605–27500kHz using DSC, telephony, and direct printing. It shall also be capable of general communications using telephony or direct printing in the band 1605–27500kHz.

2 Equipment capable of selecting any of the distress and safety DSC frequencies in the band 4000–27500kHz and maintaining DSC watch simultaneously on 2187.5kHz, 8414.5kHz and at least one additional distress and safety DSC frequency in the band.

3 Capability to initiate a distress alert from the navigating position through the polar orbiting satellite system on 406MHz (manual activation of 406MHz satellite EPIRB).

Of this array of equipment, most yachts will have the VHF installation required even if they do not have the DSC to match. A Navtex receiver is certainly a useful addition to a yacht's battery of electronic equipment. It obviates the need to listen out for warnings of gales and other navigational hazards because these are automatically printed out. It also automatically receives all distress messages. However, its cost is probably beyond the means of many yacht owners and it is unlikely to be very high on their list of equipment priorities when it only alerts them to other vessels in distress.

EPIRB Equipment

An EPIRB should certainly be somewhere near the top of the list of desirable safety equipment. The radar transponder on the IMO list is a piece of equipment for making liferafts detectable at extended ranges on the radars of searching ships.

Minimum Equipment for Yachts

So, for yachts operating mainly in inshore waters, the VHF and an EPIRB should be considered the minimum, with a Navtex receiver a useful addition. If you go outside this area and further from land, then an MF radio should be added to the list, to increase the range at which you can send distress signals. For open-ocean sailing, then either an HF radio or a satcom should be added. Both MF and HF radios must be fitted with a facility for automatically transmitting a distress signal. Simply by pressing a single button, a two-tone signal will be continuously transmitted, to be picked up by other vessels or shore stations. If they can then take a bearing of the transmission, the vessel's position can at least be estimated, if not pinpointed exactly.

EPIRBs

An EPIRB works perfectly well when floating and the light aids detection at night.

A 406 EPIRB shown here with a stowage box which can be mounted vertically or horizontally. Incorporated into the securing strap is a hydrostatic release which will allow the EPIRB to float free at a depth of around three metres and start transmitting automatically. The case offers good protection at sea, but would need to be stowed away in harbour to reduce the temptation to thieves.

To some extent, EPIRBs perform a similar function but, unlike the radios on board, the EPIRB is a fully self-contained unit which can transmit a distress signal on two or more frequencies. EPIRBs were originally developed for aircraft use and still transmit only on the aircraft distress frequencies of 121.5MHz or 243MHz.

When first introduced for marine use, they relied on the distress signal being received by overflying aircraft. However, they can now be detected by Cospas/Sarsat satellites, which gives much more reliable coverage. These satellites operate on a low polar orbit, so there can be a delay in receiving the distress signal if the satellite is not in view of both the distress transmission and its monitoring station at the same time. In this case, any distress transmission has to be saved until the monitoring station comes into view, when it can be informed. This could delay the transmission of a distress signal by an hour or two, but it does at least mean it is definitely detected when it might otherwise go unheard. The advantage of these systems is that the vessel's position can also be calculated to within about five kilometres (three miles), so that even if there is no other form of communication, the distress alert will be received and action can be focussed upon the approximate position.

The latest type of EPIRB, and the one which eventually all shipping will use, operates on 406MHz. This gives much greater efficiency, although equipment is more expensive. A further type of EPIRB operates on the L-band at 1.5GHz, and is designed to operate in conjunction with the Inmarsat satellites. Such EPIRBs do not provide any position information, although they can be linked to a GPS receiver to give this information. Many of the 406MHz type of EPIRBs not only transmit the distress signal, they also transmit a coded signal which allows the vessel to be identified by name. This, together with the approximate position, can help to ensure that not only will help be sent, but it will, as far as possible, be the right type of help for the particular vessel.

Yacht EPIRB

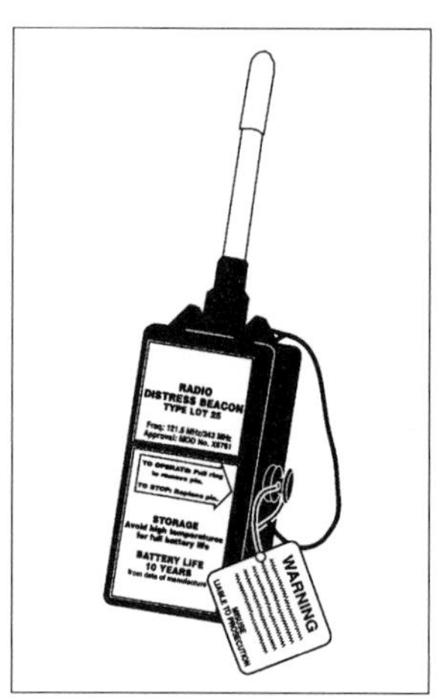

A typical small EPIRB which is fully waterproof and will work in the liferaft or even in the water. These small EPIRBs only operate on 121.5 and 243MHz.

The advantage of EPIRBs is that they can not only be activated on board the mother craft when it gets into trouble, they can also be taken with you if you have take to the liferaft. Thus a continuous signal can be sent out. Most EPIRBs have a life of at least forty-eight hours, which should give plenty of time for search and rescue units to home in on the signal. EPIRBs are mainly for manual operation, but a modern type is also designed to float free and automatically transmit a distress signal, should the mother vessel sink very rapidly.

The type of EPIRB used on most yachts is

likely to be the cheap and compact version which operates on 121.5 or 243MHz. These are now virtually pocket-sized and cost in the region of £200. The larger 406 EPIRBs can be five times this price, take up more space and are certainly less suited to the yacht environment, but for operating in offshore waters, may be considered a necessary addition to the vessel's equipment.

Radar Transponders
Before we go on to look at how to use the various types of emergency equipment, it is worth considering the other GMDSS requirement, the radar transponder. This is normally designed to be fitted to a liferaft and is triggered by an incoming radar signal from a rescue ship. It will re-transmit the signal in a coded form, which will show up on the vessel's radar as a clearly identifiable signal pinpointing the location of the liferaft or the vessel in distress. This could speed up rescue because liferafts normally present a very poor radar target, as does a small yacht. The value of such equipment must depend to a certain extent on how accurately the original position of the distress was known. These radar transponders are comparatively expensive to carry for this limited search and rescue application, but you have to balance this against the fact that, if you are out there in a liferaft, they could be a valuable means of bringing help to you quickly. An EPIRB will perform much the same function, provided the rescue vessel or helicopter is equipped with a VHF direction finder.

Sea-Marshall Man-Overboard Alarm

The Sea-Marshall man-overboard alarm is a pocket-sized unit which can initiate a distress signal. The signal can be picked up by equipment on board either as a simple alarm warning, or when combined with a directional antenna, as a bearing to the casualty. Lifeboats and SAR helicopters can also home in on the signal.

Use of Emergency Signalling Equipment
So, you have a wide variety of methods by which to indicate that you are in trouble. Your approach will obviously depend on what you have on board and what your predicament is.

Radio Emergency Signalling

In most cases you will need nothing more than a VHF radio. The big advantage of radio is that not only can you alert other vessels and shore stations to your difficulties, you can also tell them your position, the exact nature of the problem and the number of people on board. Furthermore, the station receiving your signal can acknowledge it, letting you know that it has been received, what help is being sent, and when you might expect it. This will be most reassuring in a situation which may have got out of control, and will go a long way to creating the right sort of mental attitude which, in turn, will help to ensure your survival.

Mayday

Using the radio to send a distress message, and this applies whether it is VHF, MF or HF, does require a degree of discipline. For best results you should follow the prescribed format, as follows:

MAYDAY, MAYDAY, MAYDAY,

THIS IS

YACHT......., YACHT......., YACHT.......
(substitute the vessel's name here)

MAYDAY,

YACHT.......

Then give the position, which can be a bearing and distance, a latitude and longitude, or simply an approximate location, such as 'close to such and such a buoy', whichever is the easiest to establish. After position, give the nature of the problem and the number of people on board, ending with Over to invite replies.

Let us analyse this format. The Mayday and name of the yacht are given first to alert other stations, and should be sufficient to break through any traffic already on Channel 16. Of the remaining information, you give your position first, just in case your radio stops at this stage, so rescuers will at least know where to look. Finally, you give the nature of the distress and the number of people on board, the latter so that a search can be called off with confidence if that number of people have been rescued. It is all very straightforward and logical, and it works, provided Channel 16 is kept reasonably clear. A distress message is one sent only when there is grave or imminent danger, ie where lives are, or could be, at risk.

Pan Pan

There is an alternative, called an urgency situation, which may not be life-threatening but is serious enough to warrant a warning to other shipping or to request less urgent help, as perhaps in a non-life-threatening medical emergency. This signal uses much the same format, but instead of Mayday it is preceded by Pan Pan, repeated three times.

Securité

You will also come across another type of message which is preceded by the word Security (actually the French word *securité*). This is used for gale and navigation warnings and will only come from shore stations. Other calls from shore stations, for, say, weather forecasts and traffic lists, will be preceded by a call of All Ships.

Mayday and Pan calls should be repeated at frequent intervals until you receive an acknowledgement, but do leave time in between the calls for other stations to reply. When you are desperate to get your call across, it is tempting just to keep calling, but you must discipline yourself to allow time for a reply.

With luck, you will have broadcast a distress signal before you were forced to abandon ship. Normally, once you leave the mother vessel you leave your radio behind. This is where portable VHF radios come into their own. If you have one on board, you should, of course, take it with you when you abandon ship. A portable VHF will enable you to maintain communications over, at least, a limited range, which can be vital in helping rescuers find you and in helping the rescue operation itself. It will enable you to discuss with the rescuers exactly what is going to take place, and this avoids mistakes being made at a critical stage of the rescue operation.

If you also have an EPIRB on board, it is a good idea to activate this as a secondary distress signal. In the early stages you cannot be sure that your radioed distress message is getting through. Take the EPIRB into the liferaft with you, too, because it will continue to transmit its automatic signal, which can help location. You will not get any acknowledgement

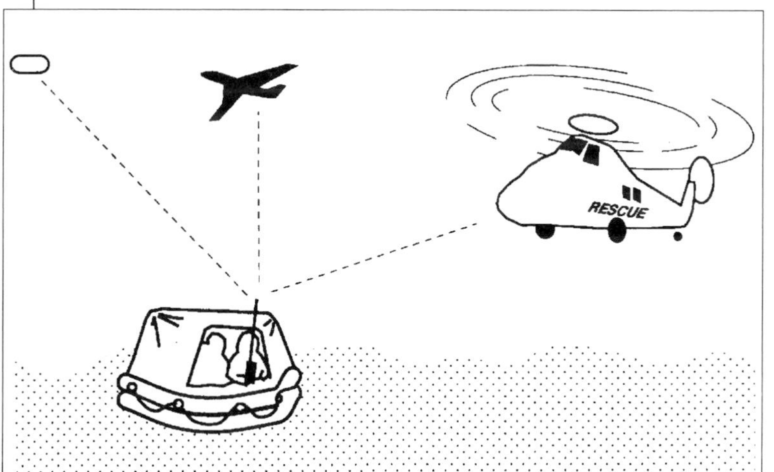

An EPIRB used from a liferaft can transmit a signal which is picked up by the Cospas Sarsat satellite and passing aircraft. Rescue helicopters can home in on the signal.

that the EPIRB signal has been received until you see the search vessels, but you can be reasonably certain that it will be detected by either an aircraft or a satellite. Equally important is the fact that an aircraft or a lifeboat can actually home in on the continuous signal.

If for any reason the radio on board is not working, perhaps because you have suffered an electrical fire, then a portable VHF radio can provide a valuable back-up. The portable VHF should preferably be of the waterproof type, or at least be in a watertight plastic container. A portable VHF radio should therefore come somewhere near the top of your list of essential emergency equipment.

Signalling with Flares

Without a working radio, to get your distress message across you would have to resort to the visual or sound signals mentioned earlier with their limited range and limited number, which will mean that you would have to be much more careful about their use. There is no doubt that, of these, the best signals to use in the first instance are the parachute distress flares because of their greater range and superior visibility.

However, you must remember that you have only a limited supply of these parachute flares, probably six at most, and nothing will be gained, and much possibly lost, by firing them all off in quick succession in the hope that one of them will be seen. Fire one off and then wait up to a quarter of an hour before firing the next one. You might fire, say, four off in this way, but always try and keep at least a couple back in case you see a passing ship or drift closer to land, where there is a better chance of your flares being seen. When you get down to your last two flares, use them only when there is a positive chance that they will be seen. It will be hard to resist the temptation to fire off flares continually, because it gives you something positive to do, and you always feel better when you feel you have done something which will apparently hasten your rescue.

If you do use up all the parachute flares, there are the hand-held flares and the smoke signals to turn to. In daylight, smoke signals are preferable because the hand-held flares will be effective day or night and they can play a vital role in guiding a rescue vessel or aircraft to your position when you know that they are on their way.

If you have to take to the liferaft, take all the remaining flares and smoke floats with you, if you possibly can. A liferaft is a tiny object at sea, and anything you can do heighten its detectability will be to your advantage. Remember, though, that pyrotechnics used from a liferaft can be extremely dangerous, so any such operations should be carried out on the lee side of the liferaft and as far away from the raft as you can possibly manage.

Use of Other Audible and Visual Signals

As for the rest of the audible and visual distress signals, your use of these will depend on the circumstances. Most of them are only useful if there are other craft in the vicinity because of their limited range and effectiveness. As mentioned previously, you may find such signals are ignored by passing vessels because they are not understood. So, if you possibly can, try and go for the more common ones which obviously indicate distress.

Anticipating Rescue Efforts

Although you might be in great difficulties, you must try and visualise what is happening at the other end. Obviously, if you can make radio contact, you will have a pretty good idea of what is going on and what is going to happen. If your VHF battery is failing, let the people on shore know so that if they cannot raise you, they will know that it is probably the radio, not some more alarming drama taking place. The same applies if you take a portable VHF radio into the liferaft. Use it sparingly, particularly for transmitting, as this uses a great deal more battery power than merely listening: try and keep your transmissions as short and sharp as possible and stick to essentials. This will also help the rescuers to understand what is going on. Provided you follow these rules, radio links during the rescue operation should be reasonably straightforward and extremely helpful.

When it comes to using visual distress signals, anticipation is much more important, and you must try and view the situation through the rescuers' eyes. For instance, if you wish to attract the attention of a passing vessel by firing a flare, look to see where the sun is in relation to the vessel. If the sun is immediately behind you, it will be right in the eyes of those on the approaching vessel, and they may not be able to see a distress flare. In this situation, it will probably pay to wait for five minutes or so until the angle of the sun and the craft involved has changed and there will probably be a much better chance of your flare being seen. The same applies when there is partial cloud. If you wait until the sun has gone behind the clouds, there will be a much better chance of a flare being seen. If you are using smoke, this will be much more visible in bright sunlight. This is the sort of anticipation you will need to make best use of the equipment you have available.

Priority of Emergency-Signalling Equipment

If you are in trouble at sea, the important thing is to let someone else know of your predicament. Without this basic information, it is impossible for anyone to help you, although you could just be lucky enough to be spotted by a passing vessel. But the aim should be to take the element of luck out of the situation. There is no doubt that electronics, in the form of radios and EPIRBs, provide by far the best means of indicating that you are in trouble. You should therefore concentrate your resources on these means. Whilst it is mandatory, or at least strongly recommended, that you carry flares, and there is no denying the value of these in extreme situations, it is the radio that can provide immediate and positive communication of your problems and also acknowledgement that the signal has been received. So, your VHF installation has a much more significant role to play than just arranging a berth in a marina.

Its vital role in safety and survival means that the radio installation should be of the highest standard, and there is a lot to be said for having an alternative circuit with a separate battery to supply the radio if the primary circuit fails. There should also be provision for an emergency antenna, particularly on sailing craft where the emergency could well be created by the mast itself coming down, complete with the VHF antenna. An emergency antenna, which can be clipped to a rail or to the stump of the mast, will restore communication and could therefore make all the difference between the success or failure of the search and rescue.

As a back-up for the primary VHF radio, portable VHF radios have a lot to commend them. Apart from its functional use for communicating with your tender when it is going ashore, the portable VHF can be taken into the liferaft if you have to abandon ship. A waterproof portable VHF radio is even better, because this can then still be used if you find yourself in the water without a liferaft. If you occasionally go out of VHF range, then an EPIRB should certainly be considered as an addition to the equipment on board, because it will provide your only means of indicating distress out in the open sea, although it should be said that in most coastal waters there is enough shipping to provide a response to a VHF radio distress call even if you are some distance from land. If you regularly go far away from land, you should consider an MF radio as an essential, preferably backed up by a VHF and an EPIRB.

The GMDSS requirements suggest that you should have, at the very least, a VHF and an EPIRB on board. If you cannot afford both, and you stick to inshore waters, a portable VHF would be a more useful and practical alternative.

For yachts, the GMDSS requirements do not at present have the force of law, and there is no suggestion that this situation is likely change. The standards set are probably excessive, given the types of voyages made, and would certainly push up considerably expenditure on safety and survival equipment, perhaps to what might be considered an unacceptable level. For most yachts, the combination of a VHF radio, a portable VHF and/or an EPIRB, and a proper complement of distress flares, is probably the best way to ensure that, if you do get into trouble, you can let somebody else know and get the help you need.

5 Search and Rescue

When you fire off a distress signal or broadcast a Mayday, the response may come from one or more of a number of sources. Having some idea of how search and rescue services operate can be important to the success of a rescue. You need to anticipate the likely reaction to your distress signals and the sort of resources which may come to your aid.

The first point of contact in any rescue operation is other vessels in the vicinity. Under international maritime law, every vessel is under an obligation to go to the assistance of any other which is indicating that it is in distress, provided that it doesn't compromise its own safety in so doing. These days, coastal waters search and rescue operations are being left more and more to the professionals – the lifeboat and helicopter services – because they are better equipped to do the job. That said, the first source of help is still other vessels in the vicinity, simply because they can probably get to the casualty before the rescue services.

If you are the casualty, you have a certain choice in the matter of who rescues you. As suggested, all vessels in the area should offer their services and help and, in theory at least, it is up to you to choose the one which seems most appropriate to your circumstances. If you find yourself in the water, you are not going to be in much of a position to choose, and you will be grateful for whatever comes along. Even in a liferaft you would probably welcome any assistance from any vessel to get you out of your predicament. The choice of a rescuer is only really likely when you are still on board your yacht in deteriorating conditions; perhaps the mast has come down but the danger is not imminent. Here there can be an element of choice because you have some time on your side.

The problem is that very few craft today are equipped to carry out rescue operations efficiently. Should one yacht try to come alongside another in a seaway, the result could be serious damage to both. This could put both craft and crews at risk and compound the situation rather than alleviate it. A rugged fishing boat might be more appropriate to the task, and whilst it may damage the casualty, this may not be particularly serious provided the crew is taken off. In many rescue situations, the best solution to the problem is to tow the casualty into harbour, and here other craft can help considerably, particularly fishing boats and some motor yachts, although a lifeboat is best equipped for this task if you can afford to wait for one to reach you.

If you are faced with a tow into harbour, you might be haunted by the possibility of a salvage claim. We will look at this factor a bit later on in this chapter, but if the situation was serious enough for you to send a distress signal, then worries about salvage should not really enter into your calculations. Saving the lives of your crew should be your prime consideration. Whilst there is always a reluctance to see your property damaged or lost, you should try and not let this influence your judgement about rescue.

Offshore Waters

Out in the open ocean away from land, other vessels will be your primary means of salvation. Search and rescue helicopters can operate up to 200 nautical miles from the shore these days, and beyond that range searching aircraft may be able to locate you. Aircraft may not be able to offer much in the way of practical assistance, but they can find you and that is the essential part of the rescue operation. But the most likely vessels to come to your aid will be ships of one sort or another, and rescue by a large ship can be a very difficult and sometimes dangerous undertaking. The problem is, of course, that these ships are often totally unsuited for rescue work, and the disparity in size between an ocean-going ship and a yacht can be make the operation extremely hazardous.

There is also a great reluctance in shipping circles to lower a lifeboat to go to the assistance of a yacht in trouble. Ships' lifeboats tend to be designed for a one-way trip and the recovery of a lifeboat at sea can itself be a difficult and dangerous operation. Few ships have crews who have experience of operating their lifeboats at sea, which means that rescue by ship is likely to be effected by the ship itself coming alongside the yacht. This requires seamanship of a high order, and careful preparation on both sides to ensure that the operation goes as smoothly as possible. For the occupants of the yacht, assuming it is disabled, seeing a large ship trying to manoeuvre alongside can be a very frightening experience, and there is the real risk of being run down if the ship's captain gets it wrong. Then there is the problem of just getting on board. A modern container ship could have a freeboard of over ten metres, which can be an impossible height to climb when you are tired and exhausted.

Rescue by ship, then, is not something to be undertaken lightly, but you may have little choice. If you are faced with this situation, it is vital that you discuss the whole operation in great detail with the captain of the rescue ship if the operation is to be successful. You may feel reluctant to suggest courses of action to the captain, but he will almost certainly be just as nervous as you are. Ships' captains generally have little practical experience of rescue work and will probably welcome any suggestions you can offer.

The best approach to this type of rescue is for the ship to stop to windward of the casualty and then let the wind blow the ship down on to it. This avoids the terrifying 'head on' approach. If the ship is say, fifty or 100 metres to windward, it will both shelter the yacht from the wind and will gradually drift downwind, alongside the yacht. It is essential that the ship has suitably sized ropes ready to pass to the yacht – to prevent the yacht drifting ahead or astern once it is alongside; as it would be impossible for the yacht to throw ropes up on to the deck of the ship. The one thing which must be avoided at all costs is the yacht getting close to the stern of the ship. Not only is there an overhang which could cause the yacht to capsize or be crushed, but the ship's propeller is obviously an added danger. The ropes passed to the yacht play a vital role in holding it alongside, and in preventing it from moving forward or aft. Having the yacht moored alongside also leaves the captain of the ship free to use the engines.

There is still, however, the problem of transferring the crew on to the deck of the ship. The pilot ladder is probably the safest way to do this, but climbing the pilot ladder up the side of the ship, even for a short distance, requires considerable physical strength. You will also need to be careful that none of the crew get crushed between the yacht and the ship as the yacht rises and falls in the waves. The secret here is to jump on to the ladder when the yacht is at the top of its rise, so that it then drops away, giving the climber a few seconds to get clear before it rises again. You will probably be able to manage to climb up the ship's side if the freeboard is three or four metres, but anything more than this can be a very daunting propect for a tired crewmember. Larger ships tend to have electric pilot hoists: you merely climb the first few feet of the ladder, to get clear of the yacht, and then hold on whilst the hoist is lifted and step on board at deck level. Another option is to be lifted on to the ship by crane or derrick, but this should only really be considered if nothing else seems to be working. Swinging on the end of a wire from a ship can be an unpleasant and dangerous experience, particularly if the mast of the yacht is still standing when there is a risk of getting tangled up in the rigging or of being struck by the swinging mast.

When you look at the many problems attendant upon getting the crew to safety, you begin to see the need for careful planning before coming alongside and you can see why this type of rescue at sea is fraught with difficulties. The situation is even worse if you are sitting in your liferaft. The drift of the liferaft may make it even more difficult for the ship to get close enough to pull it alongside. One option is for the ship to fire its line-throwing gun to make the initial contact, but this must be done with considerable care. Being on the receiving end of a rocket trailing a rope is not a pleasant experience, and it is very hard to get the line from a rocket gun to pass close to a tiny liferaft. The best means of effecting a rescue from a liferaft is for the ship to launch its lifeboat, but this is only likely to be contemplated if weather conditions are reasonable and no other solution seems to be available.

The limited rescue facilities and difficult conditions out in the open ocean demonstrate the need for a high level of self-sufficiency if you plan to make open ocean passages. There is a great deal of luck to being rescued in mid-ocean. Firstly, there is the difficulty of indicating that you are in distress; this can only be done by radio unless you happen to come within range of a passing ship when distress flares could be used. If you get your radio message across, what usually happens is that the US-based AMVER system comes into action. This is a voluntary system whereby ships report their position, speed and course every twenty-four hours. The information thus obtained is fed into a computer, so that whenever a distress message is received the nearest available vessel can be quickly contacted. The problem is that the suitability of the selected ship for rescue work is not taken into account, so you may find anything from a 275 metre long container ship to a 200,000 ton tanker coming to your rescue. Since you have little choice in the type of rescue ship sent, it is essential to be sure that there is really no other option before you summon this kind of assistance. Remember that the risks involved in being rescued in mid-ocean could be just as great as in not being rescued at all.

Inshore Waters

Fortunately, in inshore waters, where most casualties occur, there is a much wider range of rescue facilities, many of which, like lifeboats and helicopters, are dedicated solely to the task. The very number of rescue services available creates in Britain a need for co-ordination, and this role is handled by HM Coastguard.

The coastguard service is responsible for initiating and co-ordinating all civil maritime search and rescue operations around the United Kingdom and into the eastern Atlantic as far as 30°W. The United Kingdom coast is divided into six maritime search and rescue regions, each with a maritime rescue co-ordination centre. The centres are based at Aberdeen, Great Yarmouth, Dover, Falmouth, Swansea and the Clyde. Each region is divided up into districts, each of which has staffed rescue and watch stations controlled by a maritime rescue sub-centre.

The days of a visual lookout from coastguard stations are fast disappearing, although visual watch is still maintained at some stations in certain weather conditions. These days the main means of watch-keeping are VHF Channel 16 and 2182kHz MF. These radio links are combined with a network of telephone, telex and fax links which enable the coastguard station to act as a communication centre, broadcasting to and receiving information from vessels at sea and, where necessary, passing this on to the appropriate rescue authorities. The network operated by the coastguard ensures that every part of the coastline has VHF coverage, although radio links could be difficult in areas where there are high cliffs and deep inlets which prevent the line-of-sight requirements for VHF communication from being maintained. The coastguard does operate a few inshore rescue boats in selected areas, but in general its role is one of co-ordination.

It also has a responsibility for beach and cliff rescue, and, apart from co-ordinating a search and rescue operation, it can, if necessary, send out beach patrols in case there is a report of a casualty being washed ashore. Cliff rescue operations tend in the main to revolve around people who have fallen over cliffs or who have become trapped, but cliff rescue parties can also play a vital role in rescuing survivors from yachts which have blown or drifted on shore.

In addition to the vital co-ordinating role in search and rescue, the coastguard has a monitoring role. For example, you can record your passage details with the coastguard as you leave harbour. They will want to know whether your yacht is power or sail, the number of people on board, the colour of the yacht and where it is bound. This information is logged so that, in the event of your yacht becoming overdue, there is some indication of where to start a search. If you do record details of your passage in this way, it is equally important to let the coastguard know that you have arrived safely at your destination port to avoid unnecessary concern that you are still at sea and have a problem. However non-reporting of arrival is fairly common, so it is unlikely that a search and rescue operation will be initiated immediately. It is more likely that a check will be made at your destination marina or port and at other ports along the way before a full-scale search and rescue operation is put in hand.

The coastguard may be informed of emergency situations by a wide variety of sources. Obviously, it will pick up distress messages from yachts at sea transmitted over VHF, but it is also part of the 999 system, so any person on shore seeing a vessel in apparent distress can dial 999 and ask for 'Coastguard'. At sea, you could contact the coastguard in the same way using a mobile phone, but the VHF radio link is recommended. If you see a distress signal at sea, in addition to providing help and support to the casualty, you should inform the coastguard by radio so that back-up search and rescue activities can be initiated.

Information can also reach the coastguard via coast radio stations. They are a more likely source of information about casualties further out at sea, outside VHF range. The Maritime Rescue Co-ordination Centre at Falmouth is the one responsible for much of the Atlantic area, and information passed by radio will end up at this centre, which will then co-ordinate the search and rescue requirements.

When information about a vessel in distress is received by the coastguard, it will pass this on to the appropriate RNLI lifeboat station or to the Royal Navy, Royal Air Force or coastguard helicopter base. It will also broadcast a repeat of the distress message to all ships in the area via the local coast radio station. This will ensure that all vessels in the vicinity of the casualty are aware of the situation and prepared to help, and also will ensure that all other vessels keep off VHF Channel 16 or 2182Khz on MF, leaving these frequencies free for the distress radio requirements.

In addition to helicopters and lifeboats, the coastguard may call upon the services of what are known as 'shore boats' or 'auxiliaries'. These are in fact, private yachts which make themselves and their crews available to the coastguard service. They are usually asked for help in clarifying situations which do not apear to justify lifeboat or helicopter call-out but of which the shore-based coastguard needs an on-the-spot assessment before deciding on a suitable course of action.

In some areas there are also what might be termed 'private rescue organisations', such as exists in the Solent. These have invariably been set up in response to specific local requirements and are generally outside the RNLI organisation.

RNLI

Unlike the government-run coastguard, the RNLI is a charitable organisation, supported entirely by voluntary contributions. Its aim is to provide lifeboat coverage around the whole coastline of the United Kingdom and Ireland and to a distance of fifty miles offshore. There are currently around 200 lifeboat stations, about half of which have all-weather lifeboats. The remainder have inflatable or rigid-inflatable lifeboats, designed primarily for inshore work. Many of the latter type of rescue boats are only in service during the summer months, to provide coverage for the greater number of casualties which tend to occur during these months.

The lifeboats are staffed largely by volunteers, although the all-weather lifeboat stations have at least one full-time person to carry out maintenance. In most cases lifeboats can launch within five or ten minutes of a call being received. It is the honorary secretary of the lifeboat who decides whether the lifeboat should respond to a particular emergency, although obviously, advice about launching will be taken from the coastguard. Indeed, the coastguard will usually finish the message about any distress situation by advising launch of the lifeboat.

Lifeboat Design

Lifeboats come in a wide variety of shapes and sizes, to respond to different requirements, but the current trend in lifeboat design is to combine the tried and tested excellent seaworthiness characteristics with higher speeds for a faster response to casualties. This has become the paramount consideration. Most of the all-weather lifeboats now in service with the RNLI have a speed of at least twenty knots, whilst the inflatable and rigid-inflatable lifeboats can reach speeds of thirty knots, giving a response time fast enough to meet the needs of most casualties. Obviously, in extreme sea conditions it is not possible to maintain such speeds, and the lifeboat may be forced to drop down to ten knots or less. However, the combination of speed and seaworthiness found in modern lifeboat design does enable the coxswain to get the best speed in the prevailing conditions and provide the best possible response.

There is no magic about lifeboat design.The hull shape may be designed to provide the optimum combination of seaworthiness and performance, but what ensures the survival of the lifeboat in extreme conditions is that everything on board is designed to keep functioning under the most extreme sea conditions. This is a lesson which many yachtsmen could learn: that lifeboats are designed so that there is the

A United States coastguard vessel powering through sea conditions that would spell disaster for a cruising yacht.

minimum chance any of the components on board failing, which could put the lifeboat at risk. That is the secret of good lifeboat design. It has been refined over many years and is epitomised by the modern lifeboat.

The rigid-inflatable was originally designed for rescue work and, for its size, it still provides one of the most versatile and competent types of craft in the world. All the rigid-inflatables in the RNLI fleet, and all of the all-weather lifeboats, are now self-righting, which gives the crew a much better chance of survival in extreme sea conditions. The smaller D-Class inflatable lifeboats are used for rescue work in more moderate conditions. They are often launched from open beaches rather than operating from harbours.

All lifeboats are equipped with VHF radios, even the small inflatables, so if you are in a distress situation yet can maintain a working radio, this will enable you to liaise with the lifeboat and plan the rescue operation in detail, which will give it a greater chance of success. Unlike the captains of large ships, coxswains of RNLI lifeboats are experienced in rescue work and will therefore be able to make a much better assessment of your situation and optimise the rescue procedure. You can have great confidence in what they propose, rather than having to negotiate, as might be the case with a large ship with a crew inexperienced in rescue work. You should of course make them aware of any particular difficulties there might be on board before they come alongside, such as letting them know if there is debris from a broken mast or boom lying in the water near the boat, or if you have injured people on board. The more complete the information you can pass to the lifeboat, the better and more efficient will be the rescue operation. But you should never hesitate to suggest alternative possibilities if you don't like the rescue methods the lifeboat coxswain is proposing. Although they are professionals, you are the person actually on the spot, and you may be able to see the situation much more clearly and perceive particular difficulties or dangers which they will not be aware of until they come in close.

The RNLI does not claim salvage in any shape or form. The organisation is purely for saving life, not for saving property. In many cases, however, it is obviously expedient to tow a vessel to safety rather than just rescue the occupants, and whilst in this case the RNLI will not make any claim for salvage, the lifeboat crew do, as private individuals, have this option open to them. Some lifeboat stations will exercise this option and you as the casualty will have little choice in the matter because you will be more concerned with being rescued than salvaging your yacht. If you are insured then any salvage claim that might arise will be handled by your insurance company.

If one of the small D-Class inflatables comes to your rescue, there is little prospect of property salvage because these single outboard-powered boats are not suitable for towing operations, except, of course, in the case of sailing dinghies or such like. The rigid-inflatables can tow to a limited extent, whilst the powerful all-weather lifeboats tend to have a good towing capability although, in true RNLI tradition, they are primarily designed and equipped for saving life rather than property.

Air-Sea Rescue

The main alternative to rescue by lifeboat is rescue by helicopter, and in this case there are several organisations which might be involved. The coastguard itself now has a helicopter service for search and rescue work, to fill gaps in the coverage provided the Royal Navy or the Royal Air Force. There is only a limited number of dedicated search and rescue helicopter facilities around the coast. Whilst there is full coverage of the whole coastline, the time taken to reach a casualty in the more remote areas could be up to an hour in certain conditions. In general, however, the helicopter provides a quick, expedient service, partly because the crew are on standby, ready to fly at short notice, and partly because of the speed of the helicopter.

The helicopters used for search and rescue work have an all-weather capability and can also operate at night. They therefore provide a viable rescue service with a capability of operating up to 200 miles from land. At this range, of course, they would have only limited time available at the casualty itself. All search and rescue helicopters have winch-and-wire lifting capability, and the crews have developed this into a fine art. The ability to lift casualties by helicopter in extreme conditions has reduced the risk to lifeboat crews and has also brought rescue in situations which might otherwise have ended in disaster. We will look at the actual techniques of rescue by helicopter later on, but these aircraft are a graphic example of the way modern technology has been able to extend rescue capability.

Searching is obviously an important element in search and rescue, and for this function the helicopter service is supplemented by fixed-wing aircraft. The Royal Air Force operates fixed-wing search aircraft, primarily in a military role, but also in a civil rescue role. These aircraft can drop liferafts to survivors in the water and can direct ships to the rescue point. They are equipped with VHF and MF communication capabilities and their main role is to provide a search capability beyond the range of helicopters and lifeboats in the open ocean.

International Facilities

Some countries operate rescue ships with ocean-going capability. The US Coastguard is a good example of a service which has both inshore lifeboats and offshore patrol craft with a dedicated rescue facility. However, given the extent of ocean sea areas, the chances of one of these rescue ships being in the right place at the right time is remote, so their role tends to be more one of search than rescue. In other parts of the world, rescue ships tend to be associated with fishing fleets operating in a particular area, so that it is a matter of chance whether these rescue ships are available to a yacht in distress.

Most European countries operate search and rescue organisations to provide coverage along their coasts, and there is a large amount of international co-operation in this area. For example, although it is the RNLI which provides lifeboat coverage around the coasts of both Northern Ireland and the Irish Republic, there is a Marine Rescue Co-ordination Centre in the Irish Republic based at Shannon Airport. This is the co-ordination centre for the lifeboats, the Irish Army Air Corps helicopters and the Coast Life Saving Service, which is mainly concerned with beach and cliff rescue. There is no coastguard as such on the Irish coast, but the Irish Lighthouse Service provides communication and co-ordination through radio stations based at the lighthouses.

In France, search and rescue is controlled by the CROSS organisation and has three main areas of operation: one covering the English Channel, one the Bay of Biscay, and one the area of the Northern Brittany coast. There is also a further section covering the Mediterranean coast. The lifeboat service in France is also a voluntary organisation and operates in a manner very similar to the RNLI, with both inshore and all-weather lifeboats located around the coast. Rescue helicopters are operated by the military. In general, the French search and rescue organisation is similar to that in Britain in terms of co-ordination and facilities.

In Belgium, the lifeboats are administered by government organisations and the helicopters are operated by the Belgian Air Force. A sea rescue co-ordination centre is located at Oostende.

In Holland, the coastguard service not only acts as the co-ordinator, but also operates patrol craft. There used to be two separate Dutch lifeboat organisations, but these have now amalgamated and the unified organisation maintains a fleet of lifeboats and inshore lifeboats to provide coverage of all sea areas along the Dutch coast. These lifeboats are supplemented by a search and rescue helicopter base near Den Helder. The heavy concentration of shipping along the Dutch coast and in the river estuaries ensures that the coastline is closely monitored. In addition to the coastguard patrol craft, there are also police patrol craft operating in offshore waters.

The German lifeboat service is unique in operating large lifeboats – up to thirty metres in length – which also carry a daughter boat capable of working in shallow or inshore waters. These powerful, fast lifeboats are operated on a semi-voluntary basis, although there is considerable government support. Like most countries, the helicopter service is operated by the military and there is a Maritime Rescue Co-ordination Centre for search and rescue operations at Bremen.

From this catalogue of search and rescue facilities, it is obvious that, in north-west Europe at least, you will never be too far from professional help. In the Mediterranean region the rescue facilities may be rather sparse – an indication perhaps of the less severe weather conditions experienced in this region. None the less the trend is towards expanding search and rescue facilities and improving co-ordination. Both Spain and Italy are investing in their lifeboat fleets and, in Italy, a new coastguard service has been formed.

However, before any of the many search and rescue facilities available in European waters can be deployed, it is necessary for the authorities to have received some basic information: ie what is happening, approximately where, and to whom. There is increasing reliance on radio communication, both to communicate the intial distress message, and then to co-ordinate the operation as it progresses. The GMDSS has done much to provide a common system for all maritime requirements. These days, successful search and rescue operations these days depend heavily on radio communication, and yachtsmen should be very aware of just how important their VHF radio is, not only for initiating distress calls, but for following them through to a safe conclusion. It can be stated categorically that VHF radio is essential to a good search and rescue operation these days and that a back-up radio for emergencies is therefore to be considered a vital piece of safety equipment.

If you are the one needing to be rescued you will feel tempted to go along with what anybody proposes, because you need help badly and are therefore at a considerable disadvantage. However, as we saw earlier, you do have some say in the matter of how the rescue is carried out, and, in theory, you even have a choice about which rescue facility to go for, if more than one is being offered. For example, if several ships offer to come to your rescue, you can decide which one you think is the best one for the particular job, and release the others from their obligation. When it comes to lifeboat or helicopter rescue, there will be less room for discussion because you are dealing with experienced professionals who know, probably better than you, what is involved. But do remember that they are not in your shoes, and if you feel that there any factors of which they should be aware, then don't hesitate to let them know. If you have young children, or someone old and infirm, on board, it could have a significant bearing on the rescue operation, as would an injured crew member who might need a stretcher. The more information you can give the rescuers about your predicament, the better. If the yacht is lying amongst rocks, and the resue is to be by boat, point out if you can where the rocks are in relation to the yacht, and in generally keep the rescuers as fully informed as possible about the situation.

Lifeboat

Rescue by lifeboat will normally be fairly straightforward. The lifeboat will come alongside to take off your crew. The main risks involved are in the transfer from yacht to lifeboat, and it may mean the lifeboat having to make several approaches to take the crew off one at a time, rather than it being able to lie alongside and take all the crew off together. Much will depend on the prevailing sea conditions but considerable risks are involved in such an exercise, which is why it is often safer for the lifeboat to tow the yacht to safety with the crew still aboard. Even so, the lifeboat may want to put one of its own crew members on board to assist with making the tow line secure and to make sure that it doesn't chafe. The lifeboat crew are not trying to take over completely but they will feel more confident if they have on board someone who knows the procedures and what is going on. You and your crew may be traumatised by the emergency and will probably be happy to let the lifeboat crew take over and run the whole show. However, as we stated in an earlier chapter, relaxing before you are fully rescued and on dry land, or at the very least, on the deck of the rescue ship, is to be avoided at all costs. As far as you can you should stay alert and be fully involved in the rescue operation, to reduce the chance of snags or problems. The same applies to your crew, and you should impress upon them the need to concentrate on the rescue and to be alert and ready to cope with changing circumstances.

Helicopter Rescue

Helicopter rescue will be much more firmly under the control of the helicopter crew because of the considerable risks involved, not the least to the helicopter, if they don't get the right degree of co-operation. Helicopters tend to have limited range and endurance, so there is often a need for a quick rescue procedure. There are also risks involved in dealing with a sailing yacht where the mast can hamper the rescue operation quite considerably. Because of the need to keep control of the situation, the normal procedure is for one of the crew to be lowered on the end of the winch wire to take charge of the situation and organise the rescue and evacuation.

The first thing a helicopter crew needs to know when approaching an emergency is that they have the right vessel. You can help with this by indicating your position: by firing a flare, or orange smoke, or even flashing a light. Even waving will give some indication that you are the vessel involved, although yachts often wave at a passing helicopter, so this is not necessarily a positive indication. Most helicopters these days are equipped with marine band VHF, and, once again, if you can make direct communication with the helicopter, then the whole operation can be greatly simplified and properly controlled and will have a much better chance of a successful outcome.

Before the helicopter approaches there are certain things you should do if you can. On a sailing yacht, all sails should be taken down as they will be greatly affected by the downdraught from the helicopter rotors. If you have one on board, put a sea anchor out over the bow: this will help reduce the drift of the yacht and also prevent it swinging around when the helicopter is overhead. Without a sea anchor, a motorboat will tend to lie stern into the wind which can make rescue more difficult. Here the sea anchor could be of considerable benefit by allowing rescue from the stern while the helicopter pilot is still able to keep the bow in sight. During the rescue operation, the pilot will have only limited visibility below, and will be heavily reliant on one of the crew giving instructions, usually the one operating the winch for the lift. A successful helicopter rescue requires a great deal of careful co-ordination of the various crew members.

Sea Anchors and Drogues

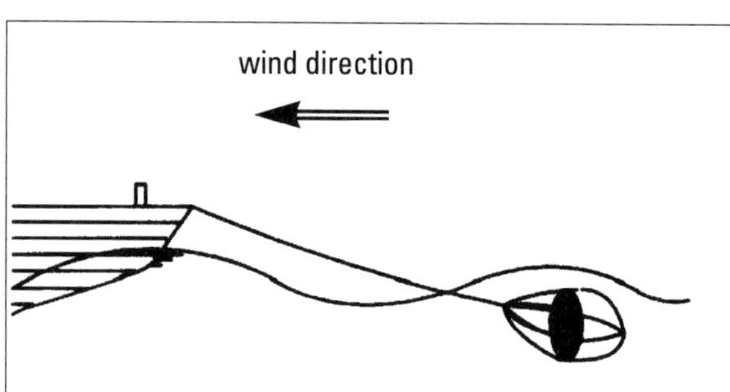

A sea anchor is streamed out from the bow of a yacht with enough scope on the line to keep the anchor well immersed. It is used to keep the yacht heading in to wind and/or to reduce drift.

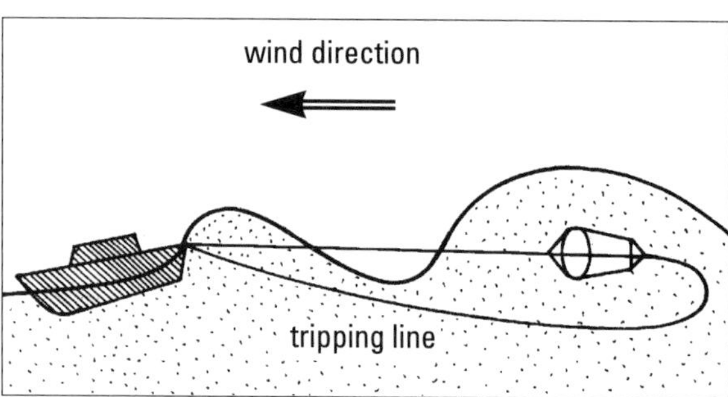

Streaming a drogue from the stern. The drogue must be kept fully in the water and the yacht must use full speed to get maximum pull on the line. A tripping line, which must be kept slack when the drogue is in use, can greatly assist recovery of the drogue.

On a sailing yacht, if the mast is still standing, it may be necessary for the yacht crew to get into a liferaft, which is then trailed astern, so the

Helicopter Lifts

A single-person lift. You need to keep your head back as the lifting wire tightens to prevent the strop hitting you in the face.

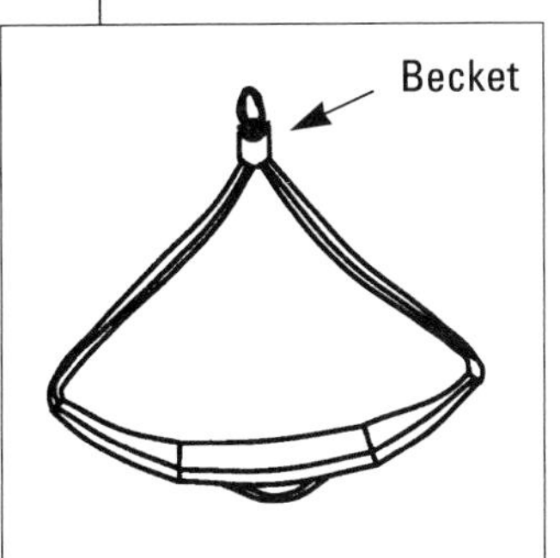

The lifting strop with the becket which is moved down to tighten it once you are in .

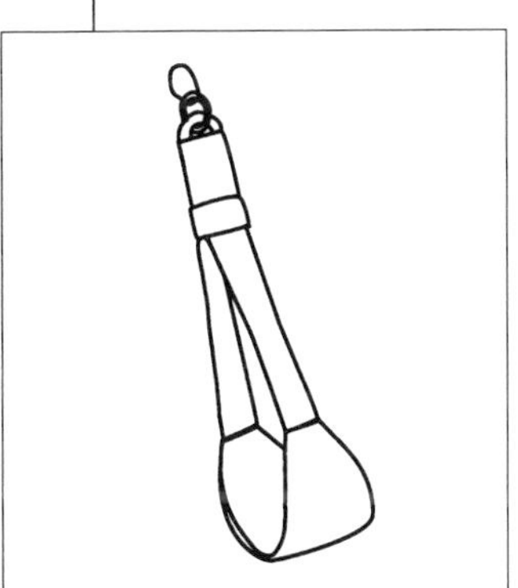

The Seattle Strop, developed as an aid to recovering casualties in a man-overboard situation.

helicopter can keep clear of the mast. The main danger is that the winch wire will get tangled up with the mast. However, if the helicopter crew want you to get into a liferaft, this will be made clear to you. If a liferaft is not available, an option is to get into the water on the end of a line and drift astern, but, once again, the instructions of the helicopter crew should be followed to the letter.

If the helicopter lowers a crewman, or just the winch wire, do not reach out to grab the man or the wire but let him first of all touch the yacht so that he can earth the static electric charge which builds up in the wire. If the wire alone is lowered, let this touch the water first. You can get quite a severe electric shock from this wire if it is not earthed correctly. Once the charge is earthed you can assist the crewman on board, from where he will organise the rescue. He will usually take the crew up one at a time in a double-lifting strop system. The survivor has a longer strop than the crewman, and is lifted lying between the crewman's legs. On reaching the helicopter, a survivor is orientated with their back towards the helicopter, and is helped into the helicopter by the winchman. If there is an injured person on board, then a Neil Robertson stretcher will be lowered into which the injured person is strapped before being lifted with the crewman.

There could be occasions when the rescue helicopter simply lowers a wire, without a crewman. If this happens, you obviously have a much greater responsibility for the course of the rescue. After earthing the wire, make sure that the wire does not foul any part of the boat as this could have serious consequences for both the helicopter and your rescue. The wire should never be made fast anywhere because this could seriously compromise the helicopter's ability to manoeuvre and may result in it having to cut the wire to ensure its own safety.

On the end of the wire there will be a webbing strop, which is put over the head and under the arms so that the padded section fits around the back. There is a sliding toggle near the lifting point which should be pulled downwards so that the strop stays closed as it is hoisted. When it is properly and comfortably fitted, the wearer or skipper should give the thumbs-up sign to the helicopter which will then start the lift, but make sure there is nothing obstructing the lift and that the wearer keeps their head back so that if the strop snaps tight it will not hit their head. The survivor can hold on to the strop if it makes him feel more comfortable. When the survivor reaches the helicopter, the crew will spin him round so that his back is towards the door and then pull him in to the helicopter backwards, slacking off the wire at the same time. Once in the helicopter, an uninjured survivor should find a seat, sit down and strap himself in, leaving the crew to get on with the rest of the rescue operation. Helicopter crews are highly trained and experienced, so this is one occasion when you can comfortably let the rescuers get on with the job and just follow their instructions.

Being a Rescuer

Being rescued is one thing, but the chances are that you could equally well be involved in a search and rescue operation as the rescuer, or at least a searcher. Here too, preparation can be of tremendous assistance to the success of the operation. Whilst you may be directed to the area you are required to search and told how to go about it, a general understanding on your part of the principles of searching at sea could greatly improve the effectiveness of the whole operation. If a search for survivors is going to be successful, it needs to be carefully planned and carefully executed. This can be undertaken in different ways. Co-ordination of a search and rescue operation may be in the hands of someone who goes under the title of the on-scene commander, but it may equally well be in the hands of the shore-based coastguard.

Let us take a situation where somebody has fallen overboard from a yacht but the loss has been undetected for several hours. You may be in the vicinity and therefore have a moral and legal obligation to help with the search and rescue operation. In this a situation the on-scene commander could be the coxswain of a lifeboat or could equally well be the commanding officer of a naval or other vessel which is in the vicinity. In the absence of anyone with some sort of authority and experience, the coastguard on shore could well co-ordinate the search operation. What is necessary is that someone who understands the principles of searching at sea plans the operation to make it as effective as possible, which means searching as large a sea area as possible in a given time, and making sure that the sea areas searched are those most likely to contain the survivor.

Areas of Probability and Possibility

The first things to understand are how to determine the area of probability, and the area of possibility. The former is the area in which it is considered most likely that the survivor will be found. This will take into account the likely effects of wind, tide, currents, and other factors which will affect the drift of the survivor from the original position. Given that the accident had gone undetected it may that the position where it occurred is not known, or only very vaguely. This will also have to be taken into account in determining the area of probability.

The area of possibility uses similar factors but takes these to extremes, which means it takes all the factors which could possibly affect the drift, and stretches their credibility to the maximum. Thus the area in which it is possible that the survivor could be found is much larger, but the extended area has a lower probability factor.

Using these two areas as the basis for a search, then you obviously go for the area of probability first and search that thoroughly. If nothing is found the search is extended to the area of possibility. Beyond that it is hard to recommend further action, except to suggest that the areas are covered once more, in case something was missed in the initial search.

The accuracy of the original position of the accident is obviously a critical factor in establishing these two areas: the more accurately this position can be pinpointed, the smaller the area that needs to be searched. Time is almost equally important: the longer the passage of time between the incident and the search, the greater the area that will have to be searched, because the various factors affecting the drift of the survivor will increase considerably. This means that as the search progresses the area to be covered will expand, whilst chances of survival will tend to diminish.

Visual Range

Another factor which needs to be taken into account is the effective range at which the survivor might be sighted. It is no good having vessels searching two nautical miles apart if it is unlikely that a survivor will be seen half a mile away. A survivor in the water is probably visible for no more than 400 metres, whereas a liferaft could be visible for double this distance, and a yacht for perhaps two miles.

The following are the sorts of distances that should be allowed to give the maximum chance of sighting survivors. Given luck and a good

Table 1: Visibility

RANGE AT WHICH DIFFERENT TYPES OF CRAFT CAN BE SIGHTED IN DIFFERENT VISIBILITY LIMITS

DIFFERENT VISIBILITY LIMITS

Visibility Range	Liferafts	Boats Under 10m	Boats 10m – 20m	Boats 20m – 30m	Ships
1	.7	.7	.7	.9	1.0
3	1.0	2.5	3.5	3.9	5.0
5	1.4	2.7	4.2	5.0	8.0
10	1.8	3.9	6.5	8.0	11.0
15	1.9	5.2	8.5	11.0	14.0
20	2.0	5.3	8.6	12.0	15.0
30	2.2	5.5	8.7	12.5	17.0
40	2.2	5.6	8.9	13.0	17.0
50	2.2	5.7	9.0	13.5	20.0

All distances given in nautical miles

lookout, it should be possible to detect them at double these distances, but you cannot be positive about this.

The weather and sea conditions will have a bearing on the search pattern. For example, in bright sunlight you will see an object very well when looking away from the sun, but not at all when looking towards the sun. In mist or fog there are obvious limits to visibility, as there are in heavy rain or snow, whilst rough seas can greatly reduce the chances of sighting survivors in the water.

When establishing the minimum distance at which survivors could be sighted during a search, you have to play it safe and go for the lowest estimate. Once an area has been searched you want to be positive that it was a 100 per cent search and be absolutely sure that the survivors aren't in that area before moving on to the next.

Patterns of Search: Single Vessel

Table 1 will give some indication of search distances. Bearing these in mind, it is possible to establish a search pattern. For a single search vessel, the best is probably a square, commencing at the most probable location of the incident. This search expands in concentric squares and is best done on a time basis, with the search vessel keeping a constant speed. The time of the initial leg would be determined by the detection range that you have already established, and would be twice this range. Thus, if the detection range is 1/4 mile, your first leg would extend to 1/2 mile, which, if you are travelling at six knots would take five minutes. At the end of this

Square Search

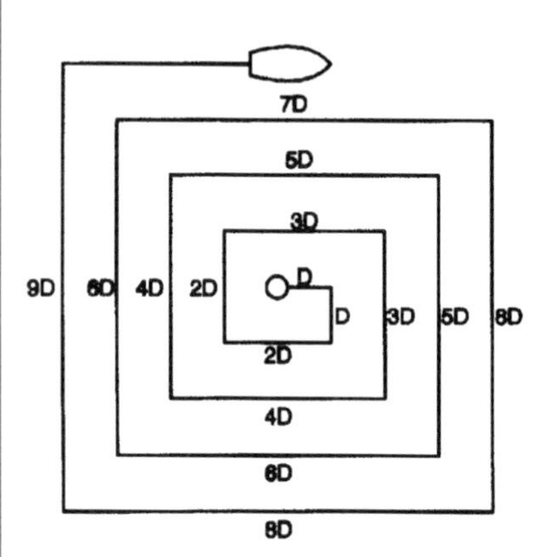

A square search where D is twice the distance at which the casualty can expect to be sighted. This pattern would normally be used when searching from a known location.

Track Crawl

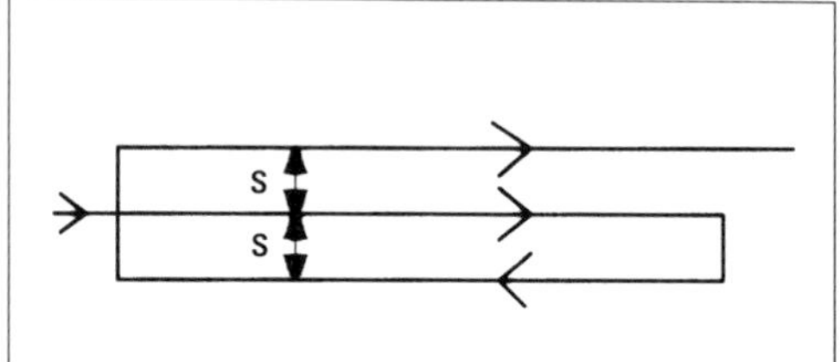

Creeping Line Ahead

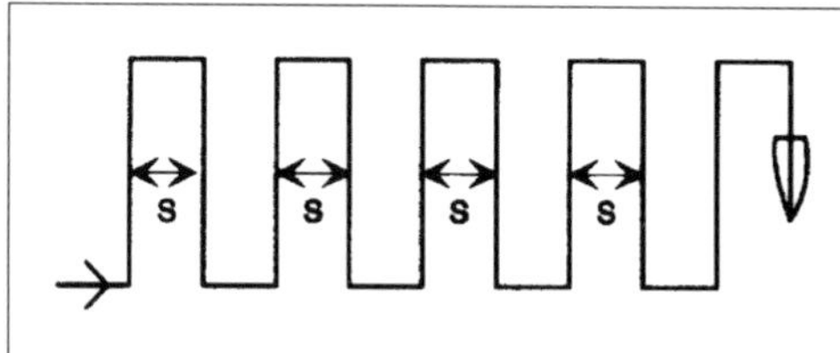

Track Crawl and Creeping Line Ahead: S equals twice the range at which the casualty can be expected to be sighted; normally used when the casualty was thought to be along a given track.

first leg, you alter course through 90 degrees and steam for the same amount of time. For the third leg, you again alter course through 90 degrees in the same direction, but this time steam for ten minutes, before altering course again through 90 degrees and steaming for another ten minutes. Every second leg you extend the time by a further five minutes, and in this way the search widens out in expanding squares as far as you want to go.

Track Crawl
An alternative is the track crawl search: you follow a given distance along a track and then double back running parallel to the initial track, but at a distance of twice the expected range of visibility from the first track. Then you cross over the initial track and run down the other side, again at twice the range of visibility from the initial track.

Creeping Line Ahead
Another type of search is the creeping line ahead search where the search area is swept back and forth on alternate headings spaced at twice the sighting distance apart. Like the track crawl search, this is more appropriate for searching long 'rectangular box' areas than the 'squares' of the expanding square search.

Table 2: Radar Visibilty Ranges

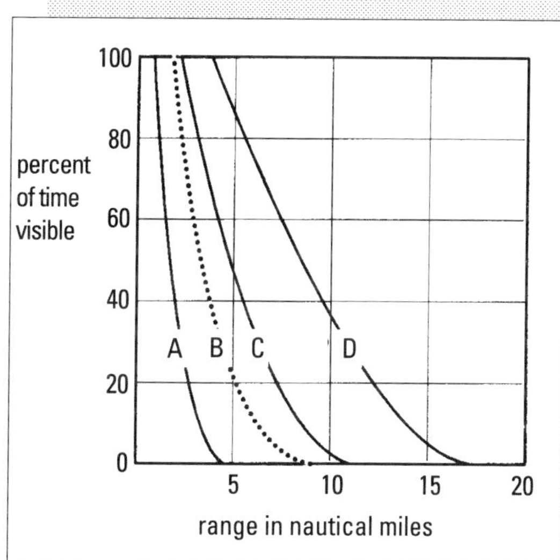

The percentage of time a target can be expected to be visible on a ship's radar screen.

A is a small yacht under 10 metres
B same yacht with radar reflector hoisted
C larger yacht around 20 metres
D moderate sized ship

Patterns of Search: Two or More Vessels

These three search patterns are more appropriate to a single search vessel, although each could be used by a single vessel covering a section of a search area in collaboration with other vessels using similar search patterns. However, when there are several vessels involved in the search, it is better to get them lined up and to sweep in a parallel formation, with each vessel twice the sighting distance apart from its neighbour. This helps to ensure that the area is fully covered and no gaps left, but it does require careful station-keeping. Unless the vessels are fitted with radar, it is not easy to get an accurate measurement of the distance from an adjacent vessel. One vessel should be allocated the position of controller and the others will keep station on this vessel, either directly or from the next vessel out.

This is much more likely to be the type of search pattern undertaken when there is an on-site commander who is also involved in the search, whereas the individual search patterns are more appropriate to a search co-ordinated from the shore where it is easy to allocate a vessel to a particular area.

The Importance of the Lookout

An important factor in any search is the quality of the lookout being kept. This should comprise at least one person on each side of the vessel, in addition to the person steering the vessel. It is very easy to believe that you are searching the sea area thoroughly when, in fact, your glance is quite cursory because there is nothing specific to focus on. You will tend to look towards the horizon rather than the near sea areas, which should be the area of your scrutiny. Anyone keeping a lookout during a search situation should be instructed to scan the sea constantly in a sweeping motion which makes you tend to focus on one point. Searching is a skill: a cursory glance is not adequate, particularly in rough sea conditions.

Night Searches

So far we have concentrated on daylight searching. This is easy compared with searching at night. It is harder to keep station on other vessels at night and it is therefore better for vessels to carry out independent searches. It is also obviously much harder to see survivors in the dark. They are only likely to be spotted if they have some means of indicating their position. The chances of actually coming close enough to hear people shouting is very remote, and could probably be discounted, but the approach to a search at night time will depend on how many hours are left till daylight, the type of casualty being searched for, and the prevailing conditions. In general, any night-time search is going to be fairly cursory and there will be a much greater element of luck in locating any survivors.

Nature of the Target

The type of search pattern employed will depend a great deal on what you are looking for. For an overdue vessel, the search would probably be a long, rectangular one, concentrating on the probable course along which the vessel was thought to be sailing. If a more positive position of the casualty is known, a square search is probably a better solution. However, in some situations a certain amount of logic can be employed. If, for instance, you come across a capsized dinghy with no one on board, then, in addition to reporting this, it would be reasonable to assume that the survivors have left the dinghy to swim towards the shore, not out to sea.

So you would concentrate your search between the dinghy and the shore. There is a third possibility: that they have already been picked up and the dinghy has been left to drift, in which case the chances are that it will be reported and you will eventually find out what has happened. If you are the target, one good reason for staying as close as possible to your boat, even though you are in a liferaft or your dinghy, it is much easier to see a boat at sea than somebody in the water, and this will greatly assist the searchers, and therefore your chances of survival.

Electronic Charts

In any search operation, an electronic chart can be of great assistance. The automatic plot of the electronic chart can display exactly the area which has been covered, so you can be sure that an area has been accurately searched.

Action on Board the Rescue Vessel

If, at any time, you are called upon not only to search but actually to effect the rescue, this will be a nerve-wracking time time for all. We have seen that it is no easy task to go in and rescue somebody at sea, whether from a dinghy that has capsized or a yacht that is dismasted.

We will look at recovering people from the water and coping with a dismasting later in this book, but the main thing to realise is that you must, first of all, stop and work out just exactly what you are going to do. The temptation is to rush straight in and do something – anything – the consequence of which is that you may overrun people in the water or damage your own boat severely by coming into contact with the stricken vessel. Stopping for a few minutes and working out a plan of action will greatly benefit all those involved – those to be rescued and the rescuers.

If, for example, you are trying to pick someone out of the water, make sure you have facilities to aid their recovery. Once you come alongside you must be ready to grab them quickly, and at least, have ropes ready to support them whilst you attempt to recover them. In coming alongside a casualty you will want to have all your fenders out at the probable point of contact, to reduce the chance of damage rather than scratches. Whilst you will need to have ropes ready, you are probably much better just to hold the boat alongside with the engines rather than attempt to tie up, and to make several approaches, taking one person off at each approach, rather than trying to grab the whole lot in one go.

Fortunately, search and rescue is something which yachtsmen are rarely called upon to do, and the same applies to most professional sailors. This means that very little training is carried out and there is very little experience to draw on. The only thing you can do is to use as much common sense as possible, and most important of all, try and work out beforehand exactly what you are going to do. If you have radio contact, make sure that the other people involved know what is expected of them, and with luck things will go reasonably smoothly and you won't get any nasty surprises!

6 Survival Equipment

In this chapter we shall be looking at those items of safety equipment which will give you a chance of survival when virtually all else has failed. Lifejackets will keep you afloat and give you a chance to survive until rescue comes, but survival suits also offer protection from the cold and therefore, when used in conjunction with a lifejacket, increase your chances of survival. Liferafts, the ultimate survival craft, give you the ability to survive for extended periods when you have had to abandon ship. The use of these three items of equipment goes hand in hand, and, if you are going to use them to best advantage, you need to get to know them intimately. However, like much of the safety equipment on board, you may have little chance to gain practical experience before you have to use it for real. So we shall look at these items in considerable detail, in the hope that it will at least give you an insight into how they should be used and what you might expect.

Liferafts and Tenders

The liferaft is a comparatively recent element in the repertoire of survival equipment, having been first introduced in its present form about fifty years ago. Before the development of the liferaft, yachts had to rely on their tenders to provide a haven if it came to abandoning ship. Even today, many yachts rely on their tenders for emergency evacuation because owners are neither prepared, nor willing, to spend the money on a dedicated survival craft. A tender, particularly if it is of the inflatable type, can provide a relatively safe haven in a crisis but, even if it is fitted with a waterproof and windproof cover, as is now often the case, it will still not provide the same level of safety and security as a liferaft. In making a comparison between tenders and liferafts you have to bear in mind that if you are ever in the dire position of having to abandon ship, it is quite likely that this will also be in extreme wind and sea conditions. It is just then that a tender could be found wanting.

A tender does not have the stability of a liferaft, which has built-in water ballast pockets underneath. It will not have the equipment built into it, although you can always have a grab-bag, packed with the necessary equipment, ready to take with you if you have to abandon ship. A tender may not have automatic inflation, as is the case with the liferaft. If you

Inflatable Dinghy in Use as Liferaft

The dinghy is converted to a liferaft by use of an inflatable canopy and other on-board equipment. In certain locations a dual-purpose dinghy of this kind is a practical and adequate alternative to a liferaft, but it does not have the stability characteristics and survival capabilities of a full liferaft. It does not meet RORC or DTp requirements.

carry it deflated, or half-deflated, to save space on board, you could waste valuable time in an emergency, particularly if the yacht is on fire. If you are going to take your safety seriously, then a fullyfledged liferaft is the only real option. If your yacht is over 13.7 metre (45 feet) long the liferaft is a mandatory requirement. It is significant that the RORC and the RYA both insist on a full liferaft and not a conversion from a tender.

Whilst not mandatory for smaller yachts in Britain, a liferaft is still highly recommended. It could be argued that you need not carry a liferaft if you sail only in crowded waters because, if you get into trouble, you will be rescued quickly. This assumes that there will always be other vessels near at hand to effect a quick rescue but you can never guarantee this. There will always be times when you are exposed to greater risk, perhaps at night, or in fog, when it may not be possible for you to be rescued quickly. The safe haven the liferaft then offers could at least see you through the night, or through a period of fog, until better visibility permits a rescue. If the alternative is to be in the water with only a lifejacket to support you, you will be at much greater risk.

Liferaft Sizes

Liferafts come in a variety of sizes, the minimum being for four people, the largest having somewhere around a sixty-person capacity. The size of the liferaft should be decided by the maximum number of people likely to be on board at any one time. A four-man liferaft is therefore not really adequate unless your yacht is less than 7.5 metre (25 feet) long. The normal liferaft carried on board would be at least a six-person raft. Where relatively large numbers of people are involved, there is something to be said for having two smaller rafts, rather than one large raft, partly because it makes stowage and handling easier, but also because it gives a degree of redundancy if one liferaft gets damaged or fails to operate properly. A liferaft is a relatively fragile piece of equipment which can be damaged, or even ripped, during launching unless care is taken, so two rafts give you a bit more security. However, two small rafts cost more than one large one and you will have double the service charges for bi-annual maintenance. And, of course, it will be a tight fit if all the crew have to get into one liferaft.

Modern Liferaft Design

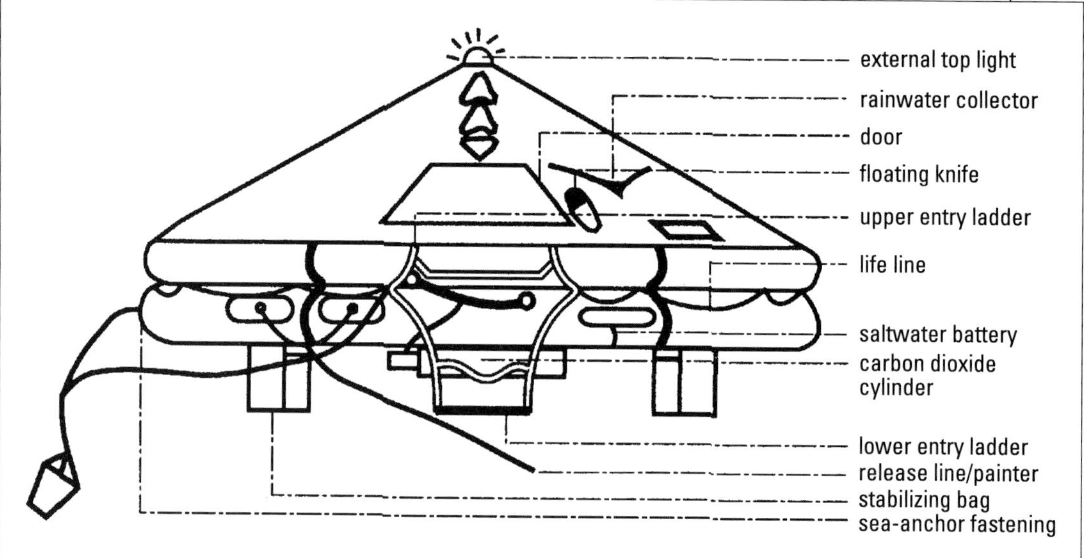

Approved Liferafts

It is obviously important that a liferaft is up to the task for which it is intended, and various bodies can 'approve' liferafts; approval denoting a satisfactorily high standard of manufacture, fitness for purpose and, in particular, level of equipment.

The two main approving bodies are the RORC and the Department of Transport. All approved liferafts have a double tube, so, that if one tube is punctured the liferaft is still quite serviceable and it will not sink. Approved liferafts also have an inflatable floor, which helps to insulate against the cold. The floor does not inflate automatically when the liferaft itself is inflated; this has to be carried out by hand once the crew are on board. The canopy is held in position by one or more inflatable tubes and is automatically deployed on inflation. This protects the crew from wind, rain and spray. The canopy and inflatable floor have been the two significant areas in liferaft development in recent years. The liferaft now not only keeps the occupants afloat, but also protects them from exposure, thus greatly increasing survival potential.

Another significant development has been the addition of water ballast pockets to the bottom of the liferaft. In very strong winds or surf liferafts have been known to capsize. The ballast pockets, which automatically fill with water when the liferaft is inflated, help to provide stability and reduce the risk of capsize. This risk cannot be eliminated altogether but ballast pockets go a long way towards extending the range of stability. If the liferaft should capsize, grab handles are fitted to the bottom of the liferaft to help the crew right it again. This is possible provided that all the crew have got out of the liferaft, although it is still difficult in rough seas. We shall look at this aspect in greater detail a bit later, when we examine abandon ship procedure in Chapter 8, (see page 137).

Keeping a Lookout

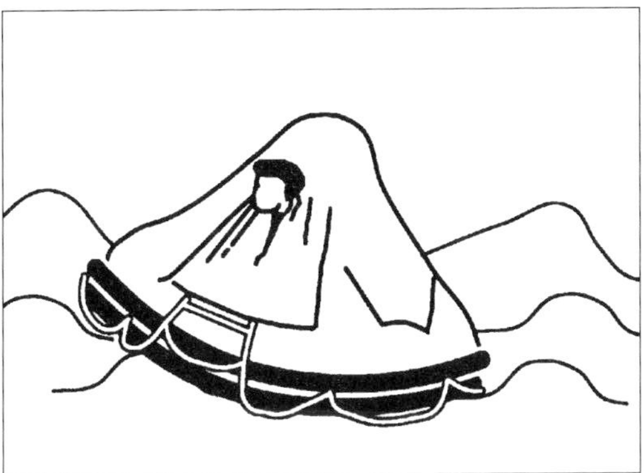

Keep the fabric doors closed as much as possible and expose as little of the body as possible to reduce the risk of hypothermia in cold weather.

When a liferaft is inflated, its canopy is automatically erected. The canopy has two entrances on opposite sides of the raft and they not only provide access to the interior, but also lookout points for the crew once they have left the mother ship and are waiting for rescue. The entrances are fitted with coverings so that, if necessary, they can be totally closed to protect the crew inside, but the coverings will also afford considerable protection from water entry, even when the opening is being used by a lookout.

Webbing ladders are fitted at each opening so that survivors can climb into the raft from the water, but flexible ladders are not easy to use. It can require a lot of effort to climb into a liferaft from the water, particularly if a lifejacket is being worn. One model of liferaft also uses inflatable tubes for the ladder. Lifelines are fitted round the outside of the liferaft so that people can hang on whilst waiting their turn to climb on board.

Liferafts are generally constructed from lightweight nylon fabric which is proofed on both sides with neoprene rubber. This fabric is glued together and stands up very well to exposure to sunlight and seawater. An alternative fabric is a polyurethane-coated nylon which can be heat-sealed instead of glued. This is an equally durable but cheaper form of construction.

Liferaft Containers

Liferaft containers come in two forms: either a rigid, moulded GRP container, which protects the liferaft and allows it to be mounted outside on deck, or a fabric valise which is something like a hold-all fitted with a lace-up section to secure the opening. Rigid containers come in different shapes, usually cylindrical or rectangular, with the latter now being the most popular for yachts because of its compact dimensions and low profile. The valise-type stowage is normally designed for locker or inside stowage where the locker itself can offer initial protection. Even when stowed, however, a liferaft should be protected from chafe and raised up from the bottom of the locker so that it does not sit in water all the time.

Stowage of Rigid Container

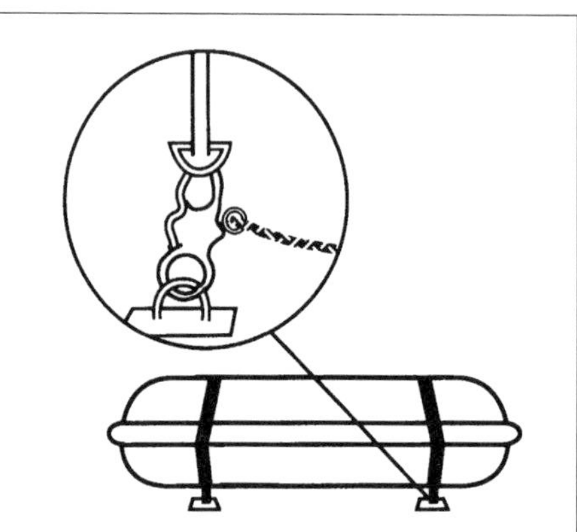

The two securing straps can be released quickly by using the slip hooks.

When stowing a rigid container on deck, there should be room for water to pass underneath. The canister is stowed on chocks and secured by a webbing strap with a quick-release mechanism. Such a stowage can make the liferaft vulnerable to theft in harbour, when it should either be padlocked in place using security chain or a wire taken below for security. With locker stowage, the locker can simply be locked in order to provide security for the liferaft.

Liferaft Stowage

Liferaft stowage needs to be considered with some care. The liferaft is quite a large piece of equipment although the container type is well shaped for easy stowage. Some yacht designs have a tailor-made stowage, but generally it is a case of finding room for the raft, somewhere where it doesn't interfere with the operation of the yacht yet is readily accessible in an emergency. The foredeck is not particularly suitable because it is exposed and is a working area, particularly on sailing boats. The coachroof is one option used by many sailing boats. On powerboats and motor-sailers, coachroof stowage can obstruct the view from the wheelhouse. The cockpit is perhaps the best place, if there is room, and is a favoured place on powerboats. Many modern sailing boat designs have special liferaft stowage on the transom, the benefit being that the liferaft can be released quickly in an emergency and doesn't have to be lifted overboard.

If the liferaft is stowed in the cockpit or on the coachroof, the container obviously has to be lifted physically and thrown over the guard rails. This looks a comparatively easy job in harbour, but out at sea, in rough conditions, lifting and throwing a liferaft over the side can demand strength and agility. The instructions on the liferaft casing make light of this aspect of the operation, simply stating, 'pick up the liferaft and throw it overboard'. Anyone who has tried this at sea will realise that it is, in fact, a very difficult task. When the GRP container is wet it becomes slippery and uncontrollable. The best way of launching it is probably to let go the lashing and let it slide overboard through the guard rails. Launching a liferaft stowed in the cockpit is really a two-person job.

A Disastrous Mistake

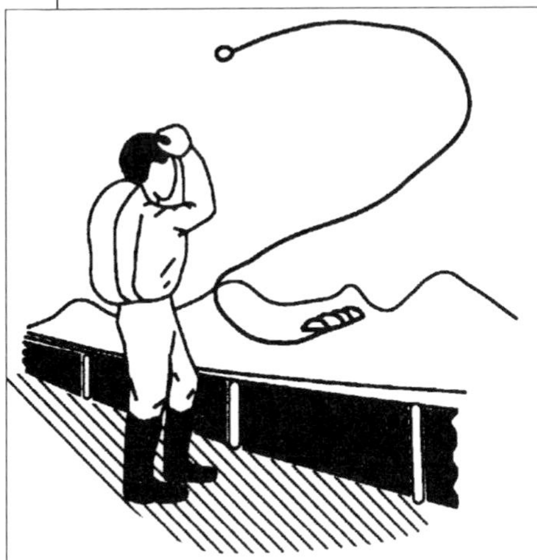

It can be a moment of despair if the liferaft is launched before the painter is made fast. It makes sense to have the painter permanently attached to avoid this happening.

At sea the liferaft painter must at all times be made fast to a secure point on the vessel. It doesn't take much imagination to picture the frustration which would result if you had struggled to get the liferaft overboard only to find that you hadn't made the painter fast and were watching it drift away. The painter line not only secures the liferaft once it is inflated, but is also the actuating trigger for the gas cylinder that inflates it. In its stowed state there are about three metres of line outside the container while the rest is stowed inside.

The painter can quite easily be pulled out from the container and, once the liferaft is overboard, you must continue pulling on the painter until you trigger the inflation mechanism. You will know when you have done this because the liferaft container will burst open and the liferaft will deploy. When you install the liferaft and tie the painter to a fixed point, you should take care not to pull out more painter than is already exposed because a sealant is incorporated into the painter at the point where it enters the container. This stops water entering the container by 'wicking' up the painter. There should be plenty of slack available without having to pull out any more rope.

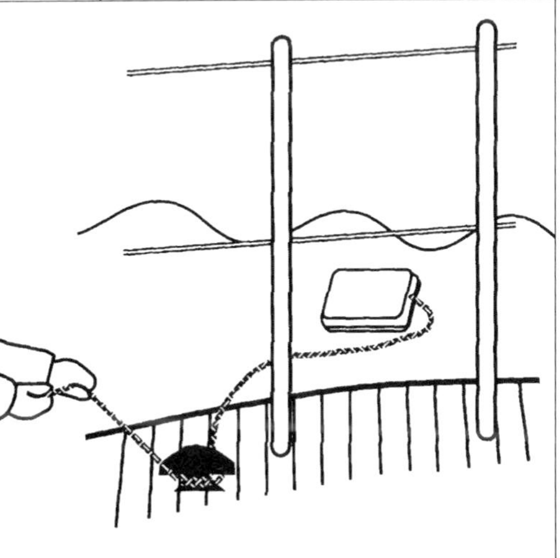

Always ensure the painter is made fast BEFORE the liferaft is launched.

The liferaft should normally be launched over on the lee side because boarding will be easier. The only exception to this might be in the case of fire when the lee side could rapidly become untenable. Launching at the

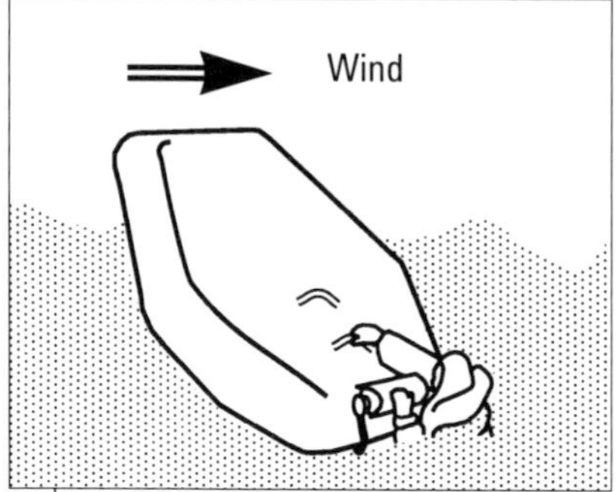

Righting a Capsized Liferaft

The inflation cylinder is kept at the bottom and the handholds can then be used to pull the liferaft over. The top of the liferaft should be facing into the wind.

bow or stern could then be the best solution. The aim is, of course, to keep the liferaft clear of the smoke and flames.

Boarding the Liferaft

Once the liferaft is in the water, the next stage is to board it. Try to arrange a 'dry' evacuation, where the crew step into the liferaft direct from the yacht. This may be difficult on yachts with a high freeboard: the bathing platform aft may be the only possible place. Avoid jumping onto the liferaft. It will deform and absorb the impact, but other occupants could be injured. If you have to jump, jump into the water and climb from there into the liferaft. However it is tackled, boarding a liferaft is not easy. The raft will be bouncing around alongside and there will be little to hold on to as you climb down from the deck. In this sort of situation previous practice would be a great advantage.

Life Onboard

In the liferaft, exposure is likely to be your greatest enemy. Boarding dry shod can help, and take any blankets and spare clothing with you that you can manage. Food and drink are great morale boosters, and any that don't require heating should be taken. Other vital things to remember when you abandon ship are the EPIRB and any portable VHF radios. Finally, if you have a grab-bag available, this should help to supplement the contents of the liferaft survival pack. A first aid kit should also be taken if one is not already in the grab-bag.

Once in the liferaft, you obviously have to try and adjust to the changed circumstances. You will no doubt feel very apprehensive about the situation. Initially there will be quite a lot to do to occupy your mind: one of the first things will be to try and find space for everybody. A four-person liferaft with four people in it is extremely crowded; there is virtually no room to move. From the point of view of survival this is good because the more you huddle together, the greater the warmth, and this reduces the risk of exposure. You should have donned lifejackets before you abandoned ship, but this of course increases the bulk of each person and reduces available space. If you also have survival suits, you are going to find things pretty crowded inside. When one person moves somebody else will have to move as well, which can make it quite difficult to get through necessary routine chores.

Once everybody and the additional survival equipment have been accommodated, you have to decide whether or not to let go from the mother ship. The fact that you are now in the liferaft would indicate that things were getting pretty desperate on board. Presumably the yacht was either seriously on fire or in danger of sinking. However, you should hang on to the parent ship for as long as possible because it will provide a much better target for the search vessels, and it will help to reduce your wind drift. If the time comes when you feel forced to let go, there is a safety knife in a pouch on the liferaft close to where the painter is attached which can be used to cut it. However, if you have time, and you can do it, pull in as much of the slack in the painter as you can before you cut, because having a good length of painter available could be useful if the craft that comes to your aid is having difficulty in getting close alongside.

When you finally let go of the mother ship and start to drift, the first thing to do is to find the sea anchor and deploy it. The sea anchor is made fast to a point on the liferaft midway between the two openings. This is so that when it is deployed with the liferaft lying downwind, the openings are located on each side and not exposed to the full blast of the wind. The sea anchor itself is stowed just inside one of the liferaft openings. Finding it may be difficult with a full liferaft, but it should be there with its line already attached, so all you have to do is to throw it out through the opening. You should be able to feel when the sea anchor is doing its job because the liferaft will suddenly change its attitude and should ride with a more comfortable motion, although its purpose is not so much to make life on board more comfortable but to reduce drift. Without it you could be a considerable distance away from the distress position within an hour or two. It will not stop drift altogether but will help to reduce it, which in turn should help speed up rescue.

The next thing to do, if possible, is to give each of the crew a seasickness tablet. Ideally, seasickness tablets should have been issued before you abandoned ship, but even the hardiest of sailors, who claim never to have been seasick in their lives, are likely to succumb to the difficult motion of a liferaft. Seasickness in a liferaft is not a pleasant experience, and crew members can rapidly lose many of their survival instincts.

Keeping the Raft Inflated

You can now begin to deal with more routine matters, such as inflating the floor of the liferaft to reduce the risk of exposure from heat loss. The canopy arch tubes should be checked to see that they have inflated properly and, if not, topped up. The bellows will be found in the equipment bag on board. There is also a repair kit for use if any of the inflatable compartments are damaged. These repair kits consist either of rubber bungs which can be pushed into holes in the tube, or a double-plate metal patch which can be put through a tear and the two parts clamped together. Tears are much more likely than the type of round hole which a bung could cope with, but neither repair is likely to prove very satisfactory. Trying to repair a damaged liferaft is almost impossible unless the damaged areas are regular and of a size to match the repair equipment. You will also find a sponge and a bailer amongst the equipment, and as far

Manual Inflation Kit

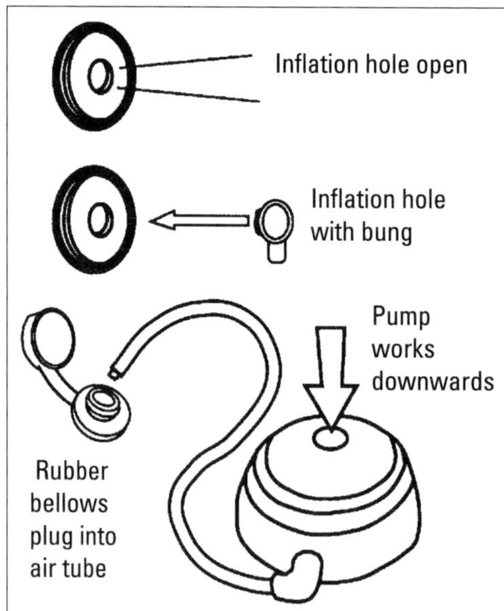

Rubber Bungs

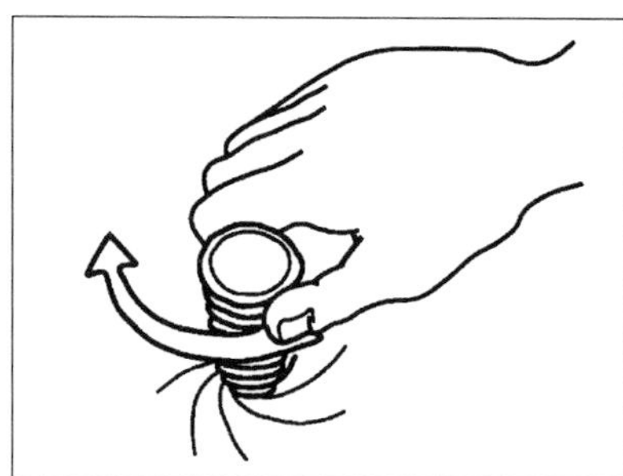

The rubber bungs are used to repair a small hole in the air tube. It can be difficult to get an effective seal unless the hole is the right shape and size.

Left: the non-return valve in the tube prevents air escaping when the bung or bellows tube is removed. The bellows are worked by hand or foot.

as possible any water inside the liferaft should now be mopped up. The bailer will cope with large quantities of water; the sponge can be used for the remainder. Keeping the inside of the liferaft, and therefore the occupants, as dry as possible helps to reduce the risk of exposure and is good for morale.

When these routine tasks have been completed you can settle down to contemplate your fate. Life inside the liferaft is not very pleasant, and in the early stages the crew will almost certainly want to put their heads out. This will be to get fresh air and reduce the effects of seasickness but, from the start, a lookout routine should be established. Flares and other distress signals should be kept ready to hand to indicate the position of the liferaft if a vessel is sighted. You will remember we have already noted that flares and smoke signals should only be fired from the lee side of the liferaft. With the sea anchor out, they can probably be fired from either opening, but the flare should be held well out and as far downwind as possible to prevent hot ash burning through the liferaft fabric.

The lookout or lookouts should be changed at frequent intervals so the person on watch stays alert. Such a regular routine helps to maintain morale and although they won't be required in the initial stages, the issue of food and drink at regular intervals can also help. You may find that a light on the outside of the liferaft has come on automatically. This is of use to help indicate your position at night. The light is activated by a seawater battery under the liferaft. The bright orange colour of the liferaft canopy should make it highly visible in daylight. For internal lighting at night, and for signalling, there is a waterproof torch in the liferaft kit, while some liferafts have internal lighting from a second seawater battery.

Risk of Exposure

In warm conditions, and in coastal waters where you are likely to be in the raft for only a relatively short time, risk of exposure is not particularly high. If you are in more exposed conditions where there is less chance of passing vessels, and where your distress signal may not have been sent or received, you should start considering the longer-term implications of your situation, particularly if temperatures are such that there could be a risk of exposure. Even in warm weather temperatures can drop dramatically at night, and every effort should be made to maintain warmth and comfort. Survival suits are obviously the number one choice, but in the absence of these the crew should take as much warm clothing, extra blankets and/or sleeping bags as they can lay their hands on.

If conditions are cold, the crew must be disciplined to keep the door openings shut at all times to maintain temperature inside the liferaft, and the occupants should huddle together as much as possible as this helps to generate and maintain warmth. Exposure can become quite a serious problem after as little as twelve hours in a liferaft unless you take the necessary precautions. Special attention should be paid to the clothing worn by the people keeping lookout who are exposed to the outside air; in particular, heads should be protected as much as possible to reduce heat loss.

Assisting your Rescue

If more than one liferaft has been used in abandoning ship, the two liferafts should be tied together to prevent them drifting apart. The painter can be used for this purpose. Keeping liferafts together gives them a much better chance of being seen and also simplifies the job of the search and rescue authorities.

In these days of radio communication and distress signals the chances of having to survive in a liferaft for more than twelve hours are quite small, in coastal waters at least, and the liferaft can certainly provide a safe haven for this length of time. The blue-water sailor, however, must expect to spend days rather than hours in the liferaft, particularly if it has not been possible to send a distress signal. In such a case careful planning and preparation in the early stages of the abandon-ship procedure can give you a much better chance of survival. In particular, you will need to conserve food and water supplies. Your liferaft should come with these as part of its standard package of equipment. (Unlike coastal liferafts which are not required to have any food and water on board.) Obviously, the more food and drink you can take with you into the liferaft the better will be your chances of survival. If you have time, try to take a pack of playing cards or some books because there is nothing worse and or soul destroying than having to just sit there and contemplate your fate.

When rescue does come, you must be ready for it. There is really little that you can physically do to help. There is a pair of paddles in the liferaft which could give you very limited manoeuvrability, one paddler operating through each door opening to make limited progress. This could just make the difference between not getting alongside and being able to cover those last few metres to the side of the rescue vessel. Otherwise, your role is limited to keeping a good lookout for the approaching rescuers, and indicating your position to them by means of flares or torch signals. They will have to do most of the manoeuvring. Fortunately, the liferaft has a built-in fender, so coming alongside should not be a problem. However, be ready to get out of the liferaft promptly once the rescue boat is alongside. Although you will probably be glad to see the back of it, try to persuade the rescue vessel to pick up the liferaft because, if it is left to float, it will be reported by other vessels and could initiate a further unnecessary and expensive search.

Lifejackets and Buoyancy Aids

Nothing is ever very simple when it comes to safety. This is particularly true of lifejackets, of which there is a wide variety on the market today. However, before we get too far into the subject, it is important to differentiate between lifejackets and buoyancy aids. The requirements for a lifejacket are laid down in British Standard 3595 and they are quite onerous: an adult's lifejacket should have a minimum buoyancy of 16kg (35lb), a child's 9kg (20lb). This aspect of the specification is quite straightforward, but more complex is the requirement that the lifejacket should support the head of an unconscious person so that the mouth is clear of the water, and that it should be able to turn an unconscious or exhausted person from the face-down position to the face-up position in less than five seconds. A lifejacket should also be fitted with a lifting becket to enable rescuers to lift the wearer from the water.

Typical Buoyancy Aid

Like a waistcoat, it does not restrict movement. It relies on inherent foam buoyancy but does not met the British Standard lifejacket requirements for buoyancy or self-righting.

In contrast, a buoyancy aid, or to give it its full title, personal buoyancy aid (PBA), has only to provide flotation and is not required to turn an unconcious person the right way up or to provide the full support and comfort of a lifejacket. A buoyancy aid is really designed for use in inshore waters, where you can expect help quickly if you do fall in the water. It gives you just enough buoyancy to keep you afloat until this help arrives. The full BS3595 lifejacket will give you a reasonable chance of survival even if you get knocked on the head by the boom as you go overboard. But even here there are limitations and compromises, and it is important to understand the various options you are being offered when choosing either lifejackets or bouyancy aids. The decision about the level of protection you need is largely a personal one, but you should understand the risks you are taking in using each of the various types of lifejacket.

Inherent Buoyancy

There are currently five types of life jacket which conform to BS3595, each with particular limitations and compromises. The first, which will be familiar to anybody who has travelled by ship, is the lifejacket which has inherent buoyancy only. Inherent buoyancy is that provided by foam (in the old days it was provided by kapok), and to provide the necessary 16kg (35lb) of buoyancy these life-jackets naturally have to be fairly bulky. They are available only in the styles found on commercial shipping and ferries, and are attach with tapes which are then tied in bows.

There is no doubt that such a lifejacket will do the job for which it is intended and will right you if you are face down and unconscious, but it would be totally unsuitable, because of its bulk, on a yacht. It would be impossible to work the yacht while wearing one. Their bulk and the difficulty of moving in these lifejackets could make them hazardous: they offer only limited protection and could, in fact, increase the risk of you going overboard.

So, for use on yachts, we can ignore the inherent-buoyancy lifejackets for practical reasons. They are not the sort of jacket you could wear before disaster struck, and wearing one when it did could greatly inhibit your ability to abandon ship in an orderly manner and to cope generally with the situation.

It should be mentioned here that if your yacht is over 13.7 metres (45 feet) in length, at which point safety equipment becomes mandatory, you have to carry either this type of lifejacket or one with partial inherent buoyancy.

DTp Lifejacket

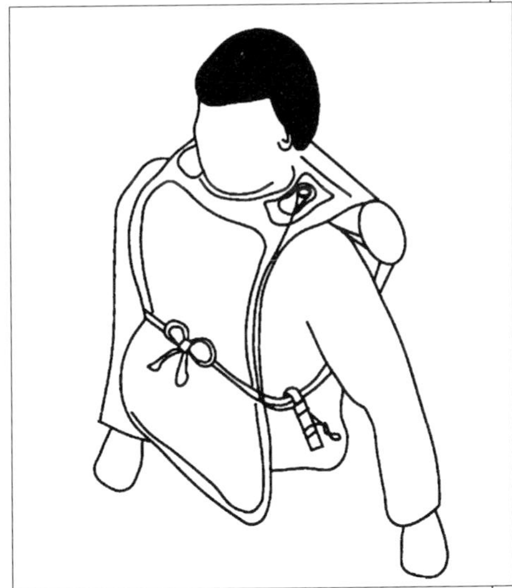

Bulky, relying entirely on inherent buoyancy. Secured with tapes tied in a bow which is not adequate for a working lifejacket.

Typical Inflatable Lifejacket

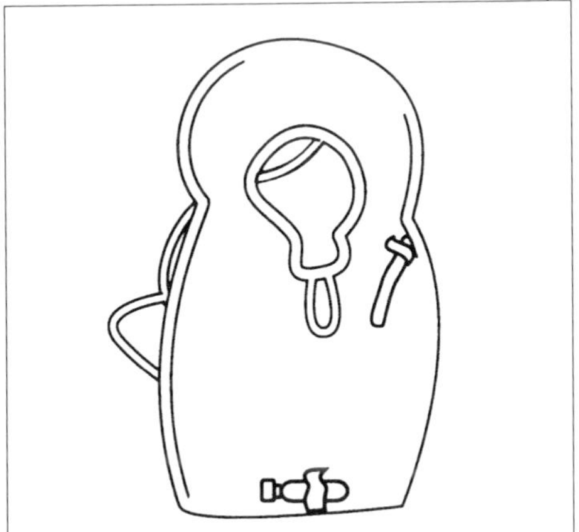

This has both oral and gas inflation. It is only a full lifejacket when inflated.

Oral Inflation

The second type works on entirely the opposite principle and uses full oral inflation to provide buoyancy. In this type there is absolutely no inherent buoyancy, the lifejacket consisting of one or more air chambers which are inflated by blowing, by mouth, through a tube. From the point of view of wearing them and working the yacht, these lifejackets offer very little restriction to movement when they are folded and you hardly notice you have them on. However, should an incident occur – a man overboard, say – you would either have to have blown up the lifejacket for some reason beforehand or be faced with the difficulty of inflating it whilst in the water. From this it is easy to see that if you were to go into the water unconscious, and you hadn't previously inflated your lifejacket, to all intents and purposes you would not be wearing a lifejacket and would be at considerable risk of drowning. But many yachtsmen opt for this type of lifejacket, largely because it is the cheapest and most compact of all those which conform to BS3595.

Full oral inflation lifejackets are available in two types: one which you put over your head like a halter and then do up the straps around the waist and the crotch; the other is put on rather like a waistcoat so that the lifejacket is divided down the front, but the harness connections are similar.

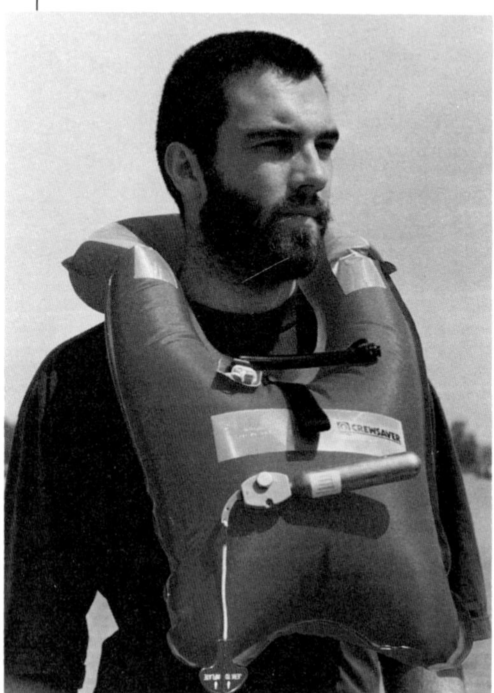

This provides a full 16kg (35lb) of buoyancy and combines both manual and gas inflation. Note the use of reflective tape.

Manual Gas Inflation

The third type has manual gas inflation. The lifejacket itself is very similar to the oral inflation type but incorporates a small carbon dioxide cylinder which is triggered to inflate the lifejacket quickly. It is easy to see the benefits of such a system: in the water you simply find the toggle and pull it and you have a full 16kg (35lb) of buoyancy, which also makes the jacket self-righting. To all intents and purposes, you have a full lifejacket capability simply by pulling on the toggle. And, of course, you can do this just as well on board the yacht if disaster looks near, so there is a degree of flexibility in this type of lifejacket. Manual inflation is also incorporated into the design, just in case the carbon dioxide cylinder fails to work. If you do inflate this type of lifejacket manually, on no account must you fire the cylinder as well, as this will result in too much pressure in the lifejacket which could then burst.

The major snag with this type of lifejacket is that if you go into the water unconcious, and with your lifejacket not inflated, you will again be unsupported. So, while it gives a slightly better capability than the full oral inflation lifejacket, it does not offer the full protection of the inherent buoyancy lifejacket. However, against this you have to weigh up the fact that it is compact, although slightly more bulky than the full oral inflation lifejacket. But you do have to be careful to ensure that the triggering toggle does not catch on anything and fire the lifejacket accidentally.

Automatic Gas Inflation

The next step up from this is the automatic gas inflation lifejacket. This is in most respects similar to the manual gas inflation type, but incorporates an automatic triggering device which is sensitive to water so, if you do fall in, the lifejacket will inflate automatically. As with the previous type, you have the option of inflating it orally. So it would seem that here you have the best of all worlds: a compact lifejacket which will inflate automatically should you do go into the water unconscious, and the full 16kg (35lb) of buoyancy. Even here, however, there is a snag. If you inflate the lifejacket orally before you enter the water, there is the risk that it will explode when the gas cylinder is triggered automatically by the water.

There is also the risk with this type of lifejacket that the automatic device could trigger if you get engulfed by a breaking wave while say working on the foredeck. The triggering device is well protected from rain or spray so it is not very likely to happen just from foul weather, but by their very nature such devices have to be sensitive so it is a possibility to be borne in mind. These lifejackets are the most expensive on the market, and with all of these fully inflatable lifejackets you tend to get the level of protection for which you are prepared to pay.

Buoyancy and Oral Type

Finally, in this round-up of lifejackets, is the type which has part inherent buoyancy and part oral inflation. This might be considered to be a good compromise because there is enough inherent buoyancy, usually about 9kg (20lb), built into the lifejacket to keep you on the surface if you go overboard. It, however, is not sufficient to give the lifejacket a self-righting capability. To do this you have to blow on the inflation tube to add the remaining buoyancy. Whilst the compromise seems logical at first, it could also be argued that you are getting the worst of both worlds with this type of lifejacket – barely enough inherent buoyancy to keep you afloat and certainly not enough to ensure you turn face up should you be unconcious on entering the water – but a lifejacket which is more bulky and cumbersome to wear than the fully inflatable type.

This illustrates the dilemma faced when trying to select the right type of lifejacket and unfortunately there is no easy solution. Personal decisions have to be made.

The Choice

The choice of a lifejacket for use on a yacht or powerboat is reasonably simple. We can rule out those with full inherent buoyancy because of their bulk which renders them impractical. This narrows down the field to those which requiring total or partial inflation. If we are going to rely on inflation to create a fully effective lifejacket, logic suggests that we may as well rely on total inflation, which excludes lifejackets with partial inherent buoyancy which also have the disadvantage of being cumbersome. This, then, leaves us with a choice between three types which rely fully on inflation to provide buoyancy, and this is where personal choice comes in. The choice is likely to be influenced as much by the cost of the lifejacket as by its effectiveness. The vast majority of yachtsmen will opt for the manual inflation type, although the manual/gas inflation type provides a viable alternative without too much increase in cost.

Lifejackets Suitable for Use on Yachts

The children's lifejackets are combined foam and air buoyancy, while the adults' jackets are fully inflatable either by manual or gas cylinder inflation.

The authorities tend to opt out of this decision-making process, merely recommending that a lifejacket should meet BS3595. The RORC requires a lifejacket which is capable of providing not less than 16kg (35lb) of buoyancy, arranged so that an unconscious person will be securely suspended face upwards at approximately 45 degrees to the water. This allows for inherent or inflatable buoyancy. So the choice of lifejacket is very much in the hands of the user or the wearer and the only time you are likely to regret your choice is when you find yourself in the water, perhaps wishing that you had chosen something better!

The Value of the Crotch Strap

Surprisingly, there is nothing in BS3595 which covers the use of a crotch strap on a lifejacket. The Offshore Racing Council recommends that a crotch strap be fitted to each lifejacket for while it may not be the most comfortable thing to wear, when you are in the water, suspended from the lifejacket, you will realise the value of this feature. On dry land a lifejacket

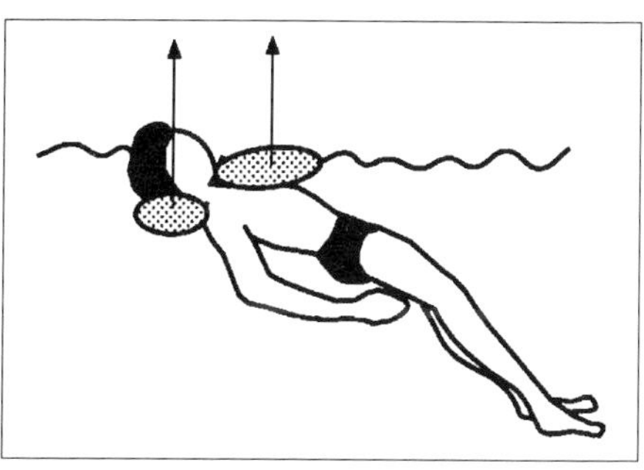

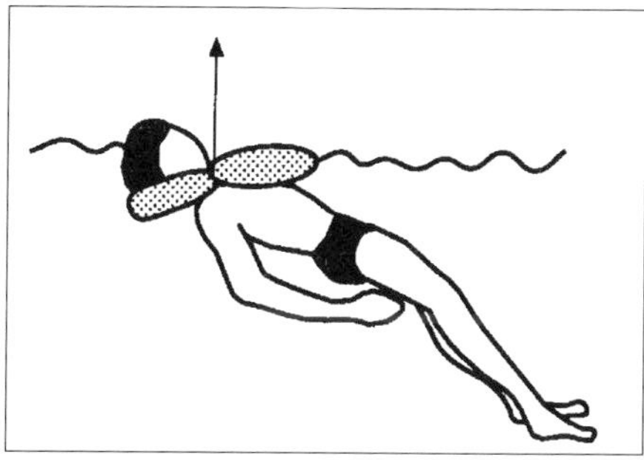

In the water you hang from the lifejacket. The harnes needs to be tight and well secured. When fully inflated the jacket will turn the wearer face upwards. The neck section is important to keep the head in the right position and to prevent the head falling sideways.

may it appear to fit snugly and comfortably, but in the water you are actually hanging from the lifejacket. So, unless there is a crotch strap, the lifejacket could ride up and become ineffective. Without a crotch strap, to prevent the lifejacket riding up, the waist strap must be secured very tightly and, particularly in the case of rotund people, it is almost impossible to get the waist strap tight enough or secure enough with the result that the lifejacket will bunch up around the head and be very uncomfortable. In extreme cases the back of the lifejacket could lift over the head, rendering the jacket virtually useless. So a crotch strap is a very desirable feature on a lifejacket. If you are going to take the trouble to wear a lifejacket, insist on a crotch strap, because only with this feature will the lifejacket be fully effective in the water.

After putting the jacket over your head you put one arm through between the waist and neck straps and then fasten the waist strap. A crotch strap (not shown) extends down from the neck strap and fastens at the front.

Trying Out Your Jacket

Trying out a lifejacket before you have to use it in a crisis is also important. If you can, try the lifejacket in the water as well as on dry land. You will then appreciate the effectiveness and importance of the crotch strap. Put on the lifejacket and inflate it manually, rather than with the gas bottle which is a one-shot item and will then need replacing. If you try to work the yacht wearing your inflated lifejacket you will have some idea of how it can impede your movement. Check whether you can get out through the forehatch whilst wearing it.

The general recommendation would be not to inflate the lifejacket when you are below, or, if it is a full inherent buoyancy type, not even to put it on because you may find it very difficult to get out of the cabin with it on.

Something else worth trying, if it can be arranged when there is a liferaft demonstration, is climbing into the liferaft with a lifejacket on. This can be a very difficult task indeed. It will certainly make you realise the importance of only inflating the lifejacket when it is absolutely necessary and will also indicate how the gas inflation types, with their one-shot inflation, may give you less flexibility in a rescue than the manual inflation type. Unfortunately, there is no such thing as a total solution to the problems of staying afloat: what is right in one situation will not be suitable in another.

Servicing Your Lifejacket

Lifejackets need to be serviced at regular intervals. This applies particularly to the inflation type, whether manual or gas inflation. Their effectiveness depends on maintaining an airtight seal in the air chamber and this needs to be checked at regular intervals. Ideally, lifejackets with any form of inflation should be checked once a year.

A full service should be carried out every two years, but it is recommended that you carry out your own check at least once a year by inflating the lifejacket manually and holding it under water. If any air bubbles are seen escaping, you have a leak in the lifejacket and it should be sent away for repair. Alternatively, simply inflate the lifejacket and check that it stays inflated over a twelve-hour period, bearing in mind that the pressure will drop if the air temperature is lowered. If gas bottle inflation is fitted, there is not a lot you can do in terms of maintenance here, except to unscrew the gas cylinder and weigh it accurately, to ensure that it remains fully charged. The weight of the gas cylinder should be stamped on the outside: any discrepancy in the weight should ring alarm bells and suggest that you replace the cylinder.

General Care and Maintenance

Lifejackets should be stowed in a dry, preferably cool place on board and the crew fully instructed in how to use them. Each crew member should have his or her own lifejacket, with the straps adjusted for a correct fit. This can make donning the lifejacket a quick and simple operation, but of course this can only be done when you have a regular crew. Children's lifejackets require particularly careful adjustment because of the wide range of body sizes.

Colour and Visibilty at Night

For maximum visibilty, lifejackets tend to be a bright orange colour. For night-time use they can be fitted with a light powered by a seawater battery which comes on automatically when immersed in water. But, like the automatic gas-inflation systems, these batteries have to be carefully protected from accidental immersion and tend to have a short life in the conditions which prevail on board the average yacht. Alternatively, there are dry-cell battery lights which have to be switched on. Probably just as effective at night, is reflective tape on the lifejacket, making the person in the water highly visible when a light is shone on them. This reflective tape obviously has to be carefully positioned so that it is on the parts of the lifejacket which remains above the water when in use.

When to be Worn

You should wear a lifejacket all the time when you are on board because there is always the chance you will need it. In practice, however, people tend to wear lifejackets only in bad weather or when there is the risk of an accident, such as when operating on the foredeck. Once again, this tends to be a personal decision, although if the fully inflatable type of lifejacket is used, there is very little discomfort in wearing this all the time. For maximum benefit, the lifejacket should be worn more as a matter of habit than when you think the conditions are bad enough to justify it.

Integral Lifejackets and Combinations of Equipment

Some of the foul weather gear currently on the market has a lifejacket incorporated into the jacket. Such an arrangement does mean that you are wearing a lifejacket every time you put your foul weather gear on, but the disadvantage is that if conditions don't necessitate the use of foul weather gear, you haven't got a lifejacket on. This is another of those compromise areas, and it is probably better to keep the lifejacket separate from the foul weather gear to give greater flexibility.

On a sailing boat it may be necessary to wear a lifejacket and safety harness at the same time, and the two harnesses could conflict or the safety harness could restrict the effectiveness of the lifejacket. If you plan to wear the two together, check that they are compatible. In most cases the safety harness should be worn underneath so that it doesn't hinder the inflation of the lifejacket. This whole problem of finding a compatible suite of equipment, comprising foul weather gear, safety harness and lifejacket, should be looked at very carefully, so that each item is effective on its own and in conjunction with the others. Compatibility can become even more important when it comes to a survival suit, which is the next item we shall look at on the list of safety equipment.

Survival Suits

Survival suits are designed to give the individual a better chance of survival in more extreme conditions. Their primary function is to limit the effects of exposure by restricting loss of body heat, both in and out of the water. In many countries, survival suits are now part of the mandatory safety equipment for fishing vessels likely to be operating in cold conditions. They are also mandatory for yachtsmen on such epic races as the Whitbread Round The World Race.

Few cruising yachtsmen contemplate the idea of a survival suit, yet it could greatly improve their prospects of survival in situations where rescue may take some time and where conditions are such as to increase the risk of exposure. This reluctance on the part of yachtsmen probably stems from the fact that early designs of survival suit were unsuitable for working in: they were only items of equipment to be put on before taking to a liferaft, if there was time to do this. Cost has also been a factor: survival suits are not cheap, generally being more expensive than a suit of foul weather gear, and the expense of the partial duplication of equipment for something which would only be used in extreme conditions was hard to justify.

Today's survival suits are more practical pieces of equipment. To a large degree, this allows them to double up as foul weather gear and thus helps to contain costs. However, for normal cruising in the summer months, foul weather gear provides adequate protection from wind and rain and the survival suit can seem a rather extreme piece of equipment to wear under such comparatively benign conditions. Yet every sailor or powerboater who considers operating in the winter months in British waters should consider a survival suit an essential item of equipment.

Wet Suit

Survival suits operate by creating a thermal barrier between the cold water, or air, outside and the warm body inside. Some designs work on the wet suit principle whereby foam rubber absorbs water, which in itself is cold but which is heated up by the warm body. Because this absorbed water is not circulating, it creates the necessary thermal barrier. Wet suits can also be quite effective against the wind, although the big snag with this type of survival suit is that it has to be close-fitting to be effective, which means taking off all normal clothing and then putting on the wet suit as a 'second skin'. Suits of this type are comparatively easy to work in but, worn over long periods, can become uncomfortable.

Foam Rubber Suits

Foam rubber can provide an effective thermal barrier and is used in many survival suit designs. Some of the early ones were little more than a partly-shaped bag of sealed foam rubber which, while effective in preventing loss of body heat, were virtually impossible to work in, and therefore brought their own dangers. They were intended for putting on over ordinary clothing and tended to be designed so that one size suited a wide variety of body shapes. Drawstrings helped to reduce some of the bulk of the fabric for thinner people. These suits were really designed to be put on either in the liferaft or immediately before having to enter the water, and could in no way be construed as meeting the ideal of a working suit which is also a survival suit.

Dry Suit

The dry suit concentrates on keeping water away from the body but relies on conventional clothing to provide the insulation. It is a practical working suit, and as such is worn by many boat operators working in more extreme conditions. Whilst dry suits are effective at preventing water ingress, which can reduce survival times, their dependence on internal insulation in the form of alternative clothing worn underneath makes them less effective as survival suits, but they are one of the possible compromises available. However, like wet suits, dry suits, if worn for longer periods, can prove quite uncomfortable, particularly around the neck and wrist seals where circulation can be restricted unless these are carefully adjusted. Dry suits do not usually incorporate the vital head protection.

Survival Suit and Foul Weather Gear

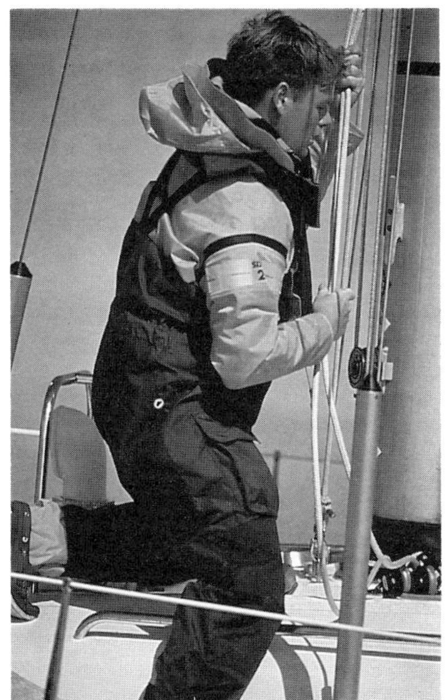

A survival suit and practical foul weather clothing. This suit is the inflatable type giving thermal protection. It incorporates an inflatable lifejacket.

The trend today is towards a suit tailored more to the individual's shape and requirements. As it is designed to double up as foul weather gear, the suit will already be in use should the wearer fall overboard or an emergency develop quickly in poor weather conditions. This can be an important consideration as emergencies rarely develop slowly, and the time needed to don first a survival suit and then a lifejacket, while still trying to retain some sort of control, may just not be available. Usually in this situation, it is the putting-on of the survival suit which suffers, so when the crew take to the liferaft, survival suits have either to be left behind or have to be put on inside the liferaft – a very difficult operation. Even putting on a survival suit in a boat which is tossing around in a rough sea can be very difficult, and some designs can take ten minutes to get on – hardly practical in an emergency!

The same suit in action. The casualty floats well up in the water with the suit providing most of the buoyancy. Note the clear plastic face mask and hood. Such a suit should allow survival for up to twenty-four hours in temperate conditions, yet when deflated is still a practical working suit.

Methods of Insulation

These modern designs obviously still need good insulating properties and there are two approaches: one being to use foam as the insulating medium, the other being to use air or gas. Even though carefully adjusted and shaped, foam suits still have a degree of bulk which can be uncomfortable if worn continuously and can develop high temperatures inside if the ambient conditions are reasonably warm. The use of air or gas as the insulating medium means that the suit can be worn deflated, which makes it little more bulky than normal foul weather gear, but can be inflated should the wearer fall into the water or conditions deteriorate. The insulation properties of carbon dioxide make it one of the best of the more common gases, but air is second best, so these suits are usually designed with a gas insulation system and optional manual inflation. Both have advantages and they can be used in conjunction as they can in a lifejacket but, once again, the problem of overinflation has to be guarded against if the gas bottle is for some reason discharged after manual inflation.

One advantage with this type of inflatable suit is that the level of insulation can be varied by the user. Obviously, the more inflation used, the less workable the suit, but it is possible for the wearer to inflate the suit to just sufficiently match the conditions. For instance, if the wearer is in the cockpit of a yacht, with no work to do, he can inflate the suit to give a measure of protection, but should there suddenly be work to do, he can quickly deflate it.

Protecting the Extremities

With survival suits, it is quite easy to protect the main parts of the body from exposure, but it is much harder to give protection to the extremities. To protect the feet, some form of boot is usually incorporated into the survival suit as an integral part so that there is no problem with water ingress at this point. The hands are a different matter as hands are often required to execute delicate tasks. Gloves are the only real solution, but these should be capable of being sealed when in use to prevent water penetration via the wrist seals, and they need to be attached by strings or other means so that they don't get lost. Protection for the head is more difficult: the survivor still needs to breath and to be able to see! Heat loss from the head is more rapid than from other parts of the body because of the large blood supply to this area. So protection here is vitally important and some form of insulated hood is essential on survival suits.

Protecting the face is the most difficult part of survival suit design, and here the usual solution is to have a clear plastic mask which can be rolled down over the face if the survivor finds himself in the water. This mask will prevent water splashing into the face but has to be open to the air to allow breathing.

Survival Suit Combined with Lifejacket

Survival suits cannot be considered in isolation: you have to look at the whole package of lifejacket and survival suit. Many designs of survival suit will trap air inside and, once in the water, this air will rise to the highest part of the suit, which could be the feet, thus upsetting the balance of the buoyancy necessary for the lifejacket to do its job effectively. If they are to work properly together, lifejacket and survival suit should be fully integrated and the current trend is to combine the two pieces of equipment into one unit. The lifejacket is built in to the survival suit as an integral part and the two are thoroughly tested and evaluated together to ensure that they are fully compatible and will work effectively under a wide variety of conditions. The face mask and hood may actually form part of the lifejacket's structure, rather than the survival suit's, but the approach to this item varies from manufacturer to manufacturer.

A tremendous amount of research work has been gone into modern survival suit design, largely funded by oil companies needing effective survival suits for the offshore oil industry. Yachtsmen are now reaping the benefit of some of this detailed research, which for the first time is producing survival suits suitable for use on sailing yachts.

Any yachtsman going to sea in the winter should seriously consider investing in a survival suit. While a good set of foul weather gear, with warm clothing worn underneath, will provide a considerable degree of insulation and protection from cold weather, it is by no means waterproof when the wearer is actually in the water, and the protection offered is very limited compared with that of a properly designed survival suit. In winter, too, there is less sea traffic around and this could increase the time you might have to spend awaiting rescue. In this situation the wearing of a survival suit could literally make the difference between life and death. In winter, wearing a survival suit and lifejacket should make it possible to survive for at least twelve hours in the water, and double that time in summer, without serious problems of exposure.

The Importance of a Co-ordinated Safety Package

It cannot be emphasised strongly enough that the various items of survival equipment we have looked at in this chapter should never be considered in isolation. A liferaft on its own does not guarantee survival, nor does a lifejacket, nor yet a survival suit. What you have on board must not only give you a reasonable chance of survival, but all the separate pieces must work together. For instance, wearing a lifejacket may keep you afloat, but it may impede your ability to climb into the liferaft. So it will pay you to look very carefully at this business of survival, to weigh up the risks involved in the type of sailing you favour, and to spend some considerable time looking at all the various options. Only by doing this will you come up with your personal optimum set of survival gear.

7 Safety on Board

In this chapter we shall look at the sorts of safety routines and equipment which are aimed equally at preventing disaster. Prevention is obviously better than cure and virtually all the equipment on a boat can affect safety in one way or another. If a halyard breaks on a sailing boat, this can make you vulnerable and put you at risk, so checking the halyards at regular intervals should be part of your safety routine. On a powerboat, if an engine water hose fails, this will let water into the boat, so checking these hoses should be an automatic part of the safety routine. But, if you want to be reasonably safe at sea, all the equipment and fittings should be checked at regular intervals. This checking should become so routine that the crew instinctively think 'safety' all the time.

A regular crew will soon get to know where the safety and emergency equipment is kept, how it is stowed and how to use it. There may be no obvious need for a safety briefing but it does no harm to have regular reminders, and every time you take a new crew member on board, a safety briefing should form an essential part of his or her induction. This will also serve to refresh the memories of the rest of the crew.

For every piece of equipment there is a right way and a wrong way, or perhaps we should say a safe way and a less safe way, of installing and using it. This is what this chapter is all about.

The Compass

It might surprise you to find the compass classified as 'safety equipment', but without this source of reference it would be easy to lose track of where you are or in which direction you are heading, particularly at night or in poor visibility. Anyone who has sailed a boat at night will know that the compass can be equally important for maintaining a heading in relation to the wind. This is particularly true when running downwind, when there is a risk of gybing. Even in a powerboat, there are severe risks of wandering off course in rough sea conditions, particularly in short, steep seas and tidal races.

If a compass is going to be used effectively it must be easy to read. You need to be able to take in the heading at a quick glance, rather than have to peer into the compass, which takes your eye off what is happening outside the boat.

Card Compasses

Compasses come in several styles, mainly to meet different installation requirements. The traditional compass is gimbal-mounted, but this type has largely been replaced by one contained within a hemispherical bowl which allows the compass card to stay level even when the boat is tilting. This compass is designed to be looked down into, which works reasonably well on sailing boats, but does have the disadvantage that you have to keep glancing down and then up again to the horizon or the sails, which is disruptive to concentration. Ideally, the compass should be mounted close to eye level and at some distance from the helmsman, so that there is a minimal change of focus and viewpoint between the horizon and the compass. An alternative type is the bulkhead compass, which is mounted in a hole in the bulkhead and can usually be viewed from either side.

Grid compasses, where a moveable pair of parallel lines on the compass housing can be set to the course to be steered, are usually found on powerboats rather than sailing boats. They provide an effective means of indicating the course, and instead of having to read the numbers, you simply keep the north/south line between the parallel lines of the grid on the casing. However, such compasses have to be mounted where can you look down into them. On powerboats, the compass tends to be mounted higher up on the dashboard and for this there are compass types which have a dished bowl which can be easier to read from a more horizontal viewpoint.

Electronic Compasses

All these types of compass are based on the traditional swinging card compass which has magnets attached to its underside. In contrast, the electronic compass has opened up new compass display possibilities. One of its big advantages is that there is no need for the display to be mounted horizontally; it can be mounted in any convenient position and, as the display is not affected by any magnetic influence, it does not have to be separate from other electronic or electrical equipment. In an electronic compass, it is only the sensor unit which is magnetically sensitive, and this can be located in any convenient part of the boat away from other magnetic influences.

Electronic compass displays are of two main types: one is fairly conventional, with a rotating needle to indicate the heading; the alternative is the LCD (liquid crystal display). The LCD type is generally less easy to read and less sensitive to precise course changes. Yet another type of heading indicator found in electronic compasses is the digital display, which is surprisingly easy to steer by once you get used it. You will often find a combination of two of these alternatives incorporated into one display.

The alternative to heading indicators is the off-course indicator. This is a simple dial with a left/right indicator. The course to be steered is set remotely and then this dial shows whether you are to the left or right of the course and indicates the way to steer to get back on to the course.

There is a lot to commend this type: you don't have to read numbers on a dial, a quick glance tells you whether you are off course and which way to steer. The problem with this type of unit at present is that most of the displays have quite small indicators which are therefore not easy to read when the compass is mounted some distance from the helmsman. Indeed, this is a criticism which can be levelled at most compass displays on the market today. There is a great need for improvement in the types of display used on both sailing and powerboats to make them easier to read, particularly at night when lighting levels are lower.

Keeping the Compass Working

The electronic compass does require a power supply to keep it working, but then the standard type of magnetic compass also needs a power supply for the lighting at night, so both are dependent on the electrical system to a greater or lesser extent. Bearing this in mind, an alternative power supply or lighting circuit should be arranged, so that the compass can remain effective even if there is a power failure. Alternatively there should be two or more compasses at the steering position, so that if one fails, the other can quickly be brought into use. A torch can provide an alternative means of illumination if the power supply fails, and the standby hand-bearing compass can be useful for emergency steering information.

Navigation Lights

Like the compass, navigation lights tend to be taken for granted, but they also have a vital safety role to play. Navigation lights are usually fitted on some of the most exposed parts of the boat, so only the highest standards of installation and maintenance will ensure their survival and continued working. You must remember that when electricity and water mix, the water always wins! Only a fully waterproof electrical circuit will do for the navigation light system. Any connecting plugs should not only be waterproof, but screwed down securely to ensure the water is kept out. Where the wire runs from its outlet into the light itself, it should be run downwards and then upwards into the light. This will allow any water on the wire to drain away from the light. Where the wire itself enters through the mast or through the pulpit rails, rubber grommets should be fitted around the entry to prevent chafe. The same applies on powerboats: where the wire exits from the superstructure mouldings a watertight gland should be fitted.

The requirements for navigation lights are laid down in the International Regulations for the Prevention of Collision at Sea. A powerboat is required to have four lights: a masthead light, a stern light, two side lights. A sailing boat is only required to have port and starboard lights, as well as a stern light, and on any yacht less than twenty metres (sixty-five feet) in length, either power or sail, the rules allow for the red and green side lights to be combined in one lantern. Yachts of less than twelve metres (thirty-nine feet), which covers the vast majority of sailing yachts on the market today, can use a single masthead light where the port, starboard and stern lights are all combined in one lantern. Such a lantern is much more likely to survive than the individual lights mounted on the pulpit and will be easily visible out in the open sea. In harbour, however, lights mounted high on the masthead can be misleading and less visible to other craft nearby. Here the side lights mounted on the pulpit are a much better proposition.

You will need to bear in mind the possibilities of bulb failure or a fuse blowing in the navigation light system and the effect on your safety. On a powerboat, only if the stern light goes out will you be left without any lights at all facing in one sector. This means that a bulb failure is not quite so critical, but you could present a confusing picture to other craft until the problem is rectified. On a sailing boat, if all the lights are combined in a masthead lantern, you could have a real problem if there is a bulb failure as you would lose all your navigation lights at once, and getting to the light to replace the bulb is difficult, if not impossible, at sea. Even if you have separate lights on the pulpit, and a separate stern light, losing one can leave you with a sector showing no lights, which could be dangerous in crowded waters.

There are several solutions available, so you need to find the one which is appropriate to your particular craft. One solution would be to have duplicate lights, fitted with a changeover switch, so that if one set fails you can switch to the other. This is an expensive solution and one which is only likely to be practicable on a powerboat. Because the lights tend to be more accessible on a powerboat, changing a bulb is not quite such a major operation as it might be on a sailing boat, so you can probably get away with a single set of lights, but it would be advisable to have a second circuit available via a changeover switch so that in the event of an electrical failure or a fuse blowing, you can rectify the problem very quickly.

On sailing boats, there is probably little you can do about a masthead light failure until you get into harbour. The remedy is to have spare port and starboard lights which can be mounted on the pulpit if required. These lights can also be used for additional clarity when you are entering or leaving harbour. Remember that with a sailing boat when you are entering or leaving harbour you will probably have the sails down, so you should be showing the lights for a power-driven vessel, which include a masthead light in addition to the side lights and stern light. These pulpit lights can perform this function, too.

Another option is to have a powerful torch, or floodlight, available, which in the event of a failure, can be shone on the sails or on the superstructure of a powerboat to give other craft some idea of your location and course while you get things fixed. Such a floodlight is useful for a wide variety of emergencies and should be considered as an essential item of safety equipment. Ideally, it should be battery-operated so that it is independent of the electrical system, but this tends to limit the power output of the light and a fully waterproof light, operating from the boat's power supply, would be acceptable. To meet visibility requirements, all navigation lights should have a bulb with a minimum power of twenty-five watts meet the visibility range requirements. Where separate lights are used, this can drain the batteries of a sailing boat, which is why the combined masthead light tends to be favoured.

Radar Reflectors

Radar reflectors are a safety aid for use in poor visibility. They enhance the radar response of a small vessel and thereby its detectability to other vessels. It is intended mainly for small yachts, particularly those of wood or GRP construction which present poor radar targets. Larger yachts in any case generate a reasonable radar return which is equal to, or better than, that generated by a radar reflector.

There are a number of different types of radar reflector on the market. The traditional one is the octahedral reflector which consists of three square metal sheets interlocked at right angles to each other. The many reflecting surfaces thus created ensure that the radar beam is reflected in a direct line back from whatever angle it strikes. Maximum reflection is obtained when the radar beam is directed into one of the internal corners of the reflector, of which there are eight. These units are efficient but not particularly practical. They are difficult to install on a yacht unless they are clamped to the mast, but here the sharp edges can snag and chafe the sails and ropes. To be effective such reflectors have to have a minimum diagonal length of 46cm (18 inches), which makes it quite a large unit for a small craft. If it is simply hoisted on a halyard, it will rattle and bang about and it is likely to chafe quickly through the halyard itself if this runs back over the reflector.

The octahedral reflector has therefore largely been replaced by the encapsulated type, which look rather like a sausage fender in a plastic case. Although it can be hoisted loose on a halyard it is better if it is permanently installed by being clamped to the mast. This type of reflector houses an array of light metal reflecting surfaces within a watertight housing, and the manufacturers claim it is more efficient than the octahedral type. It is certainly more compact and easy to install. But beware of some designs which are described as ultra-compact. Before you buy such a unit ask for some proof of its efficiency. This is not something you can easily check yourself and there have been rogue units on the market which are less effective even than the radar returns from the yacht itself.

Another thing to check when purchasing a radar reflector is that it is effective over a wide range of angles of heel, say up to 25°, because without this coverage you could, perhaps at a critical time, disappear off the radar display of approaching ships.

An effective radar reflector should make you detectable to an approaching vessel at up to five miles. This compares with the three or four mile detection range of, say, a twelve metre (thirty-nine feet) yacht and the one to two mile range of a small craft. If your boat is detected on the other vessel's radar at three miles or more, there is a good chance that it will be able to plot your position, course and speed and take any necessary avoiding action in plenty of time. The other vessel will 'see' you if you have a one or two mile detection range, but this will not allow much time to determine the best avoiding action.

The detection of small craft can be particularly difficult when there is any sort of sea running because the radar returns from the sea itself, called the sea clutter, can be just as strong as the returns from any yacht within that clutter. This could result in your not even being detected unless you have a radar reflector fitted which will allow detection outside the clutter range. This makes this type of passive defence very important for whilst you can avoid mixing with big ships by keeping to inshore shallow waters if fog comes down, many other yachts may be adopting the same tactics as you, so it is vitally important that you are detectable to each other in poor visibility.

Fog Horns

Radar reflectors are not required by the International Regulations for the Prevention of Collision at Sea. Under these rules the solution to announcing your presence in fog is the use of the ship's horn or whistle. This equipment is mandatory, like your navigation lights. You are required to sound the horn at prescribed intervals although it is surprising just how many vessels don't comply with this requirement, which could make them liable in the event of a collision. Sailing yachts are more likely to sound their fog horns because, with the helmsman out in the open, he is much more likely to hear the fog horns of approaching vessels.

On powerboats the engine noise may drown out any chance of hearing other vessels' fog horns, and operating in an enclosed wheelhouse can have a similar muting effect. These days even large vessels tend to rely on radar rather than on fog horns. The use of fog signals may be falling into disuse, but that does not exempt you from sounding them. Your insurance company will not be very pleased if you have a collision as a result of not complying with the regulations, even if you manage to walk away unscathed.

The most popular type of fog signal for yachts is the aerosol-powered portable unit. These are very practical and reasonably loud, although fairly directional. If you do rely on this type, you must keep at least one spare cylinder available because regular sounding will soon exhaust a cylinder. Powerboats have a built-in electric or air-powered horn, which will probably be more effective than the air type, but again can be directional, although they are usually pointing ahead where the greatest risk of collision is likely to be. On a sailing boat there can be just as much risk of collision from faster vessels coming up astern, so you should bear this in mind when directing your fog signals.

The traditional mouth-operated fog horn is very effective at close quarters but has little carrying power – it is unlikely to be heard more than a few hundred metres away. Your fog signal should have a range of up to one mile if it is going to break through the ambient noise on board a listening vessel.

Hand Bell

The collision regulations also require that you have a bell on board which you should sound when you are at anchor in foggy conditions. You could bang on a frying pan or make another similar noise instead of the bell, but very few yachts carry either a bell or sound fog signals when they are at anchor. These non-automatic repetitive signals fog signals can be disturbing to the rest of the crew and demand someone on watch at all times. However, if you are at anchor in poor visibility, you should have someone on watch anyway! And before deciding that you are not going to sound fog signals at anchor, think very carefully. You will almost certainly be the smaller of the two vessels involved in any collision, and the chances are that you will come off worse. This makes you vulnerable, quite apart from the legal wrangles about liability which might result.

Anchors

Anchors form a vital part of your safety equipment. They not only hold you safely when you want to anchor off a quiet beach, they can also be a last resort if your engine or sails fail, and you are drifting ashore. Any yacht should carry at least two anchors, partly because there are some situations where you may need two anchors out – to provide security or to stop the yacht swinging to the wind or the tide – but also so that there is one in reserve if the first anchor fails, or is lost. Table 3 shows the recommended weights of anchor for different sizes of yacht, applicable to both sail and power vessels.

Table 3: Anchors and Chain Sizes

Length Over All (metres)	Anchor Weight (kg)	Chain Diameter (mm)
7	7	7
8	9	7
9	11	8
10	13	8
11	15	9
12	17	9
14	22	10
16	27	11

Powerboats with a high superstructure which can greatly increase the windage, and hence the strain on the anchor line, could even have an anchor one size heavier than recommended. The problem with these recommended anchor sizes is that they are a compromise between convenience and safety. For convenience, you want an anchor as light as possible; for easy handling, particularly if it is stowed inboard and you have to lift it over the rail, but also if you have to pull the anchor line in manually. With power-assisted capstans there is not so much of a problem, but always bear in mind that there might be a power failure and you might have to resort to hauling the anchor in manually. However, the heavier the anchor the more effective it is going to be in extreme conditions such as strong winds and heavy seas. Rather than be tempted to go for the lightest possible anchor, bear in mind the emergency aspects of using the anchor and try and go at least one size heavier than the recommendations, always provided you are confident you can handle the larger size. The second anchor should preferably be the same size as the main anchor, although in most circumstances, this second, or as it is sometimes called, the kedge, anchor is invariably one size smaller because it may have to be carried away in the dinghy when it is used.

Anchors come in a variety of designs, most of which have good and bad points. Some are more effective on different types of sea bottom than others, but in an emergency situation, you probably will have little or no choice as to the sea-bed conditions in which you have to use the anchor. You want a general-purpose anchor which will be effective under all conditions.

There is no doubt that the Fisherman's anchor is the most effective for general-purpose use. It is also the one used by the RNLI on their lifeboats. However, this type of anchor is difficult to handle, is not self-stowing, and is less effective in mud and soft sand. Most yachts today go for a self-stowing type of anchor which can simply be hauled up over the special bow fairlead where it locks into position and is automatically secured. The main types available today are the Danforth, the CQR, the Bruce and the Stockless.

Danforth Anchor

The Danforth anchor is made from galvanised welded steel plate and is probably the lightest anchor relative to its effectiveness. It digs in well in soft bottom conditions and is generally effective, but the stabilising arms attached to the flukes do stick out when the anchor is stowed at the bow which means it is not very friendly in crowded marinas. Because it is made of welded steel, the Danforth anchor has to be strongly made but there are imitations of this patented design which are less robust and which can suffer bent flukes when used under stress conditions.

CQR and Bruce Anchors

The CQR anchor is rather like a plough which digs itself into the seabed. It is as effective as the Danforth, particularly in softer bottom conditions.

It stows conveniently at the bow, but the CQR is heavy in relation to some other types. The Bruce anchor is a comparatively modern design which benefits by having no moving parts to wear. The carefully shaped flukes both stabilise the anchor and encourage it to dig in. It also self-stows conveniently and is proving very popular amongst yachtsmen. It is also reasonably effective in most bottom conditions but, like the CQR and the Danforth, the Bruce anchor is not so effective when the bottom consists of rocks or large stones. This is where the Fisherman's anchor really scores.

Stockless Anchor
The Stockless anchor is rarely seen on yachts these days. It was originally developed as a self-stowing anchor for use in hawse pipes and it is heavy in relation to its effectiveness.

The Anchor Line

As important as the anchor itself is the line which connects it to the yacht. Ideally, the anchor line should be entirely of chain because, to be effective, an anchor needs a horizontal pull on the shank to encourage the flukes to dig into the seabed. Chain is far more effective than rope in getting this horizontal, or as near horizontal as possible, pull on the anchor line. The weight of the chain causes the anchor line to adopt a catenary arc, providing sufficient chain is paid out (about three times the height of tide), to ensure a near-horizontal pull. If rope is used, then this has little

Anchor Lines

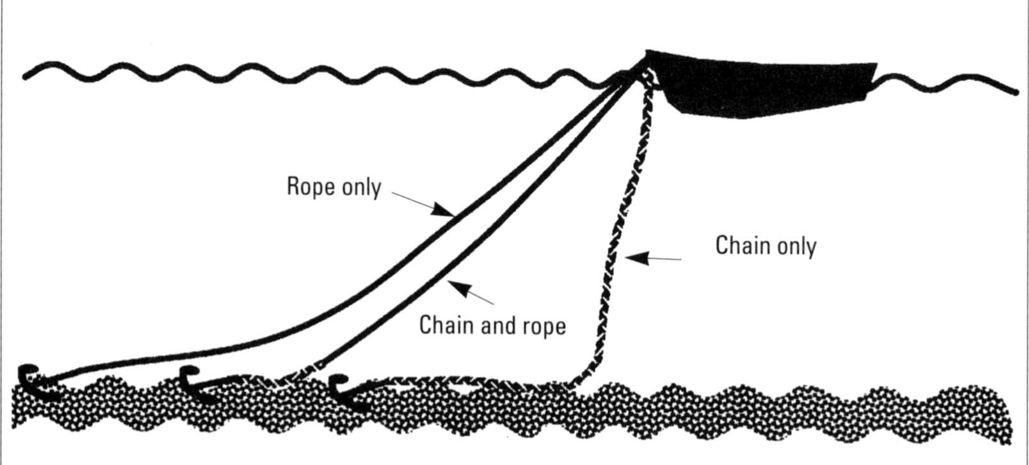

Chain gives a near-horizontal pull on the anchor. The combination chain and rope is a useful compromise. Note the long scope or length of rope anchor line needed to get a reasonable angle of pull on the anchor. In a crowded anchorage, particularly in strong winds and or tides, the boats on rope lines will swing round in a huge circle whereas the boats on chain will need much less space around them.

inherent weight and the connection made between the anchor on the sea bed and the surface is nearer to being a straight line, one which produces a partly upwards and therefore less effective pull.

On many smaller yachts a compromise is reached by using a combination of rope and chain. The first few metres attached to the anchor are usually chain, the remainder being of rope. This combination is commonly found on planing powerboats and performance sailing boats where weight is more critical. Where a capstan is used then an all-chain anchor line is preferable because the capstan can cope with this much more easily. In emergencies chain is much more effective than rope, not only because of the horizontal pull on the anchor but also the resistance to chafe on the sea bed.

Chafe can also occur at the bow fairlead, so with a rope anchor line you need to wrap rags or other material around the rope to reduce the chafe, especially if you anchor in waves or where the yacht is swinging about. Rope made from nylon is the best material because it will stretch and absorb shock loads. Chain can also absorb shock to a certain extent, obviously not by stretching, but because of the fact if enough chain has been paid out it lies in a curve. When placed under extreme load, the curve gently straightens out, then drops back when the load is reduced.

If the anchor has to be used in an emergency, then it will only be as effective as the holding power of the anchor, the strength of the anchor line at its weakest point and the attachment point of the line in the yacht. If a capstan is fitted, this is usually an adequately strong mooring point, but the mountings of the capstan should be checked to make sure that there is a good spread of the load throughout the adjacent structure of the yacht. If a mooring post or cleat is used to secure the anchor line, then this should be similarly securely attached to the structure of the yacht. In extreme conditions a turn of the line should be taken around this cleat or mooring post and the line backed up around the mast, or alternative strong point further aft in the vessel. This helps to spread the load.

Guard Rails / Lifelines

Guard rails, or lifelines as they are often called, are an essential part of the safety equipment of any boat, being designed to perform the vital function of stopping you falling overboard! If someone should fall against the guard rails when the yacht is rolling, they subject the stanchions and the rails to considerable stress and unless these fittings are strongly constructed and fastened, there is a risk of failure at the critical moment. Organisations like the RORC specify minimum requirements for guard rails and pulpits to reduce the risk of failure.

It is essential that the stanchions are firmly secured to the deck, which normally means through-bolting them, although on metal vessels they can be welded and on GRP vessels they can be bonded in. Much the same applies to pulpits and pushpits, the rigid sections of guard rails at the bow and stern respectively. The stanchions need to be as upright as possible; the RORC allows a maximum of 10° from the vertical. The required height of the lifelines is 45cm (18 inches) on vessels under nine metres (28 feet) in length and 60cm (24 inches) on vessels over nine metres in length. In the latter case, double lifelines are required. The wires have also to be a minimum size, depending on the length of the boat, and there are stipulations about the gaps between wires and the spacing of the stanchions.

Rails and Jackstays

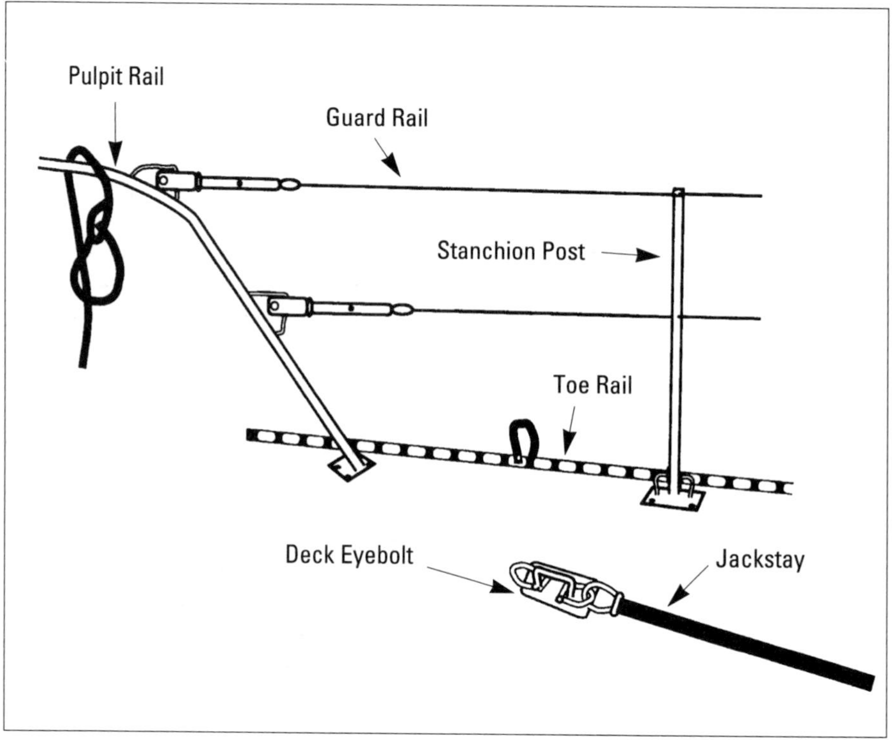

Note that with all these opportunities to clip on with a safety-harness lanyard, only the jackstay, the toe rail and, if strengthened, the pulpit can be used.

The whole aim of these regulations is to provide a secure fence around the boat which will stop people being washed overboard, even under the impetus of solid water washing across the deck. The RORC requirements are for racing boats, but they should also be considered the minimum for cruising yachts. A lifeline 60cm (24 inches) above the deck is only just adequate and will only stop someone going overboard if they have been lying or crouching on the deck. It will certainly not stop anyone who was standing up. But the guard rail will at least provide something to hang on to, which could arrest a rapid exit overboard. The pulpits and pushpits on sailing boats give added security in these work areas, particularly the pulpit which gives good security during sail changing and anchor work. It is possible that raised bulwarks may provide some of the initial protection in this area, and if these are fitted, the guard rail should be over and above the bulwark height and the total of the two combined should be at least the 60cm minimum.

On powerboats guard rails are also required, although more to provide protection when mooring up in harbour, or when anchoring, because there is little requirement for foredeck work. Guard rails and bulwarks are important around the open cockpit area aft, and here solid rails or bulwarks provide better protection than the more flexible guard rails, being much more secure to brace against if the movement of the vessel catches you unawares.

Guard rails are normally fitted by the manufacturers and are something over which the owner may have little control. However, it is still the owner's responsibility to make sure that guard rails are not only fitted and secured adequately, but are maintained in sound condition.

Toe rails fitted around the working areas of the deck also perform a valuable role by providing the crew with something to brace their feet against. They can also prevent tools and other fittings sliding off the deck, but the main requirement of the toe rail is to give the crew a foot grip around the edge of the deck, when working on the foredeck. Again, this is primarily for sailing boats. Toe rails can be moulded into a GRP deck moulding or can be added as wooden or metal strips, depending on the construction of the vessel.

Jackstays

Jackstays are another vital fitting on sailing boats as they provide the main anchorage for safety harnesses. The RORC specifies the requirements for jackstays, which should be made from stainless steel wire of 1×19 construction with a minimum diameter of 5mm, or webbing of equivalent strength specified as a breaking strain of 2,000kg.They should be attached through either bolted or welded deck plates, or similarly strong and suitable anchorages. Their main purpose is to provide a secure and sliding attachment for the safety harness clip, so that crew members can move from the cockpit to the foredeck without having to unclip the harness and put themselves at risk. On some yachts the deck layout may render this impossible, which means that there have to be double jackstays, perhaps one on the coachroof aft of the main mast, and another forward.

The strain on jackstays can be considerable if a crew member does go overboard, as his whole weight is taken by the jackstay, via the safety harness line. To be effective, jackstays need to be fitted tightly between two securing points. The pull on these anchorage points can therefore be quite considerable if the full weight of a crew member is pulling upwards or sideways on the middle point of the wire. In addition to jackstays, anchorage points for safety harnesses are required in the vicinity of working areas, such as the mast or the sheet winches. The anchorage points would normally be in the form of eyebolts through-bolted or welded into position.

Clip on at All Times

The crew can also be at risk when coming up on deck or going below. There can be a tendency, once you have got on deck, to wait before clipping on. But you could be at your most vulnerable as you get used to change of environment from below to the cockpit. This could be just the moment a wave decides to come on board, or the boat to make a heavy roll, and over you go. So some means of clipping on as you come up on deck and then of transferring the lanyard to a cockpit securing point is necessary to give the right level of security.

On powerboats there is little need for safety harnesses because there is little need to go out on deck. Provision for jackstays is not therefore normally made on powerboats, although a case could be made for people sitting in the open cockpit having to wear safety harnesses to give them some measure of protection. However, because there isn't the same need to move about on a powerboat that there is on a sailing boat, a better proposition on a powerboat could be the use of safety harnesses which are integral to each seat, rather like the safety harnesses used in cars. This type of safety harness can be particularly effective on fast powerboats where the movement can be quick and unpredictable and where any lack of concentration on the part of the crew can lead to injury.

Safety Harness and Hooks

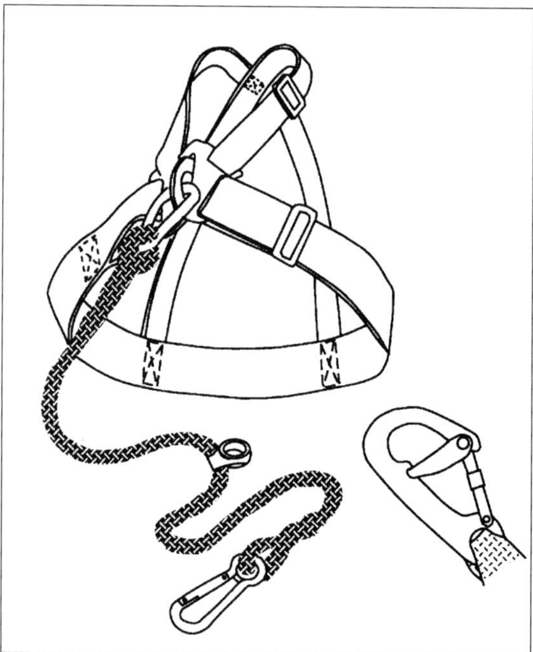

The carbine hook is often replaced by the more secure type shown bottom right which cannot capsize. The ring on the lanyard allows the harness to be secured with a bight.

The sailing boat type of safety harness, using a lanyard, is not recommended on powerboats capable of a speed of more than eight knots for if you go overboard at higher speed whilst connected by a harness, you could suffer severe back injury, or worse. It is generally argued that if you do go overboard from a fast powerboat, it is better to do so without attachment and to wait for the boat to pick you up, rather than risk being dragged along at speed, with the attendant risk of being sucked into the propeller aperture.

Safety harnesses are necessary on a sailing boat whenever the sea conditions are lively, but are doubly important in bad weather or at night, and the skipper should insist that any crew on deck wear them, if he feels that the conditions warrant it. The idea of safety harnesses is, of course, to try and prevent people going overboard. This means that the lanyard should be kept as short as possible. Harnesses are often fitted with two clips, one on a short lead and one on a longer line, giving the wearer a choice to suit the work he is doing on deck. When moving around deck, getting in and out of the cockpit, two clips also allows the second to be attached before the first is disconnected. Safety harnesses should never be clipped to the guard rails because thus attached they will not prevent the wearer from going overboard, nor are guard rails stressed to take the strain which a safety harness can exert if jerked suddenly.

British Standards for Safety Harnesses

The British Standards for safety harness construction are: adults BS4224; and for children BS4474. The RORC insists that safety harnesses comply with the BS4224 specification, or a near equivalent, and also that each harness be fitted with a crotch strap. In the case of a combination harness/lifejacket, one crotch strap for the complete unit is acceptable. Some sailing jackets incorporate a harness as do some lifejackets. Having a built-in harness can help reduce the complication of wearing harnesses, lifejackets and foul weather gear, but in fine or warm weather you will not want to wear heavy garments but will still need a harness.

It is essential that safety harnesses and their lines are checked regularly to ensure that there is no wear or tear to the fittings or the webbing straps. If harnesses are not used frequently, the snap hook hinges may need light lubrication. It is essential that safety harnesses fit tightly and snugly and therefore they should be kept, if at all possible, specific to particular crew members, not for general use.

The kind of hook normally fitted to a safety harness is the carbine hook, which is easy to hook on and off but which does suffer from the risk of 'capsizing' or opening inadvertently, when attached to a jackstay or a ring bolt. This happens when the hook turns over and, although the wire passes through the hook, it can also press on the outside of the spring-loaded moving part of the hook and open it, allowing the hook to disengage. The risk is quite small, but it could happen at a critical moment. There are alternative forms of safety harness hook which have a securing catch and are therefore much less vulnerable to opening inadvertently.

Keeping the Boat Dry

Keeping water out of the inside of the boat is an important safety measure. Boats tend to be built to take water over the bow, but in a following sea you could get water coming over the stern and you need to be prepared for such a contingency. Firstly, you need to prevent water getting below; secondly, you must ensure that any water that does come on board is cleared quickly.

Water lying in the cockpit can have an adverse effect on stability, because the increased weight tends to move the centre of gravity upwards, and because of the 'free surface effect'. Any body of water on a moving boat will run towards the low side and this can create a 'surge effect'. The amount of water in a small sailing-boat cockpit is not likely to influence stability too much, but on a powerboat with a large stern cockpit the effect could be considerable. The additional weight of water in the cockpit could also lower the stern of the boat in the water, thus making it easier for the next wave to wash on board. The cockpits on both sailing and powerboats should be self-draining.

Self-Draining Cockpits

Self-draining can be achieved in various ways, but for it to be possible the deck of the cockpit must be above the normal waterline level of the boat. Then there must be drains where the water can run away quickly. These could simply be holes in the side of the boat or the transom so long as they are of adequate size to get rid of the water quickly, particularly if the cockpit area is large.

On a sailing boat there are usually lockers at the side of the cockpit and whilst the draining of the cockpit can be achieved through the transom, the more normal method is to have large-diameter drain pipes to clear the water quickly. Because a sailing boat can spend much of its time heeled over, it is normal to have the drains arranged so that the drain from one side of the cockpit exits on the opposite side of the boat. This arrangement prevents water from running back up the pipe and into the cockpit when the boat is heeled.

Preventing Water Getting Below

If the cockpit does get flooded, then it is equally important to prevent it from getting below. A small amount of water will do no harm, unless you are particularly concerned about fixtures and furnishings, as the bilge pump should be able to cope with it. This means that you don't need absolute water-tightness and the wooden washboards used to close off the hatchway on a sailing boat should be adequate. These washboards allow the opening to be closed to various degrees while still permitting access but they should be capable of being secured in position so that they don't float out should water fill the cockpit. Washboards can be inconvenient in harbour and the trend is towards sliding or hinged doors. If doors are fitted, then at sea they have to be either open or shut – there is less chance of being able to run with them partially open as you can with washboards.

The risk of water coming on board powerboats may be less, but it can be very real if you are running in following seas. Preventing water getting into the accommodation is usually a matter of closing the outside door. Although this generally has a low sill and extensive glass, it is usually adequate to resist the pressure of water, although a little will obviously percolate through. Some water could also get in through the engine hatch which often lies under the cockpit.

A small amount of water will not cause serious problems unless it lands on parts of the electrical system. You frequently find electrical components mounted on a bulkhead immediately inside the hatch where they are convenient for access, but where they are vulnerable to water penetration which could immobilise your electrical system at a critical time. If there is a high-voltage electrical system on board using mains voltage, the water dripping through onto it can be lethal and can create a fire risk.

Bilge Pumps - Hand and Electric

Bilge pumps are the obvious answer for getting rid of such water as gets inside the boat. Most yachts have an electric bilge pump which operates automatically via a float switch. Such pumps have a quite reasonable capacity and can shift quite a lot of water in a short time, but they are designed to cope with small leaks rather than the large quantities that might come on board through a hose failure or hull damage, such as that incurred in a collision or grounding.

Correct Installation of Bilge Pumps

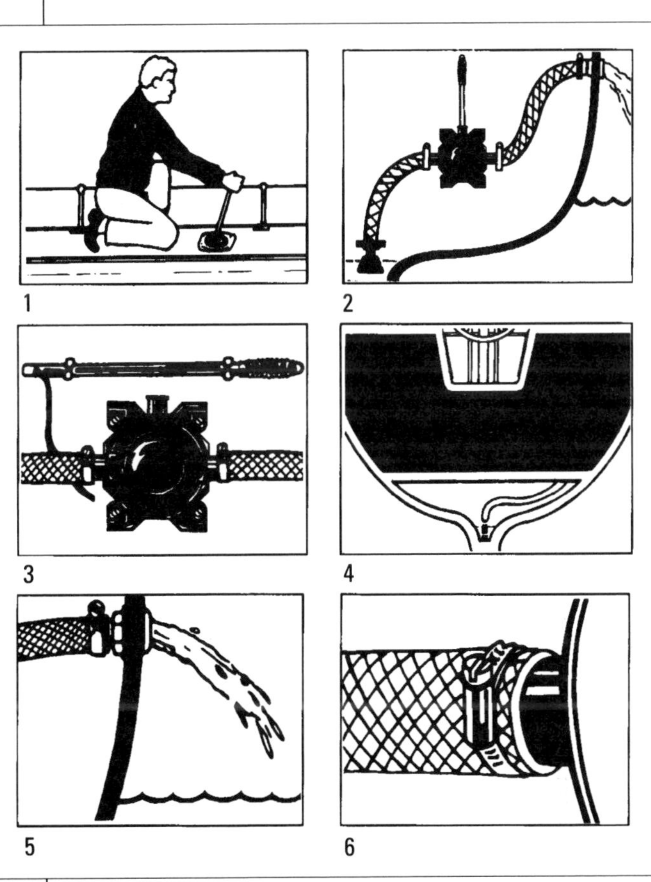

1 Install pump where it is easily accessible and can be operated comfortably.
2 For minimum pumping effort, install the pump halfway between the strainer and the outlet.
3 If the pump handle is detachable, it is recomended you secure it in a position close to the pump.
4 The suction inlet should be at the deepest point in the bilge.
5 If using through-hull discharge, ensure that the skinfitting is well above the waterline.
6 Check all fittings are of uniform bore – restricted inlet makes pumping difficult, restricted outlet can cause choking.

A useful yardstick in calculating the bilge pump capacity you need is that it should be slightly more than the amount of water that would come on board through a failure of the largest hose in the cooling system. The capacity of a bilge pump can be judged roughly by the size of its hoses, so if these hoses are larger than the largest hose in the engine cooling system, you can be reasonably confident that you have a chance of dealing with a hose failure which allows seawater to come into the boat. Do bear in mind that many bilge pumps do not produce a continuous flow. The discharge tends to be in fits and starts, whereas the flow coming in from a cooling water pipe failure will certainly be continuous.

You will be better off with two smaller manually operated bilge pumps rather than one large one. Not only does this give a measure of redundancy in the event of a pump failure, but it also allows two people to pump at the same time, thus increasing the discharge. If you have two manual bilge pumps of a combined capacity to cope with any expected water inflow from a cooling pipe failure, then the electric pump or an engine driven bilge pump will act as a bonus to supplement this capacity. Bearing in mind the low location of the batteries in many yachts, and therefore their vulnerability in a flood, you can't rely on the electric bilge pump to perform when required.

Of course, the best solution in the event of a cooling pipe failure is to have had the seacock valve extended up to deck level, so that it is readily accessible and you do not have to scrabble around in rising water to try to find the seacock handle. You should at least have a mark indicating where the seacocks can be found, and should ensure that all the crew know where and how to get to them quickly. Also ensure that the operating handles for the hand bilge pumps are either permanently installed or kept at hand, ready for use. If the boat has watertight bulkheads, you will need one bilge pump for each compartment, although you may be able to arrange for a manifold system whereby you can switch the suction from two or three compartments into a single bilge pump.

Gas Installations

If you have gas cooking or heating on board, you have the potential for a fire or explosion, which obviously needs to be guarded against. The best security is to have a properly installed gas system, with the gas bottles stowed outside the structure of the boat, and a drain leading from the stowage compartment directly overboard. The gas is heavier than air, so any leak will go into the bilges or remain in the bottom of lockers, hence the need for the overboard drain to keep any leaking gas clear of the inside of the boat.

There should be a shut-off valve at the cylinder so that the internal gas system can be isolated when not in use. The piping, which should be of copper except for areas where sections of flexible piping might be necessary, such as when leading to a gimballed cooker, should, if at all possible, be in one continuous length, without joints. The pipe needs to be carefully installed to prevent movement and chafe, but a properly installed gas system will remove much of the hazard from this fuel.

It can't, however, remove it completely and the risk of gas collecting in the bilges waiting for a spark to ignite it can be very real, which is why boats with gas systems have a gas detector, to warn of any accumulation of gas *before* you press electrical switches or put a light to gas. The gas detector head should be in the lowest part of the boat, probably the engine compartment, although if this is isolated from the gas usage area, as is often the case, you will need a second detector in the accommodation to ensure adequate protection. As of course a gas detector is only effective if it is working properly, most units have a test switch to check the circuits. This should be used regularly.

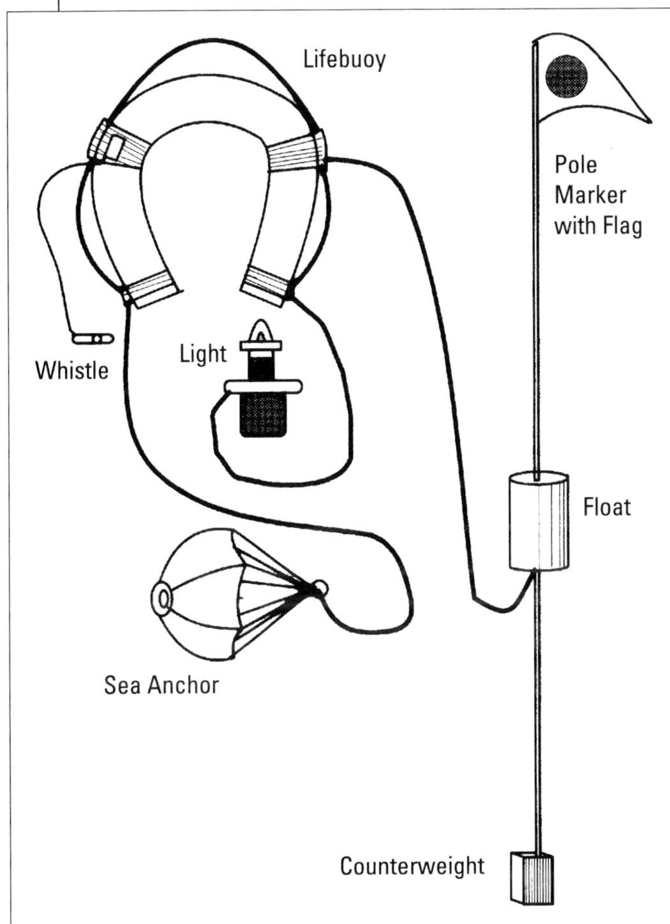

Danbuoy

'Man Overboard'

'Man overboard' is every sailor's nightmare at sea. Despite all the precautions previously described, such accidents still happen and you must have the equipment to cope. We will look at the actual procedures in Chapter 8, but the first priority is to be able to drop something over the side quickly, both to give the person in the water buoyancy support and to provide an indicator as to where he is while you prepare to recover him. The traditional circular lifebuoy can perform this function to a certain extent, but it is far from being the complete answer. The Danbuoy, as specified for offshore racing, is a much better proposition. It marks the position much more clearly and is effective at night and in poor visibility. The Danbuoy comprises a horseshoe-shaped lifebuoy (this is much easier to get into than a circular one), to provide basic support to the person in the water until help arrives, attached to which is a pole with a buoyancy block about one-third up from the bottom and a counterweight at the bottom to ensure that the Danbuoy floats upright. A flag at the top of the pole helps indicate the position – the RORC requirements insist that this flag is at least six feet clear of the water in normal conditions. Also attached to the lifebuoy is a drogue to reduce the amount of drift, and there is a battery-operated light which comes on automatically to indicate the location of the buoy at night. Finally, the buoy has a whistle attached with a lanyard, which the casualty can blow to indicate his position in poor visibility or at night time.

The Danbuoy, or if this is not available at least a lifebuoy, should be placed close to the helmsman so that it can be automatically released as soon as the helmsman becomes aware of the incident. A buoy obviously needs to be dropped as close as possible to the casualty, and most yachts have an arrangement whereby the whole thing can be released quickly by pulling on a single pin or lanyard. On a powerboat there is probably less risk of someone going overboard, simply because they tend to be inside, but there is still a risk and powerboat owners should have some means of getting initial assistance to the person overboard, either in the form of a lifebuoy or a Danbuoy.

Fire Extinguishers

Fire extinguishers are an essential fitting on yachts. In the event of a fire at sea you are on your own, and without any means to cope with it you can be in serious trouble very quickly. You are of course surrounded by water, which can be an excellent extinguisher in many cases but few yachts have the means to use this water to extinguish fires except by hauling it aboard in a bucket! A deck wash-hose could be a valuable aid in the event of a fire, particularly if fitted with a spray nozzle, but you would need to be careful just how much water was pumped on board because of its effect on stability and the danger of filling the boat up with water. But as very few yachts have the facility to pump water, the main recourse in the event of a fire is to use fire extinguishers.

There are many types of fire extinguisher available, so before we go into details of size and installation, let us first of all look at the different extinguishing media available.

Water

Water can be used on many types of fire, but should not be used in the case of burning liquids such as where cooking oil is burning, or fuel. Because the water is heavier than the oil it will tend to sink below the burning liquid and have little effect. Water should not be used if there is high-voltage electricity in the vicinity because it can produce lethal short circuits. But it is certainly less damaging than some of the chemical extinguishers and is ideal for, say, extinguishing an upholstery fire caused by a lighted cigarette. It can also be used to damp down a fire extinguished by other means and to prevent re-ignition.

Low-pressure Gas

A variety of gases can be used for extinguishing fires. Most of these are contained in pressurised fire extinguishers, stored as a liquid which vaporises on release. Amongst these gases are Halon 1211 or Halon 1301, BCF (bromo-chloro-difluoro-methane) and BTM (bromo-trifluoro-methane). All are effective as far as fire extinguishing goes but they are not particularly ozone-friendly and there is likely to be a ban on the use of these gases for fire extinguishing once suitable alternatives have been developed. They also give off dangerous fumes in confined spaces, so they can only be used in areas which have been evacuated. When one of these extinguishers has been used, areas which have been exposed to the vapour need careful ventilation before being re-entered by the crew. Fire extinguishers using these gases are comparatively light and readily portable, because the liquid gases are not kept under high pressure.

Carbon Dioxide

This cannot be said of the alternative carbon dioxide type where the gas is stored under high pressure and in comparatively heavy cylinders, which are not easy to handle in the confines of a small yacht. Carbon dioxide is, however, non-toxic and it will not damage components or fixtures, although if a compartment has been filled with this gas to the exclusion of oxygen, there is a risk of asphyxia until the compartment has been thoroughly ventilated.

Fire Extinguishers

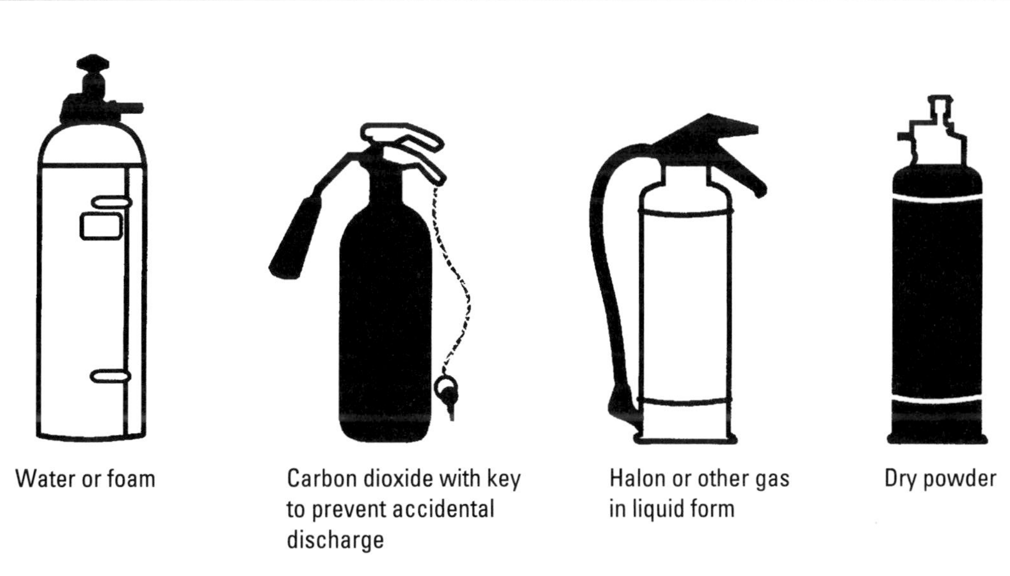

Water or foam

Carbon dioxide with key to prevent accidental discharge

Halon or other gas in liquid form

Dry powder

Dry Powder and Foam

Alternatives to gas in extinguishers are dry powder and foam. Dry powder extinguishers are operated by a small carbon dioxide cylinder which pressurises the powder and expels it through the nozzle. One of the problems with this type is that over time the vibration and movement of the boat causes the powder to compact, making them less than ideal for use on yachts. They also tend to be one-shot extinguishers, which means that, once you have triggered one, the whole contents come out, unlike the gas type of cylinder where the discharge can be controlled. Dry powder extinguishers make a useful first line of defence but should be backed up by alternative types of extinguisher.

Foam fire extinguishers are excellent for dealing with burning liquids because they form a smothering blanket over the surface of the liquid which cuts off the supply of oxygen. However, such extinguishers tend to be large and heavy and are not really practicable on small boats.

Fire Blanket

Finally in this list of fire extinguishers, we must not ignore the fire blanket which is still probably the best way of dealing with a fire in the galley area. It is simply a blanket made of fire-resistant material; it is draped over the fire and extinguishes it by cutting off the oxygen supply.

The Complete System

The fire-fighting equipment for a yacht needs to be thought about very carefully. You will need extinguishers capable of dealing with the range of types of fire you are likely to get on board, and you will need to leave something in reserve. There should be one fire extinguisher for each compartment: on a sailing yacht this will mean one for the forecabin, one for the main saloon and one for the engine compartment. They should be positioned just outside the compartment so that you do not actually have to go into the cabin to get the extinguisher. It also means that crew members can evacuate the compartment before having to deal with the fire, which means that they can place themselves in as safe a position as possible when dealing with the fire, and that they have an escape route open. These portable extinguishers should by supplemented with a fire blanket at the galley.

On powerboats, with their larger engines, it is normal to have a built-in extinguisher system in the engine compartment. This will apply particularly to petrol-engined boats, although it can be just as important on a diesel-engined boat even though the fuel is less flammable. These built-in systems normally have a large-capacity cylinder containing one of the fire extinguishing gases, Halon being a current favourite. From this extinguisher, piping leads to a series of nozzles, allowing the gas to be distributed throughout the engine compartment.

The triggering of the gas cylinder can be done automatically by means of a heat-sensitive link in the system. Alternatively, the system can be manually controlled from the dashboard. In some respects this is preferable because these are one-shot systems and for maximum effect you do need to stop the engine and, as far as possible, blank off any air inlets and outlets to the engine compartment, especially any ventilation fans.

Built-in System For Engine Compartments

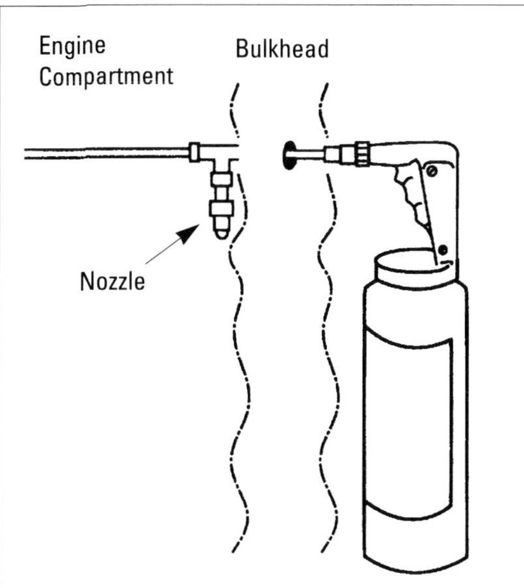

This is a manually activated system but fully automatic systems are also available. They can be activated from outside the engine compartment, removing the need to lift any inspection hatches and thereby allow oxygen in to feed the fire.

If you opt for the manually operated system then you should consider some form of early-warning alarm in the engine compartment. A manual system would be equally useful on a sailing yacht, where it could be very effective in the confined space of the average sailing yacht's engine compartment, but, again, a means of shutting off air inlets and outlets should be considered an essential part of any such system.

Like most safety equipment, fire extinguishers need checking at regular intervals. Some of the more expensive types, such as the gas-filled units, are fitted with pressure gauges which need to be checked regularly to make sure that the needle is pointing to the green sector.

Gas extinguishers can also be checked by weight to ensure there has been no leakage. The full weight is normally stamped on the outside of the container. There is no way of checking dry powder extinguishers, which is one of the negative aspects of these units. As a general rule all fire extinguishers should be sent away for checking and servicing every three years.

As I hope I have made clear, all safety equipment should be checked and serviced regularly. You may not use some of it for years on end, yet when you do come to use it you expect it to work efficiently and promptly. It is only by regular servicing and maintenance of equipment and a crew familiar with its location and use, that you will have some chance of reacting promptly and effectively when an emergency arises.

8 Coping with Emergencies

In most emergencies, the action you take in the first few minutes will determine how effectively you deal with the entire incident. If you have gone through the 'what if' routine we discussed earlier, your chances of coming up with the right course of action in those vital early minutes will be much higher. In this chapter we shall look at some of the situations you might have to cope with during your cruising or racing, and offer suggestions about how to cope. These suggestions will of necessity be general rather than specific because not only will the circumstances be unique to the incident, but the course of action chosen will be influenced by many factors, such as the size and type of boat, the number of crew and their relevant experience. However, it is hoped that these suggestions will encourage you to look around your boat and decide how you would translate these general ideas into specific solutions suitable to your particular situation.

Rate of Inflow of Water through Hole in Hull

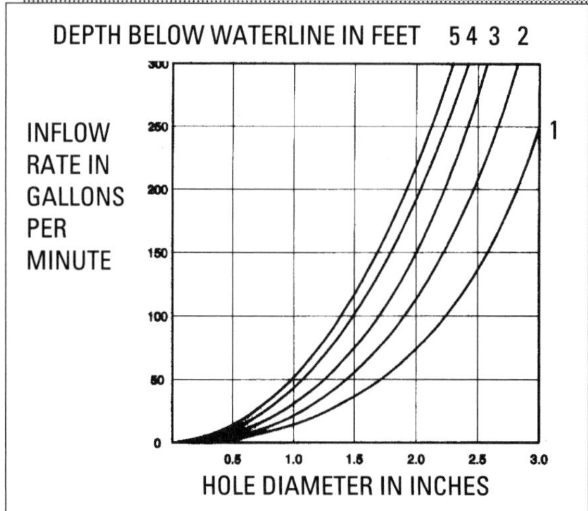

The volumes given by this graph not only serve to show just how much water can flood in quickly, but give an idea also of the capacity required by bilge pumps.

Hole in the Hull

A hole in the hull conjures up visions of a sudden and dramatic incident: a collision with a large floating object at night; running aground; or that favourite of ocean-going sailors, colliding with a whale. This third possibility is unlikely to hole a monohull; most collisions with whales resulting in damage have involved multi-hulls. The sort of hole in the hull we are going to consider here is likely to have been the result either of a collision or of running aground, and is not uncommon in sailing boat racing where sailing at speed at close quarters can lead to misjudgements and collisions.

How you cope with the hole in the hull depends on both the material from which the hull is constructed and the type of hull. With the normal type of GRP hull, you are unlikely to get a large hole unless you happen to hit a floating bulk of timber end on, or the stem of another vessel comes through your topsides. GRP tends not to give way completely and is very resistant to impact, so that a collision is likely to result in the section of the hull directly in line with the impact being pushed inward, but it is unlikely to give way completely. This means that you will probably get some water coming into the hull, but not the sudden catastrophic inflow that would result from a large hole. Obviously, if you run a powerboat onto rocks at high speed, this could create a serious hole, and powerboats, with their higher speeds, are certainly more vulnerable to larger impact holes. However, it is rare to hit anything with a direct impact, and a glancing blow, whilst serious, is more likely to push the hull structure inward, causing a number of small leaks rather than a large hole.

First Aid for Hulls

Damage of this type is best dealt with initially from the outside of the hull, if you can get access. A pillow or sail, or even a seat cushion, lashed across the outside of the hull, should help stem any major inflow of water to a level with which the bilge pumps can cope, or until you can start to tackle each individual leak. The main problem with a number of small leaks is getting access and this will probably be easier from the inside. Cushions, pillows and even mattresses can be used as a seal by jamming them in place against the hull structure. You may have to rip out some of the internal fittings, but faced with a choice between the boat sinking and getting access to the damaged area, you should not hesitate too much about breaking up lockers or other furniture. Indeed, the wood from these broken areas could be useful in wedging material in place to stem the leak.

With wood or metal hulls, the chances of an actual hole in the hull are greater. The planking of a wooden hull will tend to be pushed inward between the frames but there is also the risk of a plank springing, ie coming adrift from its fastenings, particularly at the bow or stern. This type of damage is very difficult to cope with: it can only be tackled adequately from the outside and requires very prompt action indeed to have some chance of being successfully limited. Impact damage, where the planks break inward, is easier to cope with. The immediate reaction should probably be to push a cushion or pillow into the hole to stem the flow, and then back this up with some more secure arrangement.

Much the same applies to a metal hull, although here the jagged edges of the hole could make it difficult to get something into it securely enough. Both types of hole are best tackled from the outside in the longer term, but the first aid work is probably best done from the inside.

Repair Kits

It is possible to buy special equipment to deal with holes in the hull. For example, there is an umbrella-like gadget which can be folded and pushed through the hole, and then expanded on the outside. An alternative is a collision mat such as used to be carried on merchant ships. The mat is simply heavy canvas with rope edges and lanyards attached so that it can be pulled in place over a hole. It is hard to justify carrying special equipment like this on a modern yacht. Probably the best you can do is to try to work out where holes are likely to occur, which would normally be below the waterline in the forward part of the boat, and then see how you might gain quick access and what materials are readily at hand to jam into the hole to stop the immediate flood, so buying some time to sort out a more lasting solution.

Some yachts, mainly small sailing boats and sportsboats, will not sink if holed because of built-in buoyancy, although a lot of water will still be able to get into the hull. This fixed buoyancy has to be located carefully inside the hull, usually high up, so that it doesn't upset the stability balance too much. An alternative is to have inflatable bags which can be blown up inside the hull. These are usually gas-operated for quick inflation in an emergency, and while they would keep the boat afloat and probably enable it to be salvaged in the unlikely event of severe damage, the best approach is still to try and stop the leak at source by stemming the inflow of water.

Running Aground

Damage caused by running aground is likely to be much harder to deal with, partly because rocks may intrude into the hole, making it less easy to seal off, but also because the damage will be worsening all the while the hull is being pounded. It can really only be tackled successfully once the boat has come off. When the boat is actually aground, there is little chance of it sinking, and you are more likely to be concerned for your personal survival than that of the yacht. If you are unfortunate enough to put your

Inducing an angle of heel by putting weight on the end of the boom. Unfortunately the chances are that if you were sailing, you were already heeled over.

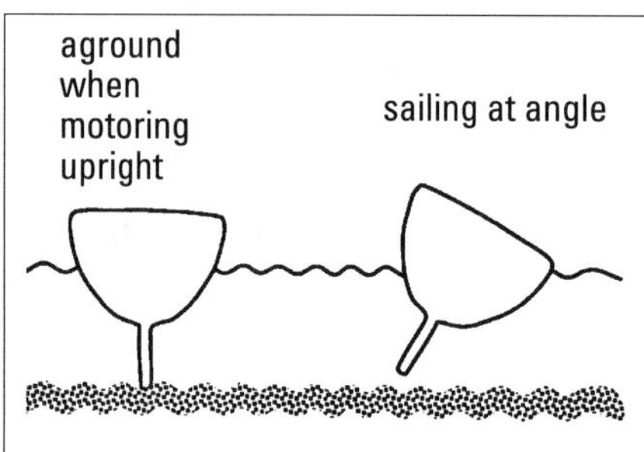

yacht aground, or have it drift ashore, damage to the hull should be coped with in a similar way to that already described for collision damage.

If a boat goes aground, the action you take will depend a great deal on the type of bottom on which it comes to rest and the prevailing sea conditions. Going aground in the confines of a harbour or an estuary is more likely to hurt your pride than your boat! It is usually a matter of running the engines astern to try and get the boat off immediately, or of waiting until the tide floods sufficiently to lift the boat off the bottom. Going aground at sea, where there is wave motion, is more serious while going aground on rocks is likely to be even more serious because of the obvious risk of hull damage. In the case of a powerboat, going aground may damage the stern gear, in which case you may have no power with which to try and get off again.

Grounding can result in a wide variety of possible situations, some immediate and serious, others requiring patience and seamanship. The first reaction on finding yourself aground is to try to get off again immediately. A sailing boat will probably be heeled over as it goes aground due to the pressure of the wind in the sails. When heeled, the draft is reduced, so by the time you get the sails down, you will be well and truly aground! Putting the engine in reverse and trying to power the boat off is unlikely to be effective. (If you have gone aground under engine alone, reversing the engine is the first step to trying to get back into deeper water.) By hanging a weight, such as the tender, or even a crewmember, on the end of the boom it might be possible to heel the boat enough for it to come off the bottom; otherwise, it is a case of waiting for the tide to float it off.

You should be able to reverse a displacement powerboat off because the propeller is adequately protected against damage and you have plenty of power. With planing hulls, however, there is a serious risk of propeller damage, so before trying to power the boat off astern, you must assess the risk of damage to the stern gear, if it is not already damaged. In the case

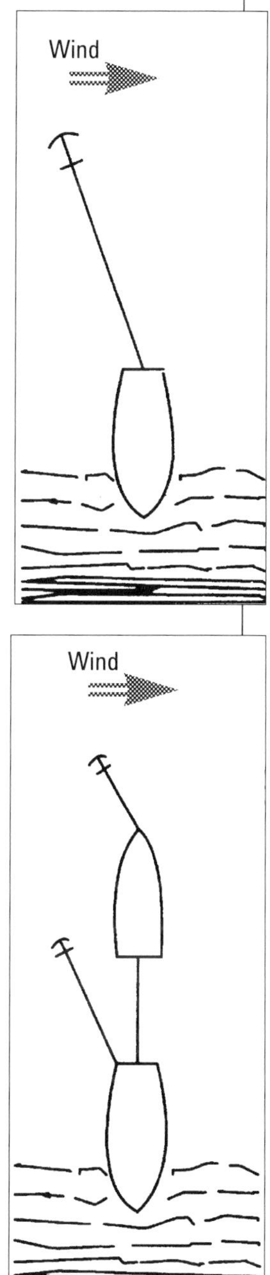

Top: a boat aground showing how the kedge anchor should be laid out in a beam wind. Bottom: how a rescue vessel might tackle the problem of towing off. By putting out its own anchor, the rescue vessel has more control of the situation. Pulling hard in on the anchor line can also help the thrust of the engines.

of a twin-screw boat which has heeled over slightly on grounding, you could use the propeller on the higher side, but where the propellers are exposed, as could be the case with stern drive units, extreme care needs to be taken to prevent further damage.

If immediate action to free the boat is unsuccessful, you will need to plan a longer-term strategy. First, you need to know what the tide is doing. If it is flooding, keeping the engine running astern will let the tide lift the boat and get you out of trouble. On a falling tide, you may be able to run out an anchor quickly in the direction of deeper water and haul yourself off, with the aid of the engine, before the tide drops too far. Laying out the anchor has to be done with the dinghy so you will have to assess the risks involved in this operation and weigh them up against the need for an anchor. The best way is to have the anchor hanging over the side of the dinghy, the chain lashed on board by a light line which can quickly be cut to let the anchor go.

If the tide is ebbing and you have been unable to free yourself, you will still need to lay out an anchor, particularly if there is a wind of any strength blowing. This will prevent the boat being blown harder aground and will hold it head to wind and secure when the tide starts to flow and it lifts off the bottom. When you do lay out an anchor, allow as much cable as possible to ensure that the anchor holds well, and keep the tension on the cable constant. As the tide gradually lifts the boat, steadily wind in the cable. You will soon find yourself water deep enough to allow you to start the engine.

If you have gone aground in a powerboat and damaged the stern gear, this is also the best solution to getting afloat again. If you don't have a dinghy available, you are going to have to seek outside help to lay out an anchor, unless you dry out completely when, of course, you can walk the anchor away. And, because your stern gear is out of action, you will have to arrange a tow once the boat refloats.

If you are stuck hard and fast and have to wait over the tide, one of the problems will be that the boat will heel over progressively as the tide drops, and here sailing boats are likely to suffer more than powerboats. If you carry legs on board, rig them so that the boat will sit upright; otherwise, it may be possible to use the spinnaker pole lashed to the gunwale. This is a rather precarious arrangement unless rigged properly, and you could find matters made worse by the boat falling over as the tide drops and the hull as well as the spinnaker pole being damaged.

Many boats will lie over on their bilge reasonably happily and incur no structural damage as long as the sea bed is fairly smooth. Of course, life on board will not be particularly comfortable. If possible, you should check that the bottom is smooth and free of rocks or other potentially damaging obstructions. You can try fixing bunk cushions or fenders at the turn of the bilge before the boat heels over to minimise any impact. But your first priority when drying out is to try and get the boat to lie head to wind and sea. Then, when the tide starts to flood, waves will not break over the side of the boat and start to fill the hull. Even so, you must be prepared for the water to rise quite alarmingly and come over the edge of the deck before the hull starts to right itself.

When the boat heels over, check that fuel is not leaking from the fuel tank breathers or fillers. Batteries should also be checked for security and leaks. If you go aground on a soft, muddy bottom, the boat will probably sit more upright as the keel will sink into the mud but, before you start the engine, check that mud has not blocked the water intake.

Going aground in the open sea, particularly on rocks, is a serious problem and broadcasting a distress call should be a top priority. You may get off without outside help but, even if you manage this, the chances are that there will be damage to the boat or hull. The knowledge that help is on its way will be very reassuring. It is always better know that help is coming, even if you don't in the end need it, than to face a rapidly deteriorating situation with no prospect of help in the offing. Going aground like this is usually either the result of propulsion failure or a mistake in navigation. In either case the method and position of your grounding will not be of your choice. The safety of your crew must be your number one priority and, whilst trying to resolve the basic problem by one or more of the methods described, you should also get safety equipment ready for immediate use and, of course, make sure that a distress call goes out.

Towing and Being Towed

It is to be hoped that yours will be the boat that does the towing rather than the boat being towed, but neither operation is an easy one if there are big waves about. Even in calm water, towing requires a considerable degree of skill if it is going to work successfully over any distance; in rough seas it can be an operation fraught with difficulty and danger.

Being Towed

If you need to be towed, it is probably because you have suffered an engine or gear failure, or both, or possibly a steering failure. With your boat immobile, all the manoeuvring has to be done by the other boat, but you can help by getting things ready and making sure that the tow line is secured fast at the first attempt. There is a heavy strain on a tow line, so you need somewhere strong to make it fast. Ideally, this should be a good, strong central mooring point at the bow, such as the anchor capstan. Even so, because of the immense strain, it is a good idea to take the end of the line back to a second securing point. On a sailing boat this will probably be the mast. This will spread the load throughout the hull instead of it being concentrated on one point towards the bow, which will give a much better chance of the inevitably heavy snatches on the line being safely absorbed.

These days, however, there is a tendency to keep the foredeck of both power and sailing boats as clear as possible, which means the absence of a strong central mooring post or capstan. In these circumstances you may have to rely on the mooring cleats on each side of the bow. On their own these may well not be strong enough, but a rope bridle, doubled if necessary, around both cleats could be a good way of securing the tow line. The bridle should be long enough to pass clear of the bows, thus avoiding chafe on either the bow roller or anchor, often stowed on or adjacent to the roller.

Once the tow line is made fast, you may be able to help with the towing operation if you have steering available. This can prevent the boat being towed from sheering about wildly, thereby increasing the strain on the tow line. The best or safest set-up for making fast a tow rope can be worked out long before the necessity occurs. On a fine day you might even like to try out the exercise, using a friendly yacht as the tow boat.

Towing

Towing a boat is not to be undertaken lightly. It calls for skilful manoeuvring and rope handling. Once you have everything ready, the first stage is to pass the tow rope across. This is best done with your stern level with the bow of the other boat. Manoeuvre close enough for the line to be thrown across, using a lighter line for the initial contact if this is going to be easier to throw. If sea and wind conditions are difficult and you are reluctant to get this close to the distressed vessel, as could be the case if it has gone aground, you could float the tow line down using a fender tied to the end of it.

When you are passing the tow line, always make sure that the rope is kept well clear of your propeller. The person handling the line on the stern of your boat must allow just enough slack to allow the line to be passed across and never allow a bight of rope to lie in the water. When you make the line fast at your stern, you may have to use a bridle to spread the load

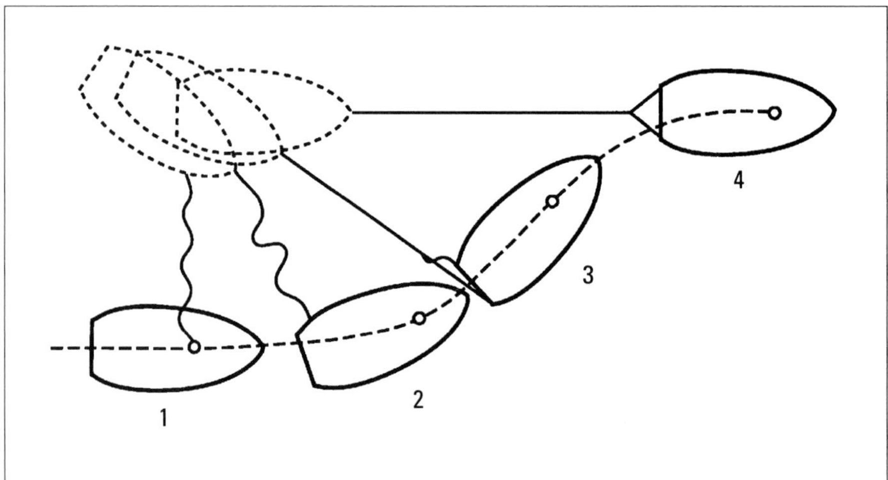

Taking a Vessel in Tow
The line is passed across at 1 and 2. At 3 it is attached to the stern bridle and as the towing boat starts to straighten out under the strain, the tow proper is commenced at 4.

between the two stern cleats. It is rare to find a good strong towing point on leisure boats these days so you may have to take a couple of turns around a stern cleat and then back these up with further turns round the mast or a bow cleat.

Take up the weight gently on the tow rope once it is fast, and try to keep the strain even – not an easy task in rough seas. Radio contact between the two boats will bring an added measure of safety to the towing operation. You should be able to find a towing speed at which both boats are comfortable without too much snatching on the line. In calmer conditions you can keep a reasonably short tow line, but in rougher conditions you will need to have a longer tow line, which will give a bit of 'spring'. You can experiment with the length of tow line to find the one which gives both craft a comfortable and compatible motion. If the boat being towed still has steering, a position somewhere just on the quarter of the towing boat can often be comfortable. Heavy sheering about of the boat being towed should be avoided because of the great strain it will put on the tow line and both boats' fittings, and the increased likelihood of chafe.

Finally, when a tow line is being secured at either end, the person handling the rope should wear a lifejacket and safety harness. The latter is probably more important than the lifejacket because he will be very vulnerable on the foredeck and will need both hands for the tow line.

Mast Down

Whilst it is not an uncommon occurrence, the dismasting of a sailing boat can be traumatic for those on board because it tends to happen very quickly. If you are faced with this problem, your prime concern will be to minimise the damage. This will mean cutting away any rigging still attached and getting rid of the mast before it can knock a hole in the hull. Before you do this, however, think about the problem a little; you may want to retain bits of the mast and rigging, particularly the sails, so that you can erect some sort of jury rig. This will certainly be the case if you are some distance from land and you don't have enough fuel to get back to harbour. So, to solve the immediate problem, you might cut away all the rigging except the fore or backstay. This will allow the wreckage of the mast and sail to drift away from the boat but remain attached and will buy you a bit of time to sort out what you want to keep and what your next step will be. One thing to bear in mind if the mast does go over the side is that, without the damping effect of the mast and sails, the motion of the boat is likely to be much more lively, making any deck activity more difficult. If you have an engine available, you can start this and point the boat up into the wind, but make sure that none of the debris gets into the propeller.

Once you have overcome the initial problem, you can think about heading for port under power, or fixing up some form of jury rig. This will only enable you to make progress with the wind astern, or at least somewhere abaft the beam which will obviously have considerable implications for where you decide to head for. How you set up the jury rig depends on what is left after the dismasting. If you are lucky and the mast broke halfway up, it is not too difficult to rig some sort of sail to what remains, but make sure that the mast is supported adequately before you impose further strain on it. It might even be possible to rig the existing main and a small jib, but an alternative is a form of square sail hung from the boom or the spinnaker pole lashed across the mast.

Typical Jury Rig

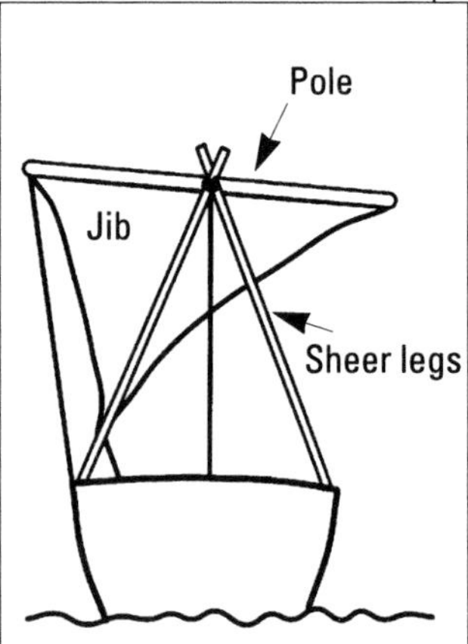

If no mast is left standing, it is not easy to rig a single pole from scratch, but you could use two spinnaker poles or part of the mast that remains to rig sheer legs, with the heel of each leg wedged against the toe rail on either side and fore and aft rigging to hold it firmly in place. The rig itself will depend on what materials you have available and what the conditions are. Jury rigs sound possible on paper, but in reality are much more difficult, often requiring hours of patient work: there are no short cuts to a sound jury rig. The chances are that when a mast goes overboard it happens in strong winds which create conditions that make rigging a replacement extremely difficult, if not impossible. If you have sufficient sea room, it is probably safer to wait until conditions moderate before attempting this operation. Assuming your yacht has an engine and you have at least a little fuel, you can use it to hold her in a comfortable position and make some progress towards land while you work out how to put together your jury rig.

Engine Failure

Powerboats, by their nature, tend to put all their eggs in one basket in terms of motive power. Machinery failure on a single-engined powerboat means that you have lost everything. One remedy is to have a stand-by outboard motor so that you have at least some form of get-you-home facility. If you do carry an auxiliary outboard, it will help if it runs on the same fuel as the main engine. Do make sure in advance that it will actually work and is powerful enough to propel the boat adequately, particularly in difficult sea conditions. In the case of a twin-engine boat it is worth establishing beforehand that it can still be steered with just one engine running. This may sound obvious, but not all boats handle well on just a single engine, and you don't want to discover this when you are already in a tight corner.

Engine failure on a single-engined boat without back-up means that the options, other than calling for help, are very limited. You could consider rigging up some form of sail, but unless the boat is fitted with a mast, you are not likely to be very successful. Provided you have adequate sea room and conditions are fair or moderate, there is not too much risk in just drifting until help arrives. However, if sea conditions are difficult, you might consider rigging a sea anchor to bring the boat round head to wind and make life on board a bit more comfortable, and perhaps safer, while you wait.

Sea Anchors and Drogues

Essentially, these two devices are means of exerting a directional force on a boat which can be used to help control it. Both use the movement of the boat through the water to exert the required pull but, apart from this single common factor, the drogue and sea anchor are very different. A drogue is towed astern, in a following sea, with the object of stabilising the steering and preventing the boat from sheering off course or broaching. Sailing boats often tow warps to achieve a similar effect. A sea anchor is used when the engines have failed or the sails are down and the boat is drifting. It is generally put out from the bow, occasionally from the stern, to keep the boat in a desired heading, usually head to wind and sea. The drogue reacts against the forward motion of the boat. The faster the boat travels the greater the pull at the stern and thus the greater the stabilising effect on the steering. A displacement powerboat should maintain full speed for maximum effect, but this in turn will demand a strongly constructed drogue to withstand the pull.

In heavy breaking seas the drogue is used primarily as a means of preventing broaching and, if used properly, the effect can be dramatic.

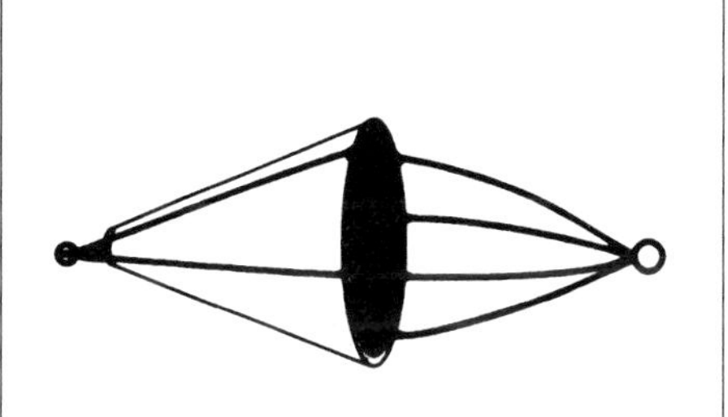

Left: a typical drogue constructed from heavy-duty canvas with the bridles made from wire rope.

Below: alternative sea anchors
1 A non-rigid parachute style.
2 A cone with a metal loop, similar but lighter than a drogue.
3 An on-board concoction made up from a storm jib hung on a pole. Note that the jib has to be weighted at the bottom.

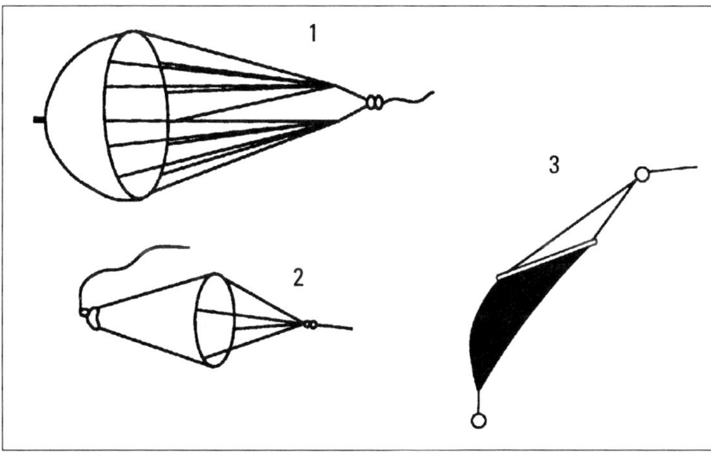

However, there are many factors which can affect the performance of a drogue, so if you consider using one it is important to understand these because bad deployment will reduce its effectiveness.

The stabilising effect of the drogue is most needed when a wave is curling ready to poop you. For the drogue to act properly, it must be well immersed; this will depend to a large extent on the length of rope which is paid out. This, in turn, will depend on the wave length; the best rope length to use is about $1^1/_2$ wave lengths, which will ensure that when a wave is close to the stern of the boat the drogue is pulling into the base of the wave behind, not the crest where it might pull clear of the water. If the waves are short and steep, a line $2^1/_2$ or even $3^1/_2$ times the wave length might be a better proposition. Too much scope will result in the rope becoming slack and the boat running forward in a series of jerks, thereby putting undue strain on the line and possibly jerking the drogue right out of the water. The objective should be to maintain a steady pull on the line at all times.

The pull on a properly rigged drogue could be in the region of three tons, so the equipment needs to be strong. A nylon drogue rope is not suitable because of its spring; it is better to use polypropylene or terylene. The strong pull on the drogue rope requires that the boat is fitted with a strong post or bollard at the stern on which to make it fast. The position of the post is not critical, but the fairlead used for the line should be as near the stern as is practicable and on the centre line, so that the pull is central. A drogue 76cm (30 inches) in diameter would be adequate for a boat up to 16 metres (50 feet) in length; a 51cm (20 inches) diameter drogue being suitable for a 6 metre (20 feet) boat. Like the line to which it is attached, the drogue should be strongly constructed and it should have negative buoyancy.

The drogue is a fairly specialised piece of equipment rarely found these days outside the realms of lifeboat work. It is not a particularly practical piece of equipment to use on a planing powerboat, which in any case should have sufficient power to be able to outrun a following sea and

Sea Anchor

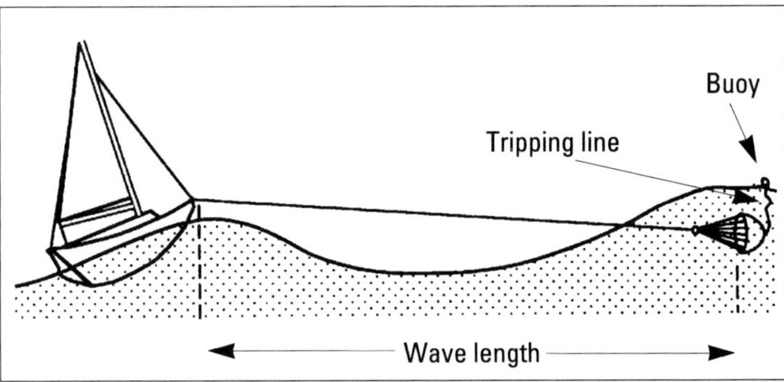

The sea anchor needs to be at least one wave length away to ensure it remains well submerged in approaching waves. The tripping line and buoy aid recovery when the need to stream the anchor has passed.

thus be relatively unaffected. On a sailing boat a drogue could be effective, but in the open sea, where breaking waves are less frequent, the use of towing warps is probably an adequate precaution and something available to both power and sailing boats. A drogue is mainly useful when entering harbour over a bar in rough conditions where its stabilising effect can be vital. But perhaps you shouldn't really be thinking of entering harbour in these conditions anyway, and would be much better waiting offshore until the conditions moderate.

The sea anchor is a means both of reducing the drift of a disabled boat and of heaving to and keeping the bow head to wind. Reducing drift could be vitally important if the boat is in danger of being blown ashore. By deploying a sea anchor you can buy time during which help might arrive or the defect be cured. Keeping the boat head to wind, or at a desired angle to the wind, can make the motion of the boat more comfortable while repairs are carried out or a jury rig assembled. The sea anchor can also be useful if, in prolonged heavy weather, the crew become very tired and desperately need a rest, and the weather was so severe as to preclude heaving-to by other means.

In construction, the sea anchor is something like a drogue but is generally larger and lighter. It needs to be larger than a drogue to exert sufficient pull to keep the bow head to wind. Whilst the stresses on the sea anchor are generally less than those on a drogue, they could rise if a heavy breaking sea engulfs the boat.

Leeway

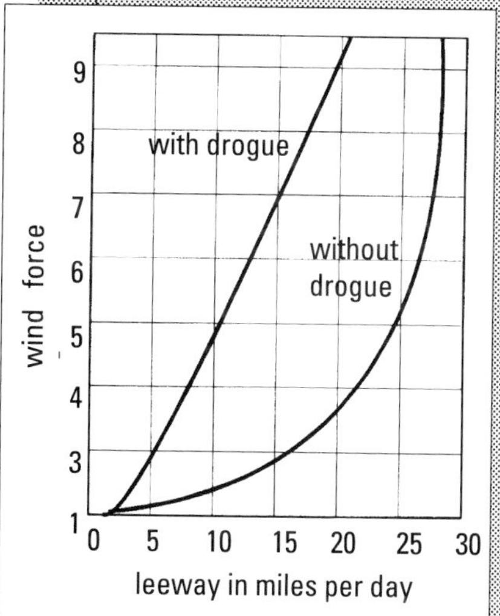

Expected rates of leeway in a liferaft with and without streaming a drogue.

The sea anchors on liferafts are primarily to stop drift and are rather like small parachutes. A liferaft's sea anchor would be far too light for use by a yacht: something more rugged is required. A metal bucket would suffice on a smaller yacht while a sail, rigged with a line to each corner, could make an effective sea anchor for a sailing boat. Unless an actual sea anchor is carried you will have to exercise a degree of ingenuity if you find yourself in need of one, and it could be a useful to consider which items of kit you have on board might suit this purpose, when you are running through a 'what if' exercise.

Loss of Steering

Loss of the steering is frustrating and potentially dangerous. On a sailing boat you could possibly steer by altering the balance in the sails, and on a twin-screw powerboat you have some chance of steering by using the engines at different speeds. In the latter case, it is better to run one engine at a steady speed below the maximum and adjust the heading by varying the speed of the second engine. With an auxiliary outboard you can have both emergency propulsion and steering.

The alternative is to try and rig some form of jury rudder, which is one of the more difficult operations that you can be faced with at sea. On a sailing boat, it might be possible to rig a spinnaker pole as a jury rudder, provided you can attach a blade of some sort to one end and run lines to each side of the stern to pull it one way or the other. It is a pretty crude set-up and may not last for too long because of chafe or other problems. A jury rudder could be even harder to rig on a powerboat.

Jury Rudder

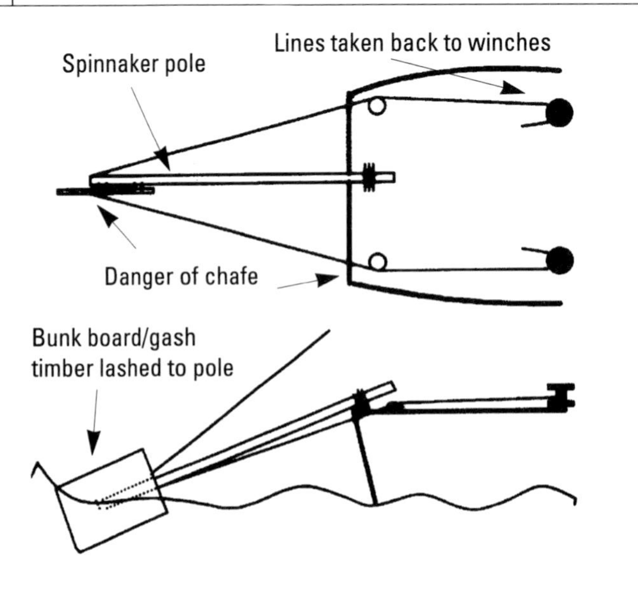

All right in theory, but difficult to achieve at sea.

Fortunately, a complete steering failure is comparatively rare these days. It is more likely that there will be a failure in some component of the steering system, such as the tiller breaking or the steering connection between the wheel and the rudder stock failing. Most rudder stocks have a square end where they enter the boat and provision is often made for a tiller to be attached at this point so that effective steering can be maintained. Check whether your yacht has this facility and work out how it could be used. In some cases only a short tiller can be fitted, so it may be necessary to rig tackles or lines from it to winches to help with the steering.

If there is no emergency tiller, you may be able to make a connection by using a large spanner clamped on to the broken tiller, or be able to disconnect the wheel steering system from the stock inside the stern and attach lines or tackles to that. Again, it is a question of looking at the possibilities of your particular boat, working out what is feasible and practical, and making sure that you have adequate equipment on board to cope with such a situation. Hand in hand with this approach should go proper maintenance and regular checking of the steering system to minimise the chance of failure. Sadly, few people seem to realise the importance of the steering system unit until it fails, when they become only too aware of its value.

Mentally rehearsing rigging up a jury system or trying to steer without the rudder can be one of those exercises to occupy 'empty time' at sea. Bear in mind that if the steering does fail, the rudder could jam in the hard-over position. This is not very likely to happen, although it is possible if you run aground, but if it does it is one of the most difficult situations to deal with. Even a twin-screw powerboat would have difficulty trying to balance the steering.

Abandoning Ship

We covered this topic in some detail in the section on liferafts, so here I wish to look at the situations leading up to abandoning ship, and the decision-making involved. There are three main situations where you may be forced to consider this extreme measure: when the vessel is on fire; when you have suffered a failure of machinery, mast or steering and the boat is drifting ashore; when the boat is holed or sinking. These are obviously all pretty desperate situations, but even so you want to save making the transition from the yacht to the liferaft until the last possible moment. Taking to the liferaft is an irrevocable step and you will always be better off staying on board the yacht whilst it remains capable of safe occupation and afloat.

Taking to the liferaft when the yacht is on fire poses particular problems. The normal practice is to put the liferaft over on the lee side, which not only helps to make boarding easier but also allows the liferaft to drift away downwind once the crew are on board. However, if the boat is on fire, the lee side is the last place you want to be, because smoke and flames will blow to leeward. If you put the liferaft over on the windward side, it will be less at risk but getting away from the side will be very difficult.

The alternative, and probably the best, solution is to launch the liferaft at either the bow or the stern, depending on where the seat of the fire is and the heading of the yacht. If the fire is in the fore part of the boat, you will want to evacuate from the stern, and vice versa. Getting into the liferaft over the bow may not be easy, but it is probably a better option than trying the same exercise amongst the smoke and flames at the stern. Even then, you will need to be particularly careful when you slip the painter, and let the liferaft drift away.

The key to successful evacuation in a fire is to take the decision to evacuate early. Almost certainly, the fire will have started down below in the accommodation rather than on deck, and if you resolve to abandon ship before it spreads to the hull and superstructure, you will have a good chance of getting out safely. If you wait until the last possible moment, when flames are raging in the cockpit, or through cabin windows, your chances of a safe evacuation are considerably reduced. The moment you realise you are losing the fight against the fire is the moment to decide to abandon ship. If you have exhausted the fire extinguishers and all other means of extinguishing a blaze and the fire is still growing, there is little more you can do except to look to your own safety, and the sooner you get into the liferaft the better. We will look at this in more detail under the 'Fire' heading.

Another situation which might prompt you to abandon ship is uncontrollably drifting down onto a lee shore through the loss of your engine and/or rig. Your last resort will be the anchor, which may just be enough to hold you when it can touch bottom. Although normally used for holding the yacht off a pleasant beach or in a sandy cove, the anchor has a vital emergency role to play if you are drifting, when it can remain the one last chance to prevent disaster. The anchor can reduce the feeling of helplessness of the uncontrolled drift and this is when you will appreciate having a larger-than-normal anchor and a good strong line. If you are already in shallow water, then the anchor should be used at the earliest possible moment to arrest the drift of the yacht. Under the stress of strong wind and choppy sea conditions, the anchor may not hold securely at the first try. However, there is a good chance it will grip as the water shoals and the sooner it does, the less stressful will be your wait for rescue.

Buying time in this way is an important consideration. You should study the chart to see whether holding conditions are better further inshore. Good holding ground in deeper water might be better than a rocky bottom in shallow water. On balance, it is good holding ground which provides the key to using the anchor in an emergency. You should also wait until the water is reasonably shallow, say down to ten metres (thirty feet), so that the anchor has a good chance of holding securely with the anchor line in a relatively shallow catenary. This is the ideal, but your choices may be limited. For example, if the coastline shelves steeply the only solution might be to put the anchor line over the side with a nearly full scope and wait, in the hope that it will catch somewhere before you actually drift on to the rocks or into the surf region. It is difficult to give hard-and-fast rules about using the anchor in this way because so much will depend on the conditions and water depths, but these are scenarios which are worth examining in safety because you may have only one chance for the anchor to hold and you need to take full advantage of it.

Once the anchor has taken hold, you can wait patiently for help to arrive, provided you have managed to send a distress message or you are reasonably confident that your plight has been observed. Alternatively, you will have to think about trying to organise your own salvation, particularly if the anchor starts to drag. When a yacht is drifting irrevocably ashore, there are really only two alternatives: one is to stay with the yacht and let that take the impact before you try and scramble through the surf or over the rocks on to dry land; the other is to take to the liferaft and try and get ashore in that. It is not an easy decision to make because you will never be able to be certain of the outcome. However, as a rule of thumb, if the coastline is rocky, it is probably best to stay with the yacht and let that take the impact of the rocks before you try to get ashore, either in the liferaft or simply by scrambling.

If it is a question of getting through a heavy surf line, the liferaft is probably the better option, although a yacht with the anchor down but dragging ashore could provide a reasonably safe passage through the surf. Liferafts are not particularly comfortable in surf conditions as the drogue line is rarely strong enough to react against the massively increased pull as the liferaft is attacked by breaking surf, and there is a risk of capsize in these conditions. One possible solution here, if you have a long enough line, is to abandon ship just outside the surf line, and drift ashore in the liferaft while still attached to the abandoned yacht, using the yacht as your sea anchor. Obviously paying out the line under any sort of control would be extremely difficult as a liferaft does not have many cleats!

Fire

Fire at sea is a frightening experience, and on board a yacht there are plenty of highly combustible materials which can fuel a fire. Prevention is obviously better than cure, an adage easier to say than to adopt. There are four main areas where fire is likely to start: in the accommodation; in the galley; in the engine compartment; in the electrical circuits.

Fire in the accommodation is most likely to be caused by smoking. Tight control of smoking on board and a strict rule that lighted cigarette ends are not left around the boat will help to prevent this occurring. Obviously there are always risks where there is a naked flame and the galley should never be left unattended when something is cooking on the stove. The confined work area of the average yacht galley also poses risks as it may be necessary to reach over the stove to pick up utensils, which could set clothing on fire and initiate a series of problems. Electrical circuits probably provide the greatest hazard on modern yachts, partly because they are hidden out of sight and you can't see what is going on. The risk comes from short circuits which generate heat and sparks. These risks will be higher on metal craft, where any break in the insulation could earth the circuit. All electrical circuits should be protected by fuses or breakers, which will greatly reduce the chance of fire because they isolate the faulty circuit automatically. One of the main risk areas is the heavy-duty battery cables, which are not protected by fuses or breakers, and these need to be very carefully installed and maintained, as do the batteries themselves.

Apart from the electrical components it is the fuel which is the greatest danger in the engine compartment, and some means of isolating the fuel tanks from outside the compartment is important. With the fuel cut off in this way, the fire will not be fed by further fuel and you have some chance of coping.

Provided it is discovered early, and you have appropriate extinguishers, the fire itself should not be too much of a hazard. The main danger is from associated smoke and fumes rather than from flames themselves. Burning cushions and furnishings can generate large quantities of toxic fumes and an electrical short circuit behind panelling could have the same effect if there is foam insulation. These fumes can be so dense that they can force the crew to evacuate the compartment, preventing them tackling the seat of the blaze and then the crisis can escalate rapidly. This is the real danger from fire on board yachts, and it highlights the need to get to a fire in its early stages and to tackle it quickly.

For a fire to burn it needs oxygen, heat and fuel. Take away one of these components and the fire will go out. For instance, water put on a fire will remove heat by generating steam, and this steam will in turn displace the oxygen, making water a good fire-extinguishing medium. As we have seen, most fire extinguishers work on the basis of excluding the oxygen, which will stop the fire burning. However, there is always the risk that once the extinguishing gas or liquid has dispersed, oxygen will be able to get back to the seat of the fire and so you could find it flaring up again after it has apparently been extinguished. This is because the other two factors required for fire, heat and fuel, have not been eliminated.

We have also seen the need for fire extinguishers to be located outside the compartment they are meant to protect. This allows you to tackle the fire from outside the compartment, which keeps your escape route open. If you suspect that the fire is electrical in origin, turn off the batteries at the main switch to try and isolate the circuits and remove the initial cause. In the case of a galley fire, try and switch off the gas or other combustible, so once again the basic fuel for the fire is removed. In the engine compartment, both fuel and electrical circuits should be isolated. If you can get to the fire early enough, an extinguisher should be enough to put it out.

But remember that, on a yacht, you are not dealing with a stable situation. On discovering a fire, one of your first reactions will probably be to stop the engine or head up into the wind. You have to try and visualise fighting a fire in a yacht which may be rolling around in heavy seas. You will need to solve a delicate balancing act between having fire extinguishers which have adequate capacity to cope with a severe fire, but which are light enough to operate one-handed – because you may need the other hand for holding on. The best type of fire extinguisher is the one where the emission can be controlled, so that you disperse just enough gas or liquid to control the fire, but have some in reserve in case it flares up again. Obviously, you will need more than one fire extinguisher, and others can be brought to the fire ready for use. The supply of fire extinguishers on a yacht is necessarily limited so you must use them as effectively as possible, always trying to keep something in reserve.

At the end of the day you are surrounded by one of the best firefighting media: water. This will cope with most fires on board, except those involving fuel, and perhaps galley fires. Whilst the fire is being tackled by fire extinguishers, have buckets of water ready in the cockpit as reinforcements. It may make a mess, but that is surely preferable to having the boat burned down to the waterline. If the fire is in a mattress or other bedding, the most expedient way of dealing with it may simply be to drag the offending item out and dump it overboard.

If toxic fumes become a major problem and prevent access to the seat of the fire, one approach is to seal off the compartment involved, blanking off as many ventilators and openings as possible, and simply let the fire burn itself out, starved as it will be of oxygen. On a powerboat, fumes could quickly reach the wheelhouse to cause further problems and it is the fumes which are almost certainly the reason why yacht fires get out of control. Fumes can be controlled to some extent, and part of the boat perhaps kept habitable, by running downwind. This will tend to keep the stern of the boat clear of fumes, and will also tend to prevent flames from reaching this area, at least in the short term, and give you a better chance to sort something out. In any fire, your priorities should be: first, tackle the fire as quickly as possible; second, send off a distress message. With an electrical fire, you will have to shut down the electrical circuits, which will cut off your capability to send a radio distress message. This demonstrates well the case for having a back-up portable hand-held radio available. Make sure that all abandon-ship equipment and items such as distress flares are taken well away from the seat of the fire and are ready for rapid use. Fire has a disconcerting habit of suddenly breaking through bulkheads or decks and flaring up with increased ferocity.

Man Overboard

At first glance, having one of your crew fall overboard seems a straightforward matter to deal with. You simply turn round, head back, pick him up and away you go. However, behind this apparently straightforward procedure lies a whole host of difficulties, amongst which are: locating the person in the water; controlling your boat and bringing it back to the person in the water, something not always easy to achieve particularly under sail; and, most difficult of all, getting the person back on board. An apparently straightforward situation can turn into a nightmare and can quickly get out of hand where lives are at risk.

The first action to take when someone goes overboard is to release or throw a marker – a Danbuoy, or failing that a lifebuoy. Even something like a cockpit cushion could help because a person in the water is very hard to keep in sight. He or she is a very small target in a very big ocean and by the time you have turned to come back again, finding that person amongst the waves can be a difficult and frustrating task. At night the problem is exacerbated by the poor visibility. The Danbuoy, with its light and flag on a pole, is a vital piece of equipment for sailing boats with their greater risk of someone going overboard. Powerboats, however, are not immune from the risks, particularly fast boats which may have a very lively motion in waves, so having equipment readily at hand to identify the position of the casualty and provide them with buoyancy is a vital first step. If a person goes overboard foreward, turning the wheel towards the side on which they went over can help keep them clear of the propellers, but you will have to be quick to have any worthwhile effect.

The next step is to post on deck one of the crew, whose sole task is to keep sight of the person in the water. This requires concentration, and the crewmember should not be distracted from this task for any reason because once you have lost sight of the man overboard finding him again will be that much more difficult. Remember that any time gap between the person going overboard and launching the Danbuoy could mean that they will be quite some distance apart.

Turning Back

Now comes the problem of turning and heading back. On a powerboat, this will normally be comparatively straightforward: you will just stop the engines and do a quick turn, possibly having moved no more than 100 metres (325 feet) from the casualty. An alternative is a manoeuvre called the Williamson Turn. This involves putting the helm hard over towards the side from which the casualty fell until the course is altered through 60° from the original heading. You then apply full opposite rudder until the boat comes round on a reciprocal course to the original course. This manoeuvre should bring you straight back to the person in the water. It was developed for use by larger vessels which cannot stop quickly. Small boats, with their rapid stopping and quick turning capabilities, should simply stop and turn round. This is good for the morale of the casualty in the water and will also make it much easier to keep him in sight. Nothing is more reassuring to the swimmer than seeing the boat stop and turn quickly as it lets him know not only that he has been spotted but that recovery is imminent. On the other hand, seeing the boat going away in a wide sweeping turn can be quite alarming and could lead to the person in the water panicking, thereby reducing his chances of survival.

The Williamson Turn for Powerboats

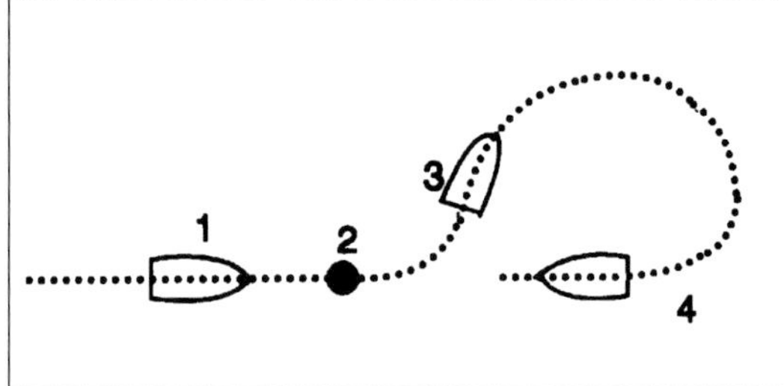

1 The initial track.
2 Point where crew member falls overboard. Helm put hard to port.
3 When compass has swung through 60° from original course, the helm is put hard to starboard.
4 Powerboat now on reciprocal course and therefore on line of original track.

Yacht Under Sail

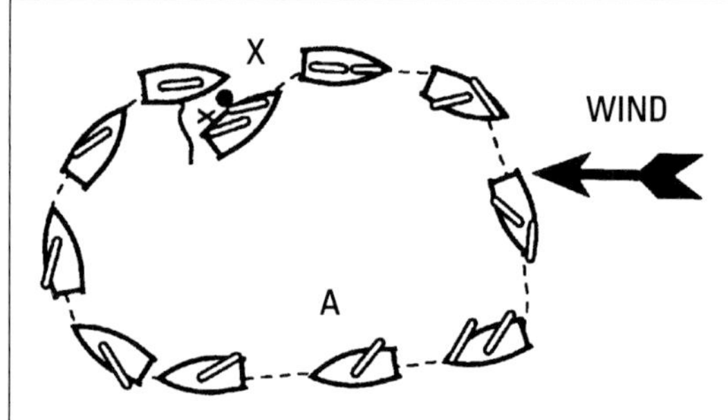

Note that the jib has been furled at A. after being backed to help the yacht turn quickly. The yacht then comes head to wind when back at casualty X.

On a sailing boat things are more complicated. The most logical way to recover someone overboard is to drop the sails and to continue under engine. This involves heading up into the wind, dropping all the sails quickly to the deck and at the same time getting the engine running. Now you have reasonable control over the situation and can make a controlled approach to the casualty in the water. Take care to ensure that in your haste, you don't get a line around the propeller.

A number of methods have been devised to bring the yacht back to the person overboard under sail alone. The classic method, when beating to windward or reaching, is to bear away downwind, gybe, and then set a course which brings the boat back close-hauled to the casualty. This enables the yacht to be rounded up head to wind as it comes alongside the swimmer. There is a risk in the gybing unless the crew are alert, but this is acceptable in the circumstances.

If the yacht is running or broad reaching when the accident occurs then getting back is more difficult, particularly if a spinnaker is set. The first thing to do is to get the spinnaker down. The boat is then brought back into the wind and sailed close-hauled back to the casualty. This manoeuvre can take the yacht a considerable distance from the casualty, which, in turn, can make keeping him in sight more difficult. Psychologically, it is not a particularly good manoeuvre because he may think his plight has not been noticed and may consequently panic.

Bringing the boat round quickly into the wind can keep the yacht closer to the casualty, but it may take a bit of time to sort out the sails before you can start sailing back and thinking about recovery. It is worth repeating here that trying to recover a person overboard under sail is a tricky manoeuvre and probably gives you only one chance to reach the casualty.

Under power you are a lot more manoeuvrable and, perhaps more importantly, you can recover the casualty when you are head to wind, which involves less risk of the boat drifting over him. You may not get close enough alongside if you try to pick him up on the weather side. These manoeuvres are fine if you can keep the person in sight, or at least the Dan marker buoy that you have put overboard. If you have an electronic position-finding receiver on board, make an immediate note of the position of the man overboard. Some of these receivers have a dedicated man overboard button which automatically records the position and gives you the course and distance back to that position. This can be a great help, particularly at night if there is no light on the casualty.

Recovering the Crewmember

Having got back alongside, you are still faced with the problem of recovery. Even if the casualty is conscious and can help himself, trying to lift a waterlogged person back on board is an almost impossible task. You should first of all secure him alongside, to make sure he stays there and he has some support, while you organise recovery. A bight of rope under the armpits and round the back and made fast on board will provide support and keep him alongside. You may then be able to get a second rope around his legs to pull him horizontal and into a position where you can think about rolling him on board. It won't be easy, particularly if you are the only person now on board or the crew members are not strong.

Alternative Methods for Recovering a Crewmember

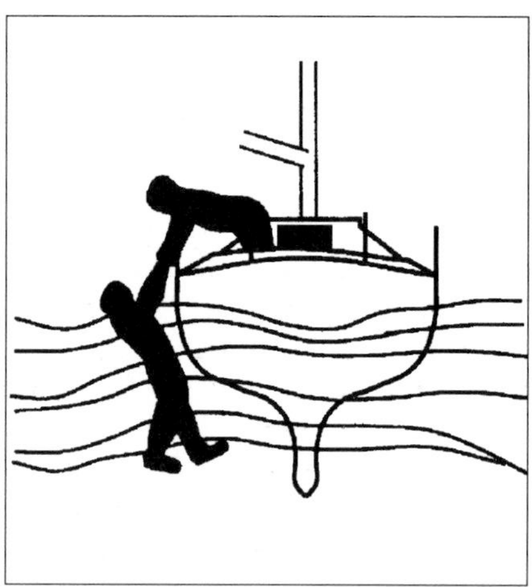

Trying to recover a casualty from the water with a straight arm lift is an impossible task for all but the very strong, even with a conscious casualty and a yacht with a low freeboard.

If you are well prepared, and in particular if the line can be easily detached, it is possible to use the main sheet tackle to lift the crewmember. Not easy if there is any sea running, and you need to attach the line firmly round the casualty before you lift.

The semi-conscious crewmember has first been secured alongside. The next stage is to take a bight of rope around the buttocks, haul in on the rope and roll the casualty on board. This will almost certainly require the bottom safety line to be cut away to have any chance of success. At least when secured alongside, mouth-to-mouth resuscitation can be attempted if necessary without having to put another crewmember in the water, assuming there is anyone else to help.

Alternatively, you can rig a tackle from the boom and lift him on this tackle. The third method is to use a sail as a sling, getting it underneath the casualty and lifting him in it. It all sounds fairly easy, but it is incredibly difficult to get someone on board, even given the comparatively low freeboard of a sailing yacht.

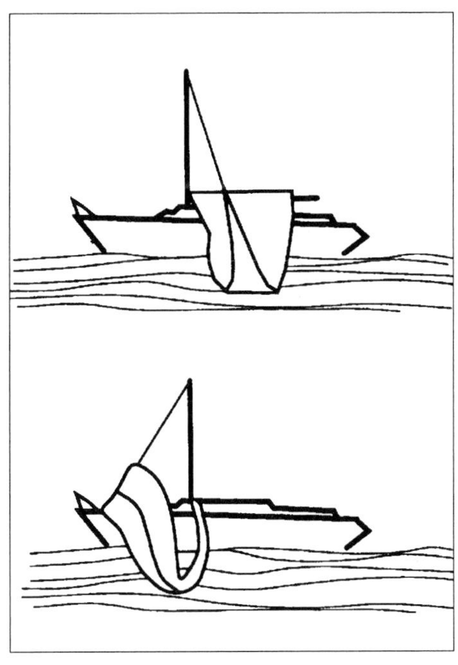

The idea is to use either the main or the jib to form a cradle under the casualty. He can then be lifted using the main halyard or the jib sheet. Getting the sail in place is the major task.

On a powerboat the situation can be even more difficult. Usually the only practical place to effect recovery is at the stern where there may be a bathing platform complete with boarding ladder. This facility might be available on a sailing boat as well, but if you use it for recovery, always bring the casualty alongside first and then take him to the stern once the engines have been stopped. Powerboats are unlikely to have any means of lifting and this, combined with high topsides, can make recovery an extremely difficult operation. If there is a dinghy on board, perhaps the best method of recovery could be to launch the dinghy and recover the casualty first into the dinghy and transfer him on board from there.

If the casualty is incapacitated, then recovery becomes that much more difficult. If he is unconscious, your priority should be mouth-to-mouth resuscitation *before* recovery, and this means somebody going into the water to help, or at least going to the casualty in a dinghy.

You can see that there is no easy and simple solution applicable to all situations. You should practise man-overboard procedures with your crew in good conditions for only then will you start to appreciate the problems involved and be able to work out possible solutions for your particular craft.

Quickstop and Life Sling

It is worth mentioning here two return and recovery systems developed by the US Sailing Safety At Sea Committee. The Quickstop recovery method involves bringing the yacht head to wind and then sailing round in an oval to arrive back at the man overboard. It is interesting to note that the recommendation is to throw cockpit cushions or lifebuoys to the casualty

The Seattle Strop

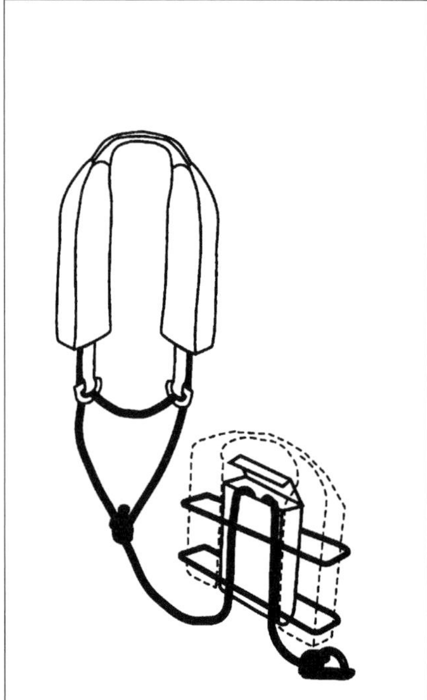

Recovery Method Recommended by the RORC

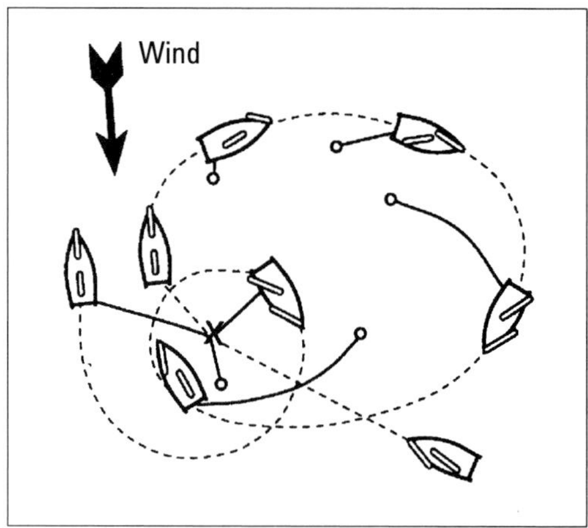

This equipment, devised in the US, has proved effective. It could be used with the recovery technique shown above. This is the method recommended by the RORC. By keeping both sails hoisted an immediate second attempt is possible, and the towed line increases the chances of making contact with the casualty.

rather than the Danbuoy, which it was felt takes too long to deploy. It is recommended that this be saved for marking the casualty's position if the first recovery attempt is not successful. This method also recommends that recovery is effected over the windward side.

The second proposed method uses what is called the life sling, or Seattle strop. The life sling is a horseshoe-shaped buoyant flexible sling on the end of a lanyard. This is trailed astern and as the yacht is turning back to the casualty the line attached to the sling passes him by so he can then grab this and put the sling over his head and under his armpits. Once in position the same sling can be used for the actual recovery. The D-rings at the front are simply hooked into a tackle attached to the main halyard, and the casualty is hoisted on deck. In the case of an unconscious person it will probably be necessary for somebody to go into the water to put the sling on the correct way for recovery. If such a system is used, recovery by this method should be practised, both to give confidence that it is going to work in a genuine emergency and to familiarise the crew with the procedures involved.

Of all the emergency procedures looked at in this chapter, man overboard is one of the most difficult. The design of modern yachts, both power and sail, does little to aid recovery: the guard rails of sailing boats can be a hindrance to the recovery of survivors from the water, which neatly demonstrates the often-conflicting requirements of safety and survival in different situations.

9 Seasickness and Survival

Seasickness is one of the most debilitating of conditions, as anyone who has suffered will testify. In Chapter 2 we noted that in some situations your survival may depend a great deal on whether or not you are seasick. Seasickness can destroy your resolve to survive in difficult conditions; even in comparatively normal conditions it can affect your judgement, both mental and physical, and make you much less aware of potential dangers and difficulties. Indeed, it could be this lack of judgement which gets you into trouble in the first place. Seasickness and safety go hand in hand, which is why a full chapter has been devoted to it.

What is Seasickness?

There are landlubbers who argue that if you go into an alien environment, you get what you deserve, ie seasickness. However, it is better described as 'motion sickness', as it can be caused by the motion of a variety of vehicles. In simple terms, your body does not like the type of motion to which it is being subjected and it reacts by triggering the stomach nerves, which make you sick. This is, of course, an over-simplification: it is a most complex affliction, in terms of both prevention and cure. It affects different people at different times and in different ways, so there is no hard-and-fast solution to the problem, except for that time-honoured remedy: stand under a tree!

Everybody has their own personal trigger for seasickness. Many yachtsmen will tell you that it is the smell of bacon which sets it off, or merely the sight of food. For others, it may be the smell of diesel oil or of the bilges, although in these cases it is much more likely to be the position in which you find yourself: down below and maybe half upside down looking into an engine compartment. There are hardened sailors who will tell you that they have never been seasick in their lives, but put them in a liferaft and they will tell a different story! Many look on seasickness as a weakness, something from which only the feeble suffer. The truth is that it is normal people who suffer from seasickness; it is those who do not who are abnormal.

What is also true is that different people are affected by seasickness to different degrees and in different ways, some being very easily and quickly affected, others only suffering in extreme conditions or perhaps when they go straight out in rough weather. Most will suffer from seasickness at some time or another – what those lucky ones who profess never to suffer from seasickness really mean is that they have not often experienced extreme situations. For more sensitive souls, for whom seasickness rears its ugly head even in moderate motion conditions, knowing what causes seasickness and how to minimise its effects can go a long way to helping you cope with this affliction, thereby making you a safer sailor.

Seasickness and Debilitation

Unpleasant and distressing as the physical symptoms of seasickness are, it is the mental effects that are by far the most dangerous. Even those mildly affected have to make a tremendous mental effort to push it to the back of their minds and concentrate on the job in hand. For those more seriously affected, it is something which can dominate their existence to the exclusion of all normal reason and precaution. It is these people who can become a dangerous liability at sea. It is very easy to say that they should snap out of it, but this is to misunderstand the near total incapacity to which seasickness can reduce sufferers. The physical incapacity is quite easy to see and recognise; much harder to spot is the mental incapacity which can impair co-ordination and judgement.

Someone who is seasick can be only too aware that something needs doing: perhaps the wind is increasing and the sails need reefing, or maybe something has come adrift and needs securing. However, acknowledging the problem is one thing, doing something about it when you are seasick is much more difficult. This is one of the less obvious facets of seasickness, but one which can have serious implications for the safety of the boat, particularly if it is the skipper who is suffering. It can take a considerable time to work up the resolve to do something about a problem, particularly if it involves physical activity, because one of the best ways of coping with seasickness is to remain as still as possible – the mere prospect of physical activity can bring on another bout of sickness. For the skipper it is sometimes easier; he is at least in a position to tell other crew members actually to do the job that needs doing.

Probably the most difficult situation in which to cope with seasickness is being on watch by yourself. You not only have to think about the problems which may be building up, but you are also there to do something about them. Here the motivation most likely to get you going is guilt at the prospect of having to face other crew members and explain why something has not been done.

Causes

There are things that can be done to reduce the chances of becoming seasick or, if you do feel seasick, at least to mitigate its effects. To evaluate these, it is helpful to understand what causes seasickness and how it affects the body. Once you know the causes, then you can find maybe not a complete cure, but ways of reducing the chances of being seasick. In many cases, knowing the causes can help even regular sufferers to cope reasonably well by eliminating as far as possible situations which would trigger or exacerbate seasickness. These precautions, combined with taking preventive tablets or other cures, will all contribute to helping you cope with the situation and enjoy life at sea in spite of a tendency to seasickness.

One of the triggers of seasickness is the balance chambers in the inner ear. These are rather like a spirit level, telling you whether you are upright, leaning forwards, or even upside down. They are your means of relating your body to the horizon or to a level or upright surface. On land, the message passed to the brain from these balance chambers will be confirmed by what your eyes can see and what the rest of your body can feel. In these 'normal' conditions the information reaching your brain from various sensors will be in harmony, and the sensors will give confirmation of the situation.

Now picture the situation on a yacht at sea. The boat is moving in the waves and your inner ear balance chamber is sending messages to your brain, informing it that the boat is moving in relation to a level surface. This will trigger your brain to send messages to the muscles of your body to make the necessary corrections to keep you upright against the movement of the boat. This is all fairly straightforward and logical, but what about the messages coming to your brain via your eyes? If you are out on deck, or in the cockpit or wheelhouse looking out towards the horizon, the message from your eyes to your brain will be similar to the message it is receiving from your balance chamber. The messages will confirm each other and everything should be fine.

But consider the situation if you take your eyes away from the horizon, perhaps to look down at the chart, or even to look up at the sails. Now the messages coming to the brain from the inner ear and the eyes will be different. The balance chamber may tell your brain that the boat is rolling, but because your eyes are focussed on something on the boat, they will give your brain a different message and suggest that you are not moving in relation to the boat. There is a conflict between the messages from the two sources, and it is these conflicting messages which create confusion in the brain. Apparently, the brain reacts by sending a trigger message to your stomach, suggesting that all is not well with the world. Your stomach reacts to this message by making you sick.

Whilst a gross over-simplification, this scenario does indicate where the main cause of seasickness lies; the conflicting messages from the two different sources create confusion, which in turn triggers sickness. The balance chambers are giving your brain the true message and the eyes the false message, although seasickness is usually blamed on inner ear disturbance caused by the constant motion of the boat.

Once you understand the cause, it is not difficult to visualise any number of situations where these conflicting sensory messages could occur. For example, it could be going down to look at the radar, which means the outside reference point for your eyes has gone. Watching a radar screen, particularly one of the older types where you have to put your head against a hood and completely shut off the outside world, can make you very vulnerable to seasickness. Going below takes away your horizon reference, and this is why people almost immediately feel much worse when they do so. The same applies if you go into the engine compartment, or even hang head-down peering into it: you have lost the visual reference point of the horizon, and the conflicting messages from the eyes and the balance chambers are coming through to your brain thick and fast.

When you are on watch in the cockpit of a sailing boat, you will tend to look at things on board because your eyes will almost automatically move to where the activity is, and this will increase the risk of seasickness. On a power boat, it is much the same: if you are shut inside the wheelhouse, there will be a strong tendency to focus on items inside rather than on the world outside. You will obviously have to concentrate to a degree on the compass, and you will no doubt be scanning the engine instrumentation and perhaps the radar and position-finding instruments. Even when you look outside, you will tend to concentrate on the bow of the boat rather than the sea beyond it. This is automatic and instinctive, because once again you concentrate on where the activity is rather than on the open view to the horizon, where there is little on which to focus.

Automatic Reactions

So here you have the basic causes of seasickness, and it is quite interesting to note how your body and your mind react almost instinctively to try to minimise its effects. When you are seasick you will feel a reluctance to go below, which would, of course, immediately increase your nausea. If on a sailing boat, you will want to stay in the cockpit, while on a power boat you will want to stay in the wheelhouse, both locations giving you a view of the horizon and therefore being the best places to minimise the effects. You will feel a reluctance even to turn round and look astern, because this can be disorientating.

However, this instinctive reaction to seasickness can produce problems, particularly in a sailing boat, because in your weakened and debilitated state the cockpit is not necessarily the best place for you to be. When you are seasick you do not hold on quite so securely, and you are certainly less reactive to spray blowing over you and to cold, both situations which can further reduce your ability to respond to sudden movements of the boat. When you are seasick you tend to go into what might be termed a sort of 'hibernation', and it takes a considerable effort of will to snap yourself out and return to the current situation.

Recognising the Symptoms

Seasickness needs a strong measure of understanding and sympathy from all on board, particularly those not afflicted. As it is often considered a sign of weakness, sufferers may try to hide the fact that they are seasick for as long as possible. This in itself can be dangerous, as the rest of the crew may not be aware that someone is suffering and may place a higher reliance on that person's mental and physical ability than the reality justifies. Seasickness is not a weakness, provided you are prepared to admit to it and take steps to try to cope with it. The weakness and the danger lie in not admitting to your reduced ability and in trying to hide it. As a skipper, you must keep a watchful eye on your crew, particularly if you go out in lively sea conditions when seasickness might be anticipated. If you see the tell-tale signs of seasickness, you must plan for the sufferers' reduced ability to cope and adjust your strategies accordingly.

In the early stages the symptoms of seasickness will be quite subtle, and will be different in different people. You may find that they will not want to talk very much and will tend to answer only in monosyllables. Another sign is that people go pale (not green!). Watch also for someone staying motionless in one particular place – there is a lack of will to move unless forced into it, so someone who sits in the cockpit with spray flying over them without complaint or without apparently wanting to move into shelter could be becoming seasick.

In more extreme cases, people will want to go below and just lie down. This is a fairly obvious giveaway, but by the time they have got to that stage they will probably have been vomiting anyway. If you see anyone exhibiting one or more of these symptoms, then a gentle question about their well-being, and possibly about feeling seasick, will probably bring about an admission, and then you can plan accordingly.

In some ways, the kindest thing to do is to send sufferers below and let them lie down, although this may not always be practicable, particularly if two or more of your crew are afflicted at the same time. You have to balance the kindness and restorative power of sending them below and relieving them of their watch against the need to keep them up on deck. Seasick people tend to think only in the short-term, and anything which will provide fairly immediate relief will be welcome. But it may not be the best long-term solution to the problem so, as skipper, you will probably have to make the decision for them.

Coping with Seasickness

If you, the skipper, are affected by seasickness, you must recognise the problem and the concomitant reduction in mental ability, and try to take steps to reduce its impact as much as possible. The same is true if you are the navigator: you know you should go below and check on the chart, but you will leave it until the last minute because this will exacerbate your sickness. If you are the skipper or navigator, or both, and you feel seasickness coming on, one of your first responsibilities is to let the rest of the crew know, not necessarily so that they can take over , but so that they can be of help and assistance to you and relieve you of some of the pressure, which will help you cope better with the seasickness.

Proprietary Anti-seasickness Remedies

Coping with seasickness should start long before you head off to sea. Many people are reluctant to take any seasickness tablets until they feel the affliction coming on. Preventative seasickness tablets are only effective if you take them *before* you start feeling ill, and at least an hour before you set sail. Part of the reluctance to take tablets stems from the fact that most of them have side effects of one sort or another, the most serious one being drowsiness, something you can well do without when you are heading off to sea. The other main effect is a tendency to dryness of the throat, which you can live with even though it is not particularly pleasant.

It is sometimes difficult to sort out cause and effect with seasickness, but the tiredness induced by some seasickness remedies can be almost as dangerous as the seasickness itself because it, too, reduces your ability to cope with difficult situations. If you are on watch and feel this tiredness wash over you, you can face a tremendous battle just to keep your eyes open: the temptation just to nod off can be very strong. Indeed, a half-hour sleep can often dispel the tiredness and leave you feeling fine. However, the feeling fine could be the prelude to the effects of the tablet wearing off, which may happen before you have had time to adjust to the movement of the boat, so seasickness may be delayed rather than avoided! The remedy is to take another tablet at this stage, rather than run the risk of seasickness.

Prescription-only Remedies

There is another form of preventive which can be much more effective but which is available only on prescription. Produced under several different trade names, it comprises a small sticking plaster-type patch which contains chemicals, and when this patch is applied behind the ear the chemicals are absorbed through the skin. These trans-dermal patches are normally applied about one hour before sailing to allow them to get to work. They tend to be slower to take effect than the tablets but have two major advantages: one is that, because the chemicals are absorbed trans-dermally rather than by mouth, the patches can be effective even after someone has started to suffer from seasickness; the second is that they tend to be effective over a much longer period, up to two or three days. So, for regular sufferers, these patches are a considerable boon.

Both tablets and patches produce the side effects already discussed. The dryness can be relieved by sips of water and the tiredness by sleep, although the latter can be a particular problem if you are the skipper and have to stay awake, perhaps during a tricky period of navigation. However, when the mind is occupied staying awake is not usually so much of a problem. As with seasickness itself, the solo watch can cause particular problems for someone experiencing remedy-induced drowsiness.

Acupuncture

There are proprietary wrist bands called Sea-Bands which, it is claimed, act on the acupuncture principle, applying pressure to points on the wrists. Some people find them effective and swear by them, but there does not seem to be universal acceptance that they are fully effective. However, their appeal is considerable because, of course, they do not involve taking drugs.

Relaxation/combatting Stress

The makers of some seasickness remedies recommend that you take the first tablet 24 hours before sailing. There is no discernible proof that this improves matters, but it does increase the sale of tablets. However, your preparation before going to sea should not just involve taking a seasickness tablet: it should also involve attempting to ensure that you are reasonably relaxed.

There is no doubt that stress plays a part in seasickness, and the hour or so before departure, combined with the hour or so needed to settle down afterwards, can be a time of considerable stress. This is particularly the case if you have a difficult harbour entrance to negotiate or weather conditions are less than favourable. If you are racing, the stress of the start and the close-quarters sailing involved can be very high indeed. Avoiding stress by a planned and considered departure can help the situation enormously, both for the skipper and for the crew, and is a good prelude to any voyage.

Compensatory Action

Any cure for seasickness can be helped considerably by what you do on the boat. Because of the importance of the horizon as a reference point, you should try to find a position where you have a clear view of it. This will certainly help, and for many people is sufficient to keep seasickness at bay. However, it has its limitations, because at night you have no effective horizon and it is not unusual to see people who have been fine all day succumb to seasickness when darkness falls.

This effect reinforces the view that seasickness is greatly dependent upon the relationship between what the eyes see and what the balance chambers feel, a theory further supported by the reluctance of seasickness sufferers to go below except to lie down. It does appear that when you are horizontal the conflicting messages to the brain are greatly reduced. No doubt this is partly due to the fact that when you are lying down you usually have your eyes shut, so the brain only gets the message from the balance chambers and not from the eyes, and you return to a more comfortable state. But there can be a rapid onset of seasickness when you have to get up again. You often see this in people who have been off watch below: they are called, and by the time they are equipped and ready to go on watch they are rushing to the heads in a frenzy of seasickness.

As skipper you will need to keep a careful watch on your crew because, as we have seen, if they are suffering from seasickness they can become a liability. On a sailing boat, the first thing to do is to make sure that they are clipped on securely so that there is no risk of their being washed overboard. This should apply in all conditions, not just in rough seas. It particularly applies if the sufferer leans over the rail to vomit, when the reduced response to the motion of the boat could easily make them fall overboard. On a power boat, assuming it is being steered from inside the wheelhouse, the ideal would be to have a forward-facing seat fitted with a safety harness into which the sufferer could be strapped, able to relax whilst still having the horizon as a focus point.

You, the skipper, must decide whether to send a seasickness sufferer down below to their bunk – probably the safest and best solution. If you do consign someone to their bunk, ensure that they have a bucket or other receptacle handy, so that they don't have to get up and move around if they want to vomit. They should be kept warm because cold is likely to exacerbate the seasickness, and they should be made as secure as possible in the bunk to aid relaxation.

Unless the passage lasts for days, any crew member sent below is unlikely to surface again until the yacht reaches calmer waters, when the recovery can be miraculous, although the sufferer will feel fatigued, rather like in the aftermath of a normal illness. Severe sufferers may not recover until they actually step ashore and it is unlikely that you will see them on board again – the misery of seasickness will outweigh any pleasure they might have got from sailing. Normal sufferers, of whom there are many, learn to cope with the problem after one or two trips, and with help and support from the rest of the crew they still derive pleasure from sailing.

Summary

During normal passage-making, seasickness is something that needs careful watching and for which sufferers need a degree of help and sympathy. It is when you come to survival situations that seasickness can become a positive danger, because of its effect on your ability to cope. The fear and incipient panic engendered by, say, having to abandon ship, will almost certainly exacerbate any tendency to seasickness and, as mentioned previously, in a liferaft seasickness can be a major handicap to survival.

The motion of a liferaft is extremely conducive to seasickness, particularly if you are shut up inside with no view of the horizon. The motion can be unpredictable and unsettling, and even people who do not normally suffer from seasickness frequently succumb. Not only does it sap your mental reserves, it can also increase the risk of exposure because the act of being sick reduces your body's heat reserves. Moreover, one person being seasick within the confines of a liferaft can rapidly result in the other occupants being affected. So, anything that can be done to reduce the effects of seasickness in a liferaft will go a long way to helping to ensure survival.

This is why it is vital to take seasickness tablets in the very early stages of any abandon ship crisis. Almost before you consider getting the liferaft over the side, seasickness tablets should be issued to all the crew. As we have already noted, they do take some time to take effect and the earlier you can get them down the more effective they are likely to be. If you are unfortunate enough to have to abandon ship, it is important to realise that seasickness can jeopardise your chances of survival, so its prevention should be one of your first priorities.

10 First Aid

It is not the intention here to cover every aspect of first aid because that would require a complete book in itself. There are some excellent first aid books for yachtsmen on the market, one of which should be an important part of your first aid equipment. You may have the best first aid kit but if you don't know how to use it, it won't be a great deal of help! But even a book on first aid is not the complete answer because, as with most safety and survival routines, you need to have *practised* first aid to be truly effective. You are only likely to be reasonably effective and, perhaps more importantly, have some confidence in what you are doing, if you have been on a recommended first aid course and taken part in practical exercises.

Medical Advice at Sea

Of course, at sea you are not alone with just the first aid kit and book – you can also get medical advice over the radio, probably the most practical solution in a medical emergency. The practical advice will normally come directly from a doctor, and it can be very reassuring to know that you are getting sound medical advice rather than having to rely solely on your own judgement. You will also be able to receive guidance about what action you should take to get the casualty ashore.

Medical advice is available free from all coast radio stations and from the coastguard, and will be given for as long as you need it. In the case of a serious accident or illness, before making your call arm yourself with a list of the symptoms manifested by the casualty as far as you are able to assess them, and check what first aid equipment and drugs you have on board. This will obviously help the doctor with his diagnosis and recommended treatment.

Accidents and Illness on Board

Accidents to your crew should be part of your 'what if' training, when you should try to visualise the sort of thing you might have to deal with. There are three main types of casualty with which you might have to deal: firstly, someone who has fallen overboard or who has been recovered from the water and requires resuscitation; secondly, someone suffering from burns as a result of a fire on board, or of hot liquids being spilt in the galley; and thirdly, someone with broken bones due to slipping and falling or being hit on the head by the boom. In each case you will need to make a quick decision about whether to treat the casualty where you find them or move them below before starting treatment. To do this, you will need to assess the apparent injuries.

When it comes to resuscitation, of course, speed is of the essence. If the person is unconscious, resuscitation should be commenced immediately, in the water alongside if you can't get the casualty on board quickly. Burns are most likely to have been incurred below, so this is the logical place for treatment as the casualty is also protected from exposure, whilst fractures should generally be treated where the casualty has fallen, provided there is no immediate risk of further injury being sustained if he remains in this position. Temporary immobilisation of the injured area will then allow the casualty to be taken below for further treatment. However, you must be particularly careful with head, neck or back injuries, where any movement can cause further damage. In such an eventuality, medical advice should be sought before any action is taken.

Apart from injuries, it is possible that one of your crew could become seriously ill at sea. Diagnosis could be very difficult, so again medical advice is essential. Not only are illnesses difficult to diagnose for the non-medic, the chances are that you will not have the drugs on board for effective treatment. Some illnesses and injuries can involve intense pain, and one of the biggest problems for the rest of the crew is not having any suitable pain-relieving drugs on board. In the case of a serious injury, you may be able to cope with the immediate problem by applying first aid, but you will feel incredibly helpless at not having anything to hand to relieve the pain. Drugs for the relief of intense pain are available only on prescription. Some, such as morphine, can be made available if you are on a long passage away from land, but because they are classified as dangerous drugs, carrying them on board can create problems with customs when you enter harbour. However, their ability to reduce the pain suffered by a seriously injured crew member certainly makes their carriage, and any problems this causes, worthwhile if you are away from direct assistance for a protracted period.

Rescue by Lifeboat or Helicopter

Faced with an injured person on board, your options are limited. In severe situations, there is the possibility that a lifeboat or helicopter can bring a doctor out to the casualty. The doctor can not only administer painkilling drugs but, perhaps more importantly from your point of view, he will also remove from your shoulders the responsibility for dealing with the patient and the decision about future action.

If his condition allows it and the nearest harbour is close enough, there is little doubt that the best course of action from the patient's point of view will be to keep him on board until you reach harbour. Transferring a patient at sea can be a risky operation; particularly in the case of injury, it is generally the rule that the less movement the better. However, both lifeboat and helicopter will carry a Neil Robertson stretcher, and once the patient is lashed into this transfer from vessel to vessel or into the helicopter can be safely carried out. Transfer into the helicopter can get the patient to hospital very quickly, but transfer into a lifeboat is probably only justified if it is much faster than your vessel, or if it can enter harbour or land on a beach to reduce the time taken to get the patient to hospital. In such situations you are usually well advised to take the advice of the various authorities involved, who will have had plenty of experience of this type of operation and will be able to cope with the situation much more efficiently. Remember, however, that the safety of the yacht is still your responsibility.

Coping on Your Own

If you are on your own and cannot call for help, either because you haven't got a radio or it has broken down, or the electricity supply has failed, then obviously you have to make all the decisions. The immediate treatment of the patient must be your first priority, but after that you must get help as quickly as possible. You may be able to get assistance by attracting the attention of another vessel in the area and getting the skipper to radio on your behalf. If you have a severely injured casualty on board, you would be justified in using distress flares to attract attention. Alternatively, you should think about getting into harbour as quickly as possible.

In this case, you will need to assess the various possibilities carefully, bearing in mind that the flow of the tide and the height of the tide in harbour entrances means the nearest harbour may not always be the quickest. Weather conditions will also have a bearing on your decision, and whilst that harbour downwind might look very attractive because you can get there more quickly with the wind behind you, you may well find the entrance too dangerous in rough conditions. Heading upwind may be an unpleasant prospect with a severely injured person on board, but it may be the safer alternative, and it could also have the merit of taking you into more sheltered waters.

Having an injured person on board can make you face some hard decisions. The main priority is to get help as quickly as possible, which generally means getting the casualty on shore and into an ambulance as fast as possible. But at the nearest harbour you may not be able to get your yacht alongside, and it may take longer there to transfer the casualty ashore by dinghy than to go to a harbour further away which has better facilities.

The First Aid Kit

You will feel a lot more confident about coping with casualties at sea if you have an effective first aid kit. The contents of these kits can be divided into two groups. There is what might be termed the 'hardware', equipment such as bandages, wound dressings and scissors, and what might be termed the 'software', actual medicines such as painkillers and seasickness tablets. For the former, you can get excellent ready-made first aid kits. If you do buy one, rather than putting one together yourself, avoid the small, almost pocket-sized ones which are more a personal first aid kit for walkers and campers, and choose a large, comprehensive one of a type necessary for dealing with the five- or six-man crew of a boat at sea.

In general, a first aid kit tends to contain equipment which can be used for a variety of purposes, rather than items for specific injuries. You never quite know what you are going to have to deal with at sea, and while some of the injury-specific equipment could be useful, it doesn't have the practical application of some of the more general-purpose equipment, such as triangular bandages and wound dressings. The guide produced by the RYA and set out below, should give you a start, but don't hesitate to add to it if you feel the need because, at the end of the day, you can never have too much first aid equipment at sea (although you have to balance this against cost and stowage).

In addition to this direct application equipment, it would be useful to have some form of splinting, but you do not need to carry special equipment for this purpose: temporary splints can be made from sail battens or pieces of wood. In the same way, although specialised thermal blankets are available for dealing with exposure victims, you will probably have sleeping bags or duvets on board which are equally effective.

Much the same advice goes for the medicines you carry on board. You will need most of the general drugs, such as you find in your first aid box at home: painkilling tablets like aspirin or paracetamol, antiseptic cream, and tablets for indigestion, diarrhoea and seasickness. You should also have creams for sunburn and chapped lips, and an antihistamine cream for bites, stings and allergies. These drugs will serve to treat minor ailments, but because you are to be away from immediate help, you should think

First aid kit recommended by the RYA

Dressings, Bandages and Hardware

3	Triangular banadages
2	Large wound dressings BPC No. 15
3	Medium wound dressings BPC No. 13
3	Conforming bandages — one each of 10 cms, 7.5 cms & 5 cms
1	Crepe bandages 7.5 cms
1	Roll 2.5 cms adhesive waterproof strapping
1	Large box assorted elastic adhesive dressings, individually wrapped
1	Eye pad
10	Sachets antiseptic wipes (eg "Mediprep")
1 pkt	Sterile Suture Strips (adhesive) eg Steristrips
2 pkts	(×5) single sterile gauze swabs 7.5 cms
10	Paraffin gauze burn dressings, individually wrapped 10 cms (eg Jelonet)
1pr	Stainless steel scissors — blunt/sharp end
1pr	Spade end tweezers — good quality
10	Protected safety pins — 5 large, 5 medium

NAME AND QUANTITY RECOMMENDED	USE	DOSE
Soluble Aspirin (100)	Pain, reducing temperature, sprains bruises and swelling	1-2 tablets, 4 hourly
	As gargle for sore throats	2 tablets dissolved in water
Paracetamol 500 mgs (20)	Alternative to Aspirin	As Aspirin
Kaolin Powder (100 gms)	Diarrhoea	1 teaspoonful in water 4 times daily
Aludrox Tablets	Indigestion	1-2 tablets, ½ hour before meals. Chew before swallowing
Kwells (50) or Stugeron tablets (50)	Seasickness preventatives	As directed on packet. Do **not** give Stugeron to pregnant women.
Caladryl cream	Sunburn and itching skin	Apply as directed on tube
Uvistat cream and lip salve	Burnt, chapped and split lips	Apply as directed on tube
Piriton tablets, 4 mgs (20)	Hay fever, insect bites and stings, Allergic conditions in general	Adult, 1 tablet 3 times daily. Children 6-12 ½ tablet 3 times daily. This drug will make you drowsy, especially if any alcohol is taken.
Tinaderm powder (1 tin)	General treatment of sweating or peeling areas of the body.	Apply liberally to affected area twice daily (You still need to wash).

The following drugs are available on prescription only. It is up to the individual owner to discuss with his own GP whether or not they should be carried.

Drugs for the relief of pain:

Codeine 30 mgs tablets (20)	Severe Pain Diarrhoea Cough suppressant	1-2 tablets, 4 hourly 1-2 tablets, 12 hourly 1-2 tablets, nightly
Distalgesic Tablets (30)	Moderate pain	2 tablets, 3 or 4 times daily. **Not** children.
DF 118 Tablets 30 mgs (30)	Moderate or severe pain. Severe coughing	1 tablet 4-6 hourly. **Not** children or asthma suffers.
Fortral Tablets 25 mgs (20)	Severe pain	Adult, 2 tablets 4 hourly. Children 6–12 1 tablet 4 hourly. **Not** children under 6 or head injuries.

Antibiotics

Magnapen tablets 500 mgs (20)	Infections	Adult 1 tablet 4 times daily. Children under 10 ½ tablet 4 times daily
Tetracycline tablets 250 mgs (20)	Infections, for patients with penicillin sensitivity. Broken bones with ends protruding	1 tablet 4 times daily. **Not** for children or pregnant women. Do not give Milk of Magnesia or Aludrox at the same time.
Chloromycetin eye ointment, 1 tube	Conjunctivitis (red eyes) and/or discharge of pus.	Small amount of ointment to each side of join of eyelids every 3-4 hours. Continue treatment for a day or so after the eye appears normal.

about extending the list with some prescription drugs. You will need to discuss your requirements with your doctor but, as a minimum, you will need some extra-strong painkilling tablets and some antibiotics. Most prescription drugs have limitations on their use in certain circumstances, which is generally why they are only available on prescription, but you should have no problem in obtaining suitable drugs provided you can assure your doctor that you will be using them in a reasonable and responsible manner. Having a first aid certificate will help to reassure him. Remember, too, that all drugs have a limited life and will not remain effective indefinitely. They should be changed at regular intervals, probably every two years, if you want them to remain fully effective and safe.

It is worth taking considerable care over your first aid kit: its contents may make the difference between being able or unable to cope with a medical emergency. If you are able to cope, it will not only bring relief to the patient but will also give you considerable peace of mind. There is nothing worse than having somebody seriously ill or injured on board and not having the means to alleviate their distress, at least temporarily.

The first aid kit needs to be kept in a cool, dry place and any items used should be replaced immediately. This sounds obvious but it rarely happens; very often you see a yacht's first aid kit half full, perhaps contaminated by a leaking bottle, or, worse still, dirty and unkempt. To be of any use in a crisis a first aid kit should be in good order and complete. Bear in mind too, when stowing the first aid kit, that you could well want to take it with you if you have to abandon ship, so it should be readily prepared and available at all times, preferably in a watertight container.

Hypothermia

Particularly if you go sailing in the winter, you need to guard against hypothermia. Any crew member falling overboard in the cooler months is likely to succumb quite quickly to severe hypothermia, emphasising why quick recovery from the water is so important in cold weather. Even in the summer months, hypothermia can be a major problem, with the possibility of death occurring after just two hours in water with a temperature of 10°C. Whilst immersion carries the greatest risk of hypothermia, the helmsman in an open

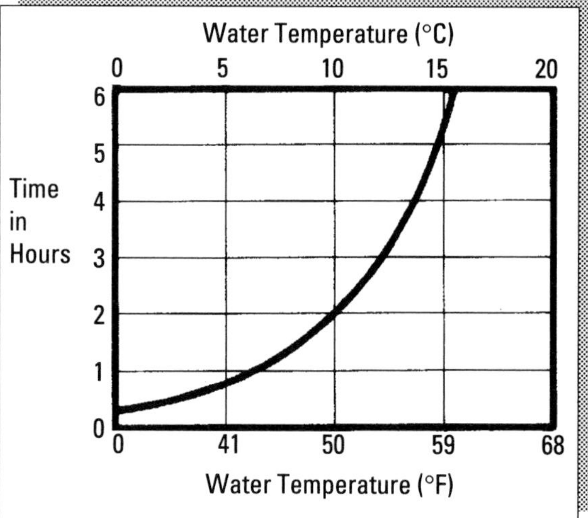

The length of time a normally clothed person could expect to remain conscious in water of different temperatures.

cockpit in winter will also be susceptible if he does not have adequate protective clothing. Strong winds can introduce a chill factor which is then exacerbated by wet conditions.

It is essential to be able to recognise the symptoms of hypothermia, although these are not always easy to identify in the early stages. They may be obvious when a casualty has been recovered from the water, but for a crew member in the cockpit the onset of hypothermia can be very gradual. The first sign is likely to be some form of confusion or indifference to surroundings. For example, the helmsman may become unable to maintain the correct course. As the condition progresses the symptoms can become something like those of a stroke: unsteadiness and stumbling; slurring of the speech; a pale skin which feels cold. Further symptoms will include shivering, although this on its own is not necessarily a sign of hypothermia; pulse weakening and becoming slower; slowing of the breathing. These symptoms are not necessarily easy to spot in someone sitting in an open cockpit swathed in foul-weather gear. The best indication that someone is developing hypothermia will be their generally unreasonable behaviour and their unwillingness to move or to participate in conversation. They may well be normally bloody-minded, but if the conditions are very cold you can't afford to take the risk, and the sooner you get them down below and into a warmer, protected environment, the better. Some of the symptoms of hypothermia are similar to those of seasickness and in their early stages the two conditions could be confused, although vomiting is not usually associated with hypothermia.

Hypothermia eventually leads to collapse and unconsciousness and, if the patient is allowed to continue to deteriorate, death. The best solution to hypothermia is prevention. Therefore, if you are out at sea in cold conditions and the crew have to spend time in an exposed cockpit or on deck, make these periods of exposure as brief as possible. Ensure that crew members in the exposed positions are changed frequently so that the risk of hypothermia is reduced. Bear in mind that thin people are much more susceptible than fat people and that the risk of hypothermia can be much reduced by wearing plenty of warm clothing. Pay particular attention to wearing adequate headgear, as this is the area where the greatest loss of heat occurs.

People who have been in water which is at all cold, say below 15°C should be treated for hypothermia, no matter how short their time in the water – do not wait for medical assistance. If the casualty has apparently stopped breathing, resuscitation should obviously take precedence over the treatment for hypothermia, although the two can go hand-in-hand to some extent. Once breathing has been restored, the casualty should be put in the coma position so that the air passages are open and free.

Mild cases of hypothermia will recover reasonably quickly if their wet clothes are removed and any surplus water mopped up by dabbing with a towel rather than vigorously rubbing, and they are then wrapped in the warmest clothing available. With hypothermia you must not rub the skin because this tends to take heat away from the body core, which has cooled down, thus causing the hypothermia. For the same reason, do not place any hot objects, such as hot water bottles, directly against the skin. Sleeping bags and duvets are an ideal way of keeping the patient warm, but if he or she is really cold another person should lie alongside to help generate the necessary heat.

A warm bath is one of the best restoratives, but there are few yachts around with this level of luxury. A warm shower could suffice, but you would certainly have to be careful that the casualty was supported upright in the shower and that his head was kept out of the water.

Never give alcohol to anyone you suspect of suffering from hypothermia or, for that matter, to anyone who has fallen overboard. Alcohol has long been the traditional cure for anybody falling overboard; a tot of rum is supposed to aid your recovery. In fact all it does is dilate the blood vessels, thereby increasing heat loss and exacerbating the condition. Indeed, alcohol should have no place in the treatment of any medical condition. As the patient recovers, and providing he is fully conscious, he can be given warm, sweet drinks, but recovery from hypothermia is a long, slow process and should not be rushed.

Even when the body temperature is back to normal and apparent recovery has taken place, the casualty should still be kept well wrapped up, dry and in a warm place, and should be landed as soon as possible for medical checks and treatment. Any case of hypothermia should be treated as a medical emergency because there is always the risk of a relapse, particularly as a yacht is far from being the ideal environment in which to recover from hypothermia.

Immersion Casualty

The same holds true where one of the crew has fallen overboard or come close to drowning, or when you pick up a survivor from the water. If you cannot detect any breathing or if they are unconscious, it is vital to start resuscitation immediately, but it can take some time to get a casualty out of the water and into a suitable position to begin resuscitation. If it appears that the casualty is unconscious when brought alongside, their best chance of survival is if an active crew member goes into the water to start resuscitation techniques there and then.

However, you must be careful when this is done that you don't end up with two casualties in the water. The crew member going overboard should be well protected, especially if the water is cold, and should be wearing a lifejacket and a safety-harness and line. Not only can someone in the water start mouth to mouth resuscitation immediately, they can also be of great assistance by placing a line or strop around the casualty to aid his recovery from the water.

With a casualty in this condition, as well as the danger of hypothermia there is also a risk of cardiac arrest. Here you have the makings of a major medical emergency on your hands, so while you are trying to carry out immediate first aid and recover the casualty from the water, one crew member should be directed to get on the radio and call for help.

Mouth-to-mouth Resuscitation

Mouth-to-mouth resuscitation involves closing off the patient's nose and blowing into the mouth with the same sort of rhythm as your own breathing. You simply pinch the nose to prevent the air you are blowing in escaping through the nose. You can, if it is easier, work the opposite way round and close off the mouth and blow down the nose.

It is vital that you don't waste any time in starting resuscitation. As soon as oxygen stops reaching the brain cells they begin to die, and the casualty will die if deprived of oxygen for too long. So the first thing, whether the casualty is in the water or has been brought on deck, is to try to get two or three good breaths of air into his lungs. If it has to be done in the water, hold the nose, tip the head back and cover his mouth with yours, breathing out at the same time. When you have got some breath into his lungs then you can think about removing false teeth, mucus or vomit from the mouth and ensuring that the tongue is not obstructing the throat, after which you can get on with the serious business of regular resuscitation. Resuscitation is not an easy operation in the water, but if you can get the odd breath into the casualty's lungs now and again, it may just be enough oxygen to keep him going until regular resuscitation can be carried out on deck.

Full resuscitation, with the casualty lying flat, involves lifting up the chin, which will tilt the head backwards and thereby ensure that the air tubes will not be blocked by the tongue. Now you can close off the nose by pinching both nostrils between your thumb and forefinger, take a deep breath, place your mouth over the casualty's mouth and breathe out so that the air from your lungs enters their lungs. You may not be pumping in the best quality air, but it still contains enough oxygen to keep the casualty alive and you should see his chest rise as you blow. After blowing in, take your mouth away. The casualty should expel the air naturally and you should see the chest fall. This procedure should be repeated every five seconds; after every five or so cycles you should check the pulse in the

The head is gently tipped back to ensure clear air passages before starting mouth-to-mouth.

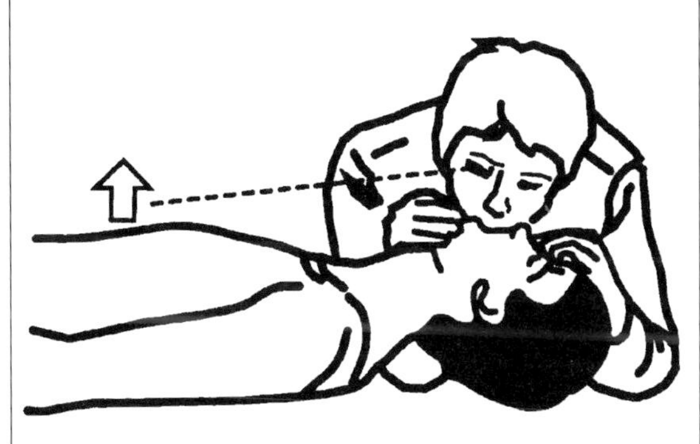

Every time you blow into the mouth you should be able to see the chest rise. A lack of movement could indicate that the airway is blocked.

patient's wrist. If you feel a pulse, continue the mouth-to-mouth resuscitation at the same rate, about 12 times every minute.

Cardiac Massage

If you can't feel a pulse, it is time to start cardiac massage. If there are two of you available, this can be done in conjunction with the mouth-to-mouth resuscitation. If there is only one of you, you must breathe into the mouth and then immediately try the cardiac massage. For this you first have to locate the casualty's breastbone, which runs down the centre of the chest, ending in an inverted V. Kneel beside the casualty, facing the chest, and place your right hand on the centre of the chest, approximately on the lower third of the breastbone. Place your left hand on top of your right hand, and rock forward with your arms held stiff so that your weight presses down on the breastbone (you will feel the breastbone move downwards under this pressure), then rock back, allowing the breastbone to spring back.

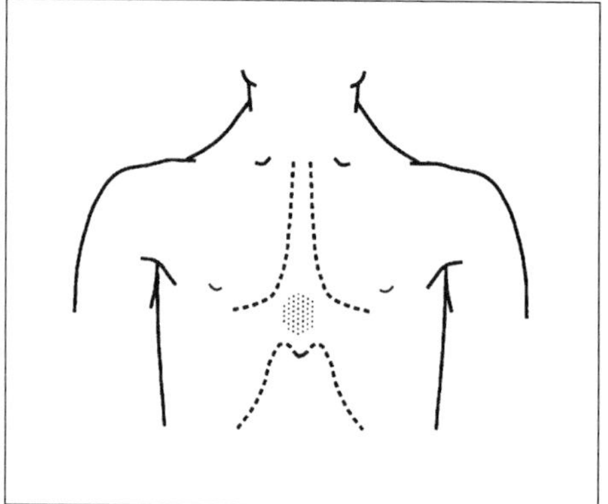

Apply pressure at the shaded area.

If you repeat this procedure every second you will, with luck, get the heartbeat going again. If you are on your own, then carry out five cardiac massage pressures followed by one cycle of the artificial resuscitation procedures. Check the pulse every few minutes, and once you can feel it beating strongly, at somewhere between 50 and 100 beats a minute, you can stop the cardiac massage and concentrate on the mouth-to-mouth resuscitation. If the two procedures are being performed properly then, even though the casualty is not breathing on his own and has no discernible heartbeat, his colour will gradually improve and you will know that at least he is getting enough blood to the brain, and therefore enough oxygen to keep

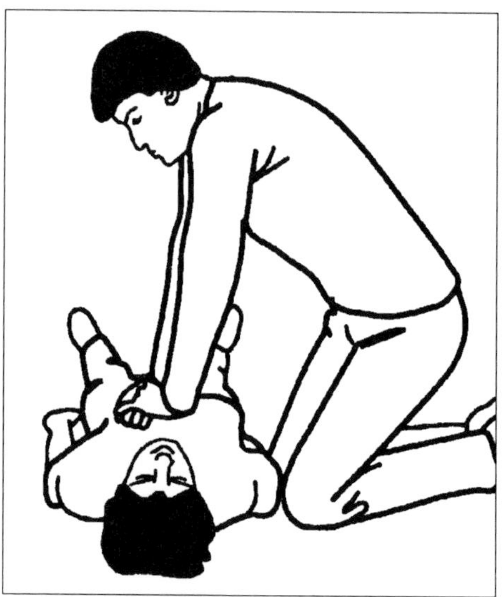

The posture for cardiac massage. It requires physical strength to deflect the breastbone but if overdone may break a few ribs. It is extremely tiring to keep this manipulation going. Mouth-to-mouth can be carried out with the patient in same position.

him alive. This doesn't mean to say that you can stop, however. Artificial resuscitation may have to be continued for an hour or more before the casualty has recovered adequately to be able to function independently.

The best indication that the casualty is recovering is the colour of the inside of the mouth and the tongue. When you begin, this may be blue, indicating lack of oxygen, but it should quickly turn to a more healthy-looking pink if your actions are successful. Even though the skin may remain blue or grey and unhealthy-looking for several hours, if the colour inside the mouth improves you can be confident that recovery is under way. Although the casualty may not actually regain consciousness for several hours, once he is breathing on his own he must be put in the recovery position and watched very carefully to ensure that there is no relapse and that pulse and breathing continue to strengthen. He can now be treated for hypothermia.

You must make every effort to get the casualty ashore as quickly as possible because he will still need a full medical check-up, and there is the risk of a relapse or complications setting in after such a traumatic experience. Hospitalisation is necessary for at least 24 hours to ensure that survival will continue. If you are several hours from harbour then you must obviously consider the possibility of transfer to helicopter or lifeboat. Do not assume that because the patient has apparently made a complete recovery all will be well, but if there is no means of getting the him to hospital quickly, once he regains consciousness he can be given small sips of water or hot drinks – but no solid food.

With luck you will never have to deal with such a medical emergency, but you should be prepared to do so. A casualty's chances of survival could be entirely in your hands and what you do, particularly in the early stages, could mean the difference between life and death. This is an awesome responsibility and it is likely to be thrust upon you at very short notice.

I hope I have demonstrated to you the need for thorough training in all aspects of first aid. When an accident occurs the time for learning is past and it is time for action, and how you perform your first aid can have a profound and permanent effect on the life of the casualty.

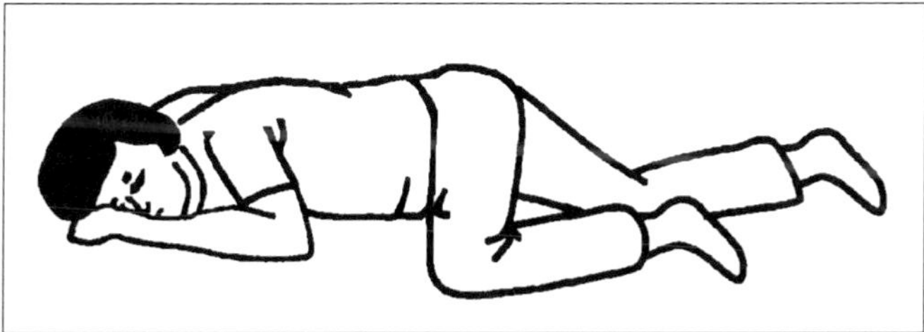

Casualty placed in the 'recovery' position once breathing again.

11 Rules and Regulations

There are not too many rules and regulations governing yachting. You are reasonably free to go where you want, and how you want, whether under power or sail. You are not even under any obligation to carry basic safety equipment if your craft is under 13.7 metres (45 feet), which covers the majority of pleasure craft in the United Kingdom. Only when your boat exceeds this figure are there mandatory requirements concerning the level of safety equipment.

However, although there is no legal requirement, you are certainly under a moral obligation to make adequate safety provision for you crew and to ensure your craft is in a seaworthy condition. Your insurance company will also be interested in the condition of your craft and the equipment carried on board. If you look at the small print on your policy, you will find an exclusion of liability clause unless your craft is maintained in a sound and seaworthy condition and carries recommended safety equipment. Depending on the information on the proposal form and, in certain cases, a surveyor's report, you may find you are restricted to UK coastal waters only. So, whether it is a legal requirement or not, you should have both a seaworthy and well-maintained yacht and carry adequate safety equipment.

The best safety equipment in the world is worthless unless you and your crew know how to use it. Just having safety equipment on board does not make you safe. There are no rules and regulations regarding training in its use, and it is down to the skipper to act in a responsible manner and ensure his crew know where the equipment is stowed and how to use it in an emergency. After all, the skipper is as prone to going overboard as anyone else.

Racing

An entirely different situation applies when you go racing. When you submit a race entry form you agree to follow the rules set by the body responsible for organising the event. These rules do not carry the force of law but they do carry the force of race organisers, be they the Royal Ocean Racing Club, the Ocean Racing Council, the Royal Yachting Association, or the Union Internationale Motornautique. These bodies set standards for the provision of safety equipment, and in many cases for the construction of the craft itself, and if you want to race you have to meet these requirements. Boats are usually visited by a 'scrutineer' before each race and detailed checks are made of the boat and its equipment – failure to meet the standards means you are automatically excluded from taking part. In one sense the crew may also be tested, as the scrutineer may request a demonstration that a liferaft stowed below can be ready for launching on deck within a specified time period.

Racing Standards

The safety standards devised by the various authorities responsible for organising races are not arbitrary, but have been developed from hard-won experience, including such tragedies as the infamous 1979 Fastnet Race. Although some of the rules are devised to stop cheating, eg to prevent yachts having a particular advantage in the way they are constructed or operated, most form a sound and sensible basis for a cruising yacht to follow. If you are genuinely interested in safety, it will pay great dividends to examine carefully the standards set by these race organisers.

Standards Set by the Royal Ocean Racing Club

The RORC has developed detailed requirements for racing yachts based on experience that stretches back to 1925. First, races are divided into four categories dependent on such factors as where the race is to be held, how long the race is to last and the type of craft involved. There then comes a highly detailed list of requirements, some common to all race categories, others specific to particular categories. Thus yachts racing across oceans have different requirements to meet from those for inshore races for small yachts. The four categories are as follows:

Category 0 race. Trans-Ocean races, where yachts must be completely self-sufficient for very extended periods of time, capable of withstanding heavy storms and prepared to meet serious emergencies without the expectation of outside assistance.

Category 1 race. Races of long distance and well offshore, where yachts must be completely self-sufficient for extended periods of time, capable of withstanding heavy storm and prepared to meet serious emergencies without the expectation of outside assistance.

Category 2 race. Races of extended duration along or not far removed from shorelines or in large unprotected bays or lakes, where a high degree of self-sufficiency is required of the yachts but with the reasonable probability that outside assistance could be called upon for aid in the event of serious emergencies.

Category 3 race. Races across open water, most of which is relatively protected or close to shorelines, including races for small yachts.

Category 4 race. Short races, close to shore in relatively warm or protected waters normally held in daylight.

Some of the requirements are listed on the following pages, together with the race categories to which they apply.

THE RORC REQUIREMENTS FOR RACING YACHTS

ORC SPECIAL REGULATIONS DIAGRAMMATIC GUIDE

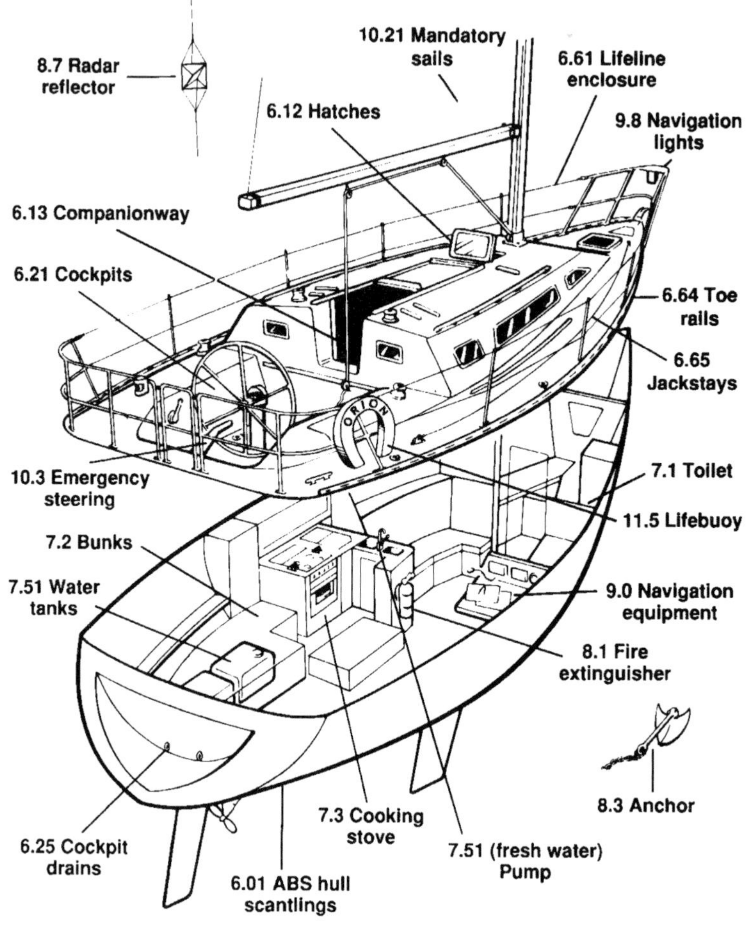

THE RORC REQUIREMENTS FOR RACING YACHTS

SPECIAL REGULATIONS

OFFSHORE RACING COUNCIL

JANUARY 1992

SPECIAL REGULATIONS GOVERNING OFFSHORE RACING

Note to the 1992 edition: Editorial and layout changes have been made to the Regulations to improve ease of use. Significant changes are indicated by a thick bold line in the left margin. Editorial changes are indicated by a thin single line in the left margin. An alphabetical index is provided at the back of this booklet.

Definitions

Hatch	the term hatch includes the entire hatch assembly and also the movable closure(s) ie. the cover(s) or door(s).
Monohull	Hull in which the hull depth in any section does not decrease towards the centre-line.
Age Date	month/year of first launch
Series Date	month/year of first launch of first yacht of the production series
LWL	(length of) loaded waterline
LOA	length overall not including pulpits, bowsprits, boomkins etc.

In these Regulations the terms L, B and FA shall be taken as defined by IOR or IMS (as appropriate) when the yacht is IOR or IMS rated. When the yacht is not IOR or IMS rated, the alternative terms (in brackets) shall apply.

1.0 PURPOSE AND USE

1.1 It is the purpose of these Special Regulations to establish uniform minimum equipment and accommodation standards for monohull yachts racing offshore.

1.2 These Regulations do not replace but rather supplement the requirements of governmental authority and the Racing Rules. The attention of owners is called to restrictions in the Rules on the location and movement of equipment.

1.3 The Offshore Racing Council strongly recommends the use of these Special Regulations by all organisations sponsoring offshore races. Race Committees may select the category deemed most suitable for the type of race to be sailed.

2.0 OWNER'S RESPONSIBILITY

2.1 The **safety** of a yacht and her crew is the sole and inescapable responsibility of the owner, or owner's representative who must do his best to ensure that the yacht is fully found, thoroughly seaworthy and manned by an experienced crew who are physically fit to face bad weather. He must be satisfied as to the soundness of hull, spars, rigging, sails and all gear. He must ensure that all safety equipment is properly maintained and stowed and that the crew know where it is kept and how it is to be used.

2.2 Neither the establishment of these Special Regulations, their use by sponsoring organisations, nor the inspection of a yacht under these Regulations in any way limits or reduces the complete and unlimited responsibility of the owner or owner's representative.

2.3 It is the **sole and exclusive responsibility** of each yacht to decide whether or not to start or continue to race.

3.0 INSPECTION

3.1 A yacht may be inspected at any time. If she does not comply with these Special Regulations her entry may be rejected, or she will be liable to disqualification or such other penalty as may be prescribed by the national authority or the sponsoring organisation.

THE RORC REQUIREMENTS FOR RACING YACHTS

4.0 CATEGORIES OF OFFSHORE EVENTS

4.1 In many types of race, ranging from long-distance ocean races sailed under adverse conditions to short-course day races sailed in protected waters, five categories of races are established, as follows, to provide for the differences in the standards of safety and accommodation required for such varying circumstances.

4.2 Category 0: Trans-Ocean races, where yachts must be completely self-sufficient for very extended periods of time, capable of withstanding heavy storms and prepared to meet serious emergencies without the expectation of outside assistance.

4.3 Category 1: Races of long distance and well offshore, where yachts must be completely self-sufficient for extended periods of time, capable of withstanding heavy storms and prepared to meet serious emergencies without the expectation of outside assistance.

4.4 Category 2: Races of extended duration along or not far removed from shorelines or in large unprotected bays or lakes, where a high degree of self-sufficiency is required of the yachts but with the reasonable probability that outside assistance could be called upon for aid in the event of serious emergencies.

4.5 Category 3: Races across open water, most of which is relatively protected or close to shorelines, including races for small yachts.

4.6 Category 4: Short races, close to shore in relatively warm or protected waters normally held in daylight.

	5.0 BASIC REQUIREMENTS	**RACE CATEGORY**
5.1	All required equipment shall: **Function properly** **Be readily accessible** **Be of a type, size and capacity suitable and adequate for the intended use and size of the yacht.**	**0 1 2 3 4**
5.2	Yachts shall be **self-righting**. They shall be strongly built, watertight and, particularly with regard to hulls, decks and cabin trunks capable of withstanding solid water and knockdowns. They must be properly rigged and ballasted, be fully seaworthy and must meet the standards set forth herein. "Properly rigged" means (inter alia) that shrouds shall never be disconnected.	**0 1 2 3 4**
5.3.1	**Inboard engine installations** shall be such that the engine when running can be securely covered and that the exhaust and fuel supply systems are securely installed and adequately protected from the effects of heavy weather. When an electric starter is the only provision for starting the engine, a separate battery shall be carried, the primary purpose of which is to start the engine.	**0 1 2 3 4**
5.3.2	Each Yacht fitted with a propulsion engine shall carry a **minimum amount of fuel** in a **permanently installed fuel tank**. This minimum amount of fuel may be specified in the Notice of Race but if not, shall be sufficient to be able to meet charging requirements for the duration of the race and to motor at (square root of LWL in feet = minimum speed in knots) for at least 8 hours.	**1 2 3 4**
5.3.3	Organising clubs are recommended to apply their own **minimum fuel requirements**.	**0**
5.4	**Ballast and Heavy Equipment**. All heavy items including inside ballast and internal fittings (such as batteries, stoves, gas bottles, tanks, engines, outboard motors etc.) and anchors and chain shall be securely fastened so as to remain in position should the yacht be capsized 180°.	**0 1 2 3**
5.5	**Yacht equipment and fittings** shall be securely fastened.	**4**

THE RORC REQUIREMENTS FOR RACING YACHTS

RACE CATEGORY 0 1 2 3 4

5.6 **National Letters and Numbers** (sail numbers) on sails shall be carried in accordance with IYRR 25, except that:-

(a) Letters and numbers shall also be carried on every spinnaker and every jib of which the perpendicular distance from the clew to the luff exceeds 130% of the base of the foretriangle.

(b) Letters and numbers may be allotted by a national or state authority.

(c) Letters and numbers of the size carried on the mainsail shall be either permanently displayed on each side of the hull, or shall be carried on a **portable cloth** suitable for display when none of the numbered sails is set.

6.0 STRUCTURAL FEATURES

ABS

6.01 The following yachts shall have been built in accordance with ABS approved plans under the **ABS Guide for Building and Classing Offshore Yachts**. An IMS or IOR certificate may be endorsed by the Rating Authority to confirm ABS approval, when the owner should hold an ABS certificate (see Appendix IV). Alterations and repairs to yachts requiring plan approval shall also have such approval. 0 1 2

Race Category	LOA	earliest of Age or Series date	ABS Approval?	ABS Certificate on board?
0 1	any	{before 1/86	no	no
		{1/86 to 12/90	yes	no
		{1/91 and after	yes	yes
2	under 40ft	{before 1/88	no	no
		{1/88 to 12/90	yes	no
		{1/91 and after	yes	yes
2	40ft and over	{before 1/87	no	no
		{1/87 to 12/90	yes	no
		{1/91 and after	yes	yes
3 4	any	any	no	no

Metric equivalent: 40ft = 12.19m

6.1 **Watertight integrity of hull.** The hull, including, deck, coach roof, windows, hatches and all other parts, shall form an integral, essentially watertight, unit and any openings in it shall be capable of being immediately secured to maintain this integrity. **Centerboard and daggerboard trunks** shall not open into the interior of the hull. 0 1 2 3 4

6.12 **Hatches**. No hatches forward of the maximum beam station shall open inwards excepting ports having an area of less than 110sq in (710 sq cm). Hatches shall be so arranged as to be above the water when the hull is heeled 90°. All hatches shall be permanently fitted so that they can be shut immediately and will remain firmly shut in a 180° capsize. 0 1 2 3 4

6.13 **Hatches and Companionways**. Companionways, if extended below the sheerline, shall be capable of being blocked off up to the level of the local sheer line when the companionway shall continue to give access to the interior of the hull. The main companionway hatch shall be fitted with a strong securing arrangement which shall be operable from above and below. **All blocking arrangements** (eg washboards) shall be capable of being secured in position with the hatch open or shut and shall be secured to the yacht (eg by lanyard) to prevent their being lost overboard. 0 1 2 3 4

THE RORC REQUIREMENTS FOR RACING YACHTS

		RACE CATEGORY
6.21	**Cockpits General.** Cockpits shall be structurally strong, self-draining quickly at all angles of heel and permanently incorporated as an integral part of the hull. They must be essentially watertight, that is, all openings to the hull must be capable of being strongly and rigidly secured. Every cockpit sole must be at least 2% L above LWL (2% LOA above LWL). Every bow, lateral, central or stern well will be considered as a cockpit for the purposes of 6.22, and 6.23 and 6.24.	0 1 2 3 4
6.22	**Cockpits opening aft to the sea.** The lower edge of the companionway shall not be below main deck level at the local sheerline. Openings aft shall be not less in area than 50% maximum cockpit depth x maximum cockpit width (see 6.64 for details of lifelines).	0 1 2 3 4
	For yachts with age 4/92 and after: The determination of lowest coamings in 6.23 and 6.24 shall not include any aft of the FA station and any extension of the cockpit aft of the working deck shall not be included in the calculation of cockpit volume.	
6.23	**The total volume of all cockpits** below lowest coamings shall not exceed 6% L x B x FA (6% LWL x maximum beam x freeboard abreast the cockpit).	0 1
6.24	**The total volume of all cockpits** below lowest coamings shall not exceed 9% L x B x FA (9% LWL x maximum beam x freeboard abreast the cockpit).	2 3 4
6.25	**Cockpit Drains**	0 1 2 3 4

Race Category	LOA	earliest of Age or Series date	minimum drain size after allowance for screens
0 1 2 3 4	under 28ft	any	2 x 1" diameter or equivalent
0 1 2 3 4	28ft and over	before 1/72	2 x 1" diameter or equivalent
3 4	28ft and over	1/72 to 1/77	2 x 1" diameter or equivalent
0 1 2 3 4	28ft and over	1/72 to 1/77	4 x 3/4" diameter or equivalent
0 1 2 3 4	28ft and over	after 1/77	4 x 3/4" diameter or equivalent

Metric equivalents: 28ft = 8.53m 1" = 25mm 3/4" = 19mm

6.51	**Sea cocks or valves** on all through-hull openings below LWL, except openings for integral deck scuppers, shaft log, speed indicator, echo sounder and the like, for which openings a means of shutting off their through-hull openings shall be provided.	0 1 2 3 4
6.52	**Soft wood plugs,** tapered and of the appropriate size, to be attached or adjacent to the appropriate fitting.	0 1 2 3 4
6.53	**Sheet winches** shall not be mounted in such a way that an operator is required to be substantially below deck.	0 1 2 3 4
6.54	**Mast step.** The heel of a keel stepped mast shall be securely fastened to the mast step or adjoining structure.	0 1 2 3 4
6.55	**Bulkhead.** The hull shall have a watertight bulkhead within 15% LOA from the bow and abaft the forward perpendicular.	0
6.6	**Life-Lines, Stanchions, Pulpits and Jackstays**	0 1 2 3 4
6.61.1	**Life-line materials, lifeline enclosure minimum strength.** Life-lines shall be stranded	0 1 2 3 4

THE RORC REQUIREMENTS FOR RACING YACHTS

RACE CATEGORY

stainless steel wire of minimum diameter as given below. Grade 316 stainless wire is recommended.

Race Category	LOA	Minimum Wire Diameter
0 1 2 3 4	under 28.0 ft	$^1/_8$" (3mm)
0 1 2 3 4	28-43.0 ft	$^5/_{32}$" (4mm)
0 1 2 3 4	over 43.0 ft	$^3/_{16}$" (5mm)

Metric equivalents: 28ft = 8.53m 43ft = 13.0m

A taut lanyard of synthetic rope may be used to secure life-lines provided the gap it closes does not exceed 4" (100mm). All wire, fittings, anchor point fixtures and lanyards shall comprise a life-line enclosure system which has at all points at least the breaking strength of the required life-line wire.

6.61.2 **Stanchions profile and materials.** Within the first 2" (50mm) from the deck, stanchions shall not be displaced horizontally from the point at which they emerge from the deck or base by more than $^3/_8$" (10mm). Stanchions shall not be angled at more than 10° from vertical at any point above 2" (50mm) from the deck. 0 1 2 3 4

Race Category	LOA	earliest of Age/Series date	detail
0 1 2 3 4	any	before 1/87	Carbon fibre is not recommended in stanchions, pulpits and lifelines.
0 1 2 3 4	any	1/87 to 12/87	Stanchions, pulpits and lifelines shall not be made of carbon fibre.
0 1 2 3 4	any	1/88 and after	Stanchions, pulpits and lifelines shall not be made of carbon fibre. Stanchions shall be straight, except that one bend is permitted in the first 50mm above deck.

6.61.3 **Stanchions and pulpits - fixing.** Pulpits and stanchions shall be securely attached. 0 1 2 3 4

- When there are sockets or studs, these shall be through-bolted, bonded or welded. The pulpit(s) and/or stanchions fitted to these shall be mechanically retained without the help of the life-lines.

- Without sockets or studs, pulpits and/or stanchions shall be through-bolted, bonded or welded.

THE RORC REQUIREMENTS FOR RACING YACHTS

RACE CATEGORY

6.62 **Lifelines, stanchions and pulpits - general arrangements**

- Provided the complete lifeline enclosure is supported by stanchions and pulpit bases within the working deck, lifeline terminals and support struts may be fixed to the hull aft of the working deck. **0 1 2 3 4**

- Fixed bow pulpit (forward of headstay) and stern pulpit (unless lifelines are arranged as to adequately substitute for a stern pulpit). Upper rails of pulpits shall be at no less height above the working deck than upper lifelines. Upper rails in bow pulpits shall be securely closed while racing.

- Lifelines shall be permanently supported at intervals of not more than 7ft (2.13m) and shall not pass outboard of supporting stanchions.

- The bases of pulpits and stanchions shall not be further inboard from the edge of the working deck than 5% of maximum beam or 6" (152mm), whichever is greater. Stanchion bases shall not be situated outboard of the working deck.

- Lifelines need not be fixed to the bow pulpit if they terminate at, or pass through, adequately braced stanchions set inside and overlapping the bow pulpit, provided that the gap between the upper lifeline and the bow pulpit does not exceed 6" (152mm).

- Lifelines shall be effectively continuous around the working deck but may be substituted by appropriate horizontal rails in pulpits.

Race Category	LOA	earliest of Age/Series date	Detail
0 1 2 3 4	under 28ft	before 1/92	Taut single lifeline, at a height of not less than 18" (457mm) above the working deck, however no vertical opening shall exceed 22" (560mm) and additional lifelines shall be fitted if required to achieve this.
0 1 2 3 4	under 28ft	1/92 and after	As above for under 28ft before 1.92 except that when an intermediate lifeline is fitted, no vertical opening shall exceed 15" (380mm).
0 1 2 3 4	28ft and over	before 1/92	Taut double lifelines, with upper lifeline at a height of not less than 24" (609mm) above the working deck. No vertical opening shall exceed 22" (609mm).
0 1 2 3 4	28ft and over	1/92 and after	As above for LOA 28ft and over before 1/92 except that no vertical opening shall be greater than 15" (380mm).

Metric equivalent: 28ft = 8.53m

6.64 **Toe Rails**

A toe rail of minimum height 1" (25mm) shall be permanently fitted around the foredeck from abreast the mast, except in way of fittings and not further inboard from the edge of the working deck than one third of the local beam. **0 1 2 3**

THE RORC REQUIREMENTS FOR RACING YACHTS

RACE CATEGORY

The following variations are acceptable:-

Race Category	LOA	earliest of Age/Series date	detail
0 1 2 3	any	any	an additional lifeline of minimum height 1" (25mm) and maximum height 2" (50mm) is acceptable in lieu of a toe rail (but shall not count as an intermediate lifeline required in SR6.62)
0 1 2 3	any	before 1/81	a toe rail minimum height of 0.75" (19mm) is acceptable.

6.65 **Jackstays**

Jackstays shall be fitted on deck, port and starboard of the yacht's centre line to provide secure attachments for safety harnesses. Jackstays shall comprise stainless steel 1x19 wire of minimum diameter $^{3}/_{16}$" (5mm), or webbing of equivalent strength (4,400lb (2,000kg) breaking strength webbing is recommended). Jackstays shall be attached to through-bolted or welded deck plates, or other suitable and strong anchorages. The jackstays shall, if possible, be fitted in such a way that a crew member, when clipped on, can move from a cockpit to the forward and to the after end of the main deck without unclipping the harness. If the deck layout renders this impossible, additional lines shall be fitted so that a crew member can move as described with a minimum of clipping operations. **0 1 2**

A crew member shall be able to clip on before coming on deck, unclip after going below and remain clipped on while moving laterally across the yacht on the foredeck, the afterdeck, and amidships. If necessary, additional jackstays and/or through-bolted or welded anchorage points shall be provided for this purpose.

Through-bolted or welded anchorage points, or other suitable and strong anchorage, for safety harnesses shall be provided adjacent to stations such as the helm, sheet winches and masts, where crew members work for long periods. Jackstays should be sited in such a way that the safety harness lanyard can be kept as short as possible.

7.0 ACCOMMODATIONS

7.11 **Toilet,** securely installed. **0 1 2**

7.12 **Toilet,** securely installed or fitted bucket. **3 4**

7.2 **Bunks,** securely installed. **0 1 2 3 4**

7.3 **Cooking stove,** securely installed against a capsize with safe accessible fuel shutoff control capable of being safely operated in a seaway. **0 1 2 3**

7.4 **Galley facilities.** **0 1 2 3 4**

7.51 **Water tank(s)**, securely installed and capable of dividing the water supply into at least three compartments and discharging through a pump. The quantity of water to be taken aboard is left to the discretion of the organising authority but 2 gallons (9 litres) per person per 1,000 miles may be taken as the minimum. **0**

7.52 **Water tank(s)**, securely installed and capable of dividing the water supply into at least two compartments and discharging through a pump. **1**

7.53 At least one securely installed **water tank** discharging through a pump. **2 3**

THE RORC REQUIREMENTS FOR RACING YACHTS

		RACE CATEGORY
8.0	**GENERAL EQUIPMENT**	
8.1	**Fire extinguishers,** at least two, readily accessible in suitable and different parts of the boat.	0 1 2 3 4
8.2	**Bilge pumps and buckets**	
	8.2.1 No **bilge pump** may discharge into a cockpit unless that cockpit opens aft to the sea. Bilge pumps shall not be connected to cockpit drains.	0 1 2 3 4
	8.2.2 **Unless permanently fitted, each bilge pump handle** shall be provided with a lanyard or catch or similar device to prevent accidental loss.	0 1 2 3 4
	8.2.3 **Two manual bilge pumps**, securely fitted to the yacht's structure, one operable above deck, the other below deck. Each pump shall be operable with all cockpit seats, hatches and companionsays shut and shall be provided with permanently fitted discharge pipe(s) of sufficient capacity to accommodate sumiltaneously both pumps.	0 1 2
	8.2.4 One **manual bilge pump** operable with all cockpit seats, hatches and companionways closed.	3
	8.2.5 One **manual bilge pump**.	4
	8.2.6 Two **buckets** of stout construction each with at least 2 gallons (9 litres) capacity. Each bucket to have a lanyard.	0 1 2 3 4
8.3	**Anchors** shall be carried as follows:-	0 1 2 3 4

Race Category	LOA	Detail
0 1 2 3	28 ft and over	2 anchors with cables
0 1 2 3	under 28ft	1 anchor with cable
4	any	1 anchor

Metric equivalent: 28ft = 8.53m

8.41	**Flashlights,** one of which is suitable for signalling, water resistant, with spare batteries and bulbs.	0 1 2 3
8.42	At least one **flashlight**, water resistant, with spare batteries and bulb.	4
8.5	**First aid kit and manual.** National authorities are encouraged to state titles of recommended first aid manuals.	0 1 2 3 4
8.6	**Foghorn.**	0 1 2 3 4
8.7	**Radar reflector**. If a radar reflector is octahedral it must have a minimum diagonal measurement of 18in (457mm), or if not octahedral must have a documented "equivalent echoing area" of not less than 108 sq ft (10 sq m).	0 1 2 3 4
8.8	**Set of international code flags** and code book.	0 1
8.9	**Shutoff valves on all fuel tanks.**	0 1 2 3 4

THE RORC REQUIREMENTS FOR RACING YACHTS

RACE CATEGORY

9.0 NAVIGATION EQUIPMENT

9.1 **Compass,** marine type, properly installed and adjusted. 0 1 2 3 4

9.2 **Spare compass** 0 1 2 3

9.3 **Charts, light list and piloting equipment.** 0 1 2 3

9.4 **Sextant, tables and accurate time piece.** 0 1

9.5 **Radio direction finder or an automatic position fixing device.** 0 1 2

9.6 **Lead line or echo sounder.** 0 1 2 3 4

9.7 **Speedometer or distance measuring instrument.** 0 1 2 3

9.8 **Navigation Lights** 0 1 2 3 4

Navigation lights shall be shown as required by the International Regulations for Preventing Collision at Sea, (Part C and Technical Annex 1) and:

- navigation lights shall be mounted so that they will not be masked e.g. by sails or the heeling of the yacht
- navigation lights shall not be mounted below deck level and should be at no less height than immediately below the upper lifeline
- spare bulbs for navigation lights shall be carried
- all yachts shall exhibit sidelights and a sternlight at the required times

Race Category	LOA	Minimum bulb power which should be used
0 1 2 3 4	under 39.6 ft	10 watts
0 1 2 3 4	39.6 ft and over	25 watts

Metric equivalent: 39.6ft = 12m

10.0 EMERGENCY EQUIPMENT

10.1 **Emergency navigation lights and power source.** Emergency navigation lights shall have the same minimum specifications as the navigation lights in 9.8 with a separable power source and separate wiring from that used for the normal navigation lights. 0 1 2 3

Emergency navigation lights shall not be used if the normal navigation lights (under Rule 9.8) are operable.

10.21 The following specifications for **mandatory sails** give maximum areas; smaller areas may suit some yachts. Sheeting points on deck shall be provided for these sails.

10.21.1 One **storm trysail** of area not greater than 17.5% mainsail luff length x mainsail foot length, sheeted independently of the boom and without headboard and battens. The yacht's national letter(s) and sail numbers shall be placed on both sides of the trysail in as large a size as practicable. 0 1 2

Aromatic polyamides, carbon fibres and other high modulous fibres shall not be used in the storm trysail.

10.21.2 One **storm jib** of area not greater than 5% height of the foretriangle squared, and luff maximum length 65% height of the foretriangle. 0 1 2

THE RORC REQUIREMENTS FOR RACING YACHTS

		RACE CATEGORY
	Aromatic polyamides, carbon fibres and other high modulous fibres shall not be used in the storm jib.	
10.21.3	One **heavy-weather jib** of area not greater than 13.5% height of the foretriangle squared area without reef points.	0 1 2
	The ORC recommends that the heavy-weather jib does not contain aromatic polyamides, carbon fibres and other high modulous fibres.	
10.22	One **heavy-weather jib** as in 10.21.3 (or heavy-weather sail in a boat with no forestay) and either:	3 4
	(a) a **storm trysail** as in 10.21.1; or	3 4
	(b) **mainsail reefing** to reduce the luff by at least 40% of a mainsail which does not contain aromatic polyamides, carbon fibres and other high modulous fibres.	3 4
10.23	**Any storm or heavy-weather jib** if designed for a seastay or luff-groove device shall have an alternative method of attachment to the stay.	0 1 2 3 4
10.24	No mast shall have less than two **halyards** each capable of hoisting a sail.	0 1 2 3 4
10.3	**Emergency Steering Equipment**	
10.31	An **emergency tiller** capable of being fitted to the rudder stock.	0 1 2 3
10.32	Crews must be aware of **alternative methods of steering** the yacht in any sea condition in the event of rudder failure. At least one method must have been proven to work on board the yacht. An inspector may require that this method be demonstrated.	0 1 2 3 4
10.4	**Tools and spare parts,** including adequate means to disconnect or sever the standing rigging from the hull in the case of need.	0 1 2 3 4
10.5	**Yacht's name** on miscellaneous buoyant equipment, such as lifejackets, oars, cushions, lifebuoys and lifeslings etc.	0 1 2 3 4
10.51	**Marine grade retro-reflective Material** shall be fitted to lifebuoys, lifeslings, liferafts and lifejackets.	0 1 2 3 4
10.61	**Marine radio transceiver.** When this is VHF it shall have a minimum power of 25W, shall be provided with a masthead antenna and co-axial feeder and should include Channel 72 (an international ship-ship channel which, by "common use", could become an accepted yacht-yacht channel for ocean racing yachts anywhere in the world). An emergency antenna shall be provided when the regular antenna depends upon the mast.	0 1 2
	Note: from 1/93 SR 10.61 will extend to Category 3.	
10.62	In addition to 10.61 a waterproof **hand-held VHF transceiver**.	0 1
10.63	**In addition to 10.61 Radio receiver** capable of receiving weather bulletins.	0 1 2 3 4
10.64	**EPIRB**. Emergency Position Indicating Radio Beacon transmitting on 121.5, 243 or 406 MHz.	0 1
10.7	At least 2 gallons (9 litres) of **water** for emergency use carried in one or more containers.	0 1 2 3

THE RORC REQUIREMENTS FOR RACING YACHTS

RACE CATEGORY

11.0 SAFETY EQUIPMENT

11.1 **Lifejackets**, one for each crew member. Each lifejacket shall have a whistle. In the absence of any specification, the following definition of a lifejacket is recommended: 0 1 2 3 4

"A lifejacket should be of a form which is capable of providing not less than 35lb (16kg) of buoyancy, arranged so that an unconscious man will be securely suspended face upwards at approximately 45° to the water surface."

The ORC recommends that a crotch strap should be fitted on each lifejacket.

11.2 **Safety harness**, one for each crew member, in accordance with Appendix I. Each yacht may be required to demonstrate that two thirds of the crew can be adequately attached to strong points on the yacht. **The ORC recommends that a crotch strap should be fitted on each safety harness.** 0 1 2 3

11.4 **Liferaft(s)** in accordance with Appendix II, capable of carrying the entire crew, as follows:- 0 1 2

11.4.1 **Stowage** shall be **either**

(a) on the working deck; **or**

(b) in compartment(s) opening immediately to the working deck containing liferaft(s) only, provided that:
(i) each compartment is watertight or self-draining (self-draining compartments will be counted as part of the cockpit volume except when entirely above working deck level); and
(ii) the cover of each compartment is capable of being easily opened under water pressure; **or**

(c) packed in valise(s) each not exceeding 88lbs (40kg) securely stowed below deck adjacent to the companionway.

11.4.2 **Recovery Time** Each raft shall be capable of being got to the lifelines within 15 seconds.

11.4.3 **Certificate** Each raft shall have a valid annual certificate from the manufacturer or an approved servicing agent certifying that it has been inspected, that it complies with these requirements and stating the official capacity of the raft which shall not be exceeded. The certificate, or a copy shall be carried on the yacht.

11.4.4 **Liferaft cover** The National Authority or Notice of Race should specify whether or not a cover (Appendix II (d)) is required.

11.4.5 **Insulated Floor** The National Authority or Notice of Race should specify whether or not an insulated floor (Appendix II(k)) is required.

11.51 **Lifebuoy with a drogue** OR **Lifesling (without a drogue)** equipped with a self-igniting light within reach of the helmsman and ready for instant use. (see Appendix V). 0 1 2 3 4

11.52 In addition to 11.51 **one lifebuoy** within reach of the helmsman and ready for instant use, equipped **with a whistle, dye marker, drogue, a self-igniting light, and a pole and flag.** The pole shall be either permanently extended or be capable of being fully automatically extended in less than 20 seconds. It shall be attached to the lifebuoy with 10ft (3.048m) of floating line and is to be of a length and so ballasted that the flag will fly at least 6ft (1.828m) off the water. 0 1 2

THE RORC REQUIREMENTS FOR RACING YACHTS

RACE CATEGORY

11.6 **Pyrotechnic signals** conforming to SOLAS Regulations Chapter VII Visual Signals and not more than 3 years old stowed in waterproof container(s):- 0 1 2 3 4

Race Category	Red parachute flares SOLAS Regulation 35	Red hand flares SOLAS Regulation 36	White hand flares *	Orange smoke SOLAS Regulation 37
0 1	12	4	4	2
2 3	4	4	4	2
4	-	4	4	2

* Specifications (except colour and candela rating), should comply with SOLAS Regulation 36.

11.7 **Heaving Line** 50ft (15.24m) minimum length readily accessible to cockpit. 0 1 2 3 4

12 **Weight Jackets** (IYRR 61.2) are not permitted. 0 1 2 3 4

Standards for Powerboat Racing

The rules for offshore powerboat racing have been developed by the Royal Yachting Association and again, although some are to prevent cheating, many of the requirements are of relevance for the average planing powerboat. Even though you may not be interested in racing, it is still worth looking at the racing requiremnts as they cover constructional details and saftey equipment in a comprehensive manner and many of the items listed would be worth looking at on the conventional powerboat.

The rules occupy many pages and as with the requirements of the RORC they change over time. It is essential therefore, should you decide to enter a race, to obtain the latest full set of regulations. Some of the requirements are set out on the following pages to give you an idea of nature and detail of the regulations.

THE RYA REQUIREMENTS FOR POWERBOAT RACING

LIGHTS FOR MOTOR YACHTS

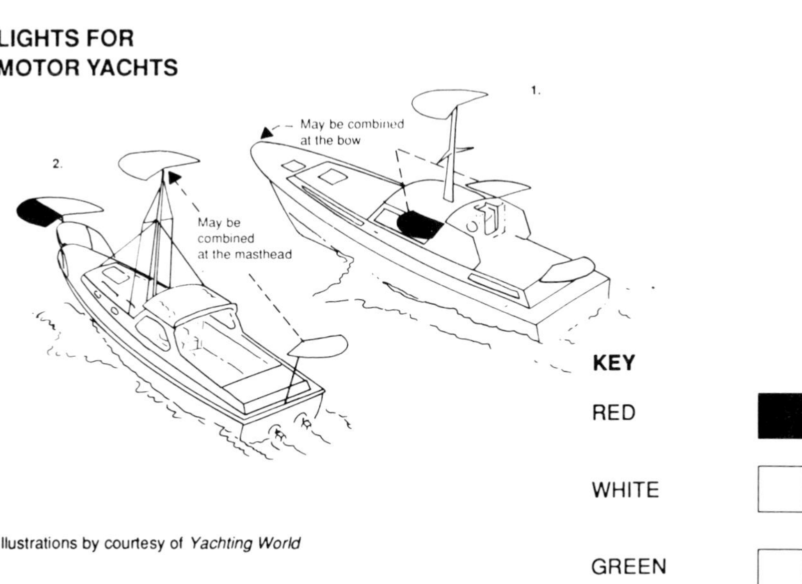

Illustrations by courtesy of *Yachting World*

B10. WINDSHIELDS/WINDSCREENS/CANOPIES (if fitted)

(a) Shall be well secured.
(b) Shall be of non-splintering material. The use of glass for windscreens is forbidden in Classes I & II. Replacement Cruiser screens should be of a safe material providing that the profile is not altered from standard.
(c) Shall be masked by rubber or plastic on any bare edges.
(d) Shall not be so designed that it would restrict the driver from being ejected.
(e) Windshields shall be so constructed as to present no hazard if the crew is thrown forward.
(f) Safety Belts are banned unless the installation conforms to criteria approved by the UIM.

B11. SHARP EDGES

All mascots, lights, bow fittings and other sharp edges, shall be adequately protected or removed.

B12. STEERING

(a) The steering wheel and drum shall be secured and locked on to the shaft.
(b) The steering wheel unit shall be fixed to, or through the dash panel, or a steering mounting bar, and shall be through bolted and locked.
(c) The steering wheel strength shall be checked; if the wheel is split or cracked, the wheel shall be rejected. Wheels of the laminated rim type shall be checked for weakness caused by the breakdown of the laminations. Plastic composition wheels shall be checked for early fatigue where the spokes join the boss to ensure the wheel cannot be forced to spin on the internal boss.
(d) Where shackles or such devices are used to attach the steering to outboard engines, they shall NOT be of non-ferrous metal. Scrutineers shall satisfy themselves that this is so even if the shackles are painted.
(e) Pulleys shall operate freely and shall be through bolted with positive locking.
(f) The steering wires shall be in good condition and shall be free running throughout

THE RYA REQUIREMENTS FOR POWERBOAT RACING

their path, with adequate tension throughout their travel.

(g) Wires shall be secure and, where double to form an eye, shall be around a thimble and shall be secured with two bull-dog clips or the equivalent.

(h) Lock wiring on all shackles, stretching screws, etc. in the system shall be secure.

(i) There shall be no undue degree of play in the steering system but steering wires shall not be over-tightened in a "piano-wire" fashion.

(j) All steering and throttle controls and linkages, quadrants and any fitting to the stock shall be in good condition and secure.

(k) Engine and rudder controls shall operate with full and free movement.

(l) Rudder assemblies, glands, keys, etc. shall be in good condition and secured with lock nuts and/or tight split pins.

(m) Rack and pinion steering shall be in good mechanical condition with no excessive backlash. Casings should also be checked.

(n) All pulleys with rivetted pins of non-ferrous material shall be rejected or the pins shall be replaced by a positively locked steel bolt. Pulleys should also, if possible, incorporate a bush.

(o) All pulleys with any tension shall not cause the yoke to clamp down on the pulley wheel.

(p) All attachment hooks shall be closed.

(q) Sheathed steering cables shall not be permitted.

(r) Wires to the steering wheel running across the front of the dashboard and wires running fore and aft inside the cockpit shall all be effectively shielded.

(s) Tiller steering is not permitted.

(t) Hydraulic steering shall be fully operative, hoses and unions shall be free of leaks and adequately protected.

(u) Boats with more than one shaft shall be capable of maintaining a course in a set direction on any one propeller.

(v) Single push-pull steering cable is not permitted.

B13. CONTROL CABLES

All control cables shall be taped or screwed down securely.

B14. ENGINE CUT-OFF

Class I, II, III (+ NCC/OCR drivers)

(a) Engine cut-off devices for connection to crew are mandatory (first man out shuts off engine). An emergency override system to restart engine shall be mandatory. The lanyards used must not exceed 120cm between driver and the boat. The emergency cut-off devices must be positioned so when they operate the lanyard and cap (or clip) will not catch or foul. The lanyard shall be attached to all crew members at all times when the boat is at racing speeds. For craft where the driver and co-driver are separated, a means must be provided for starting and control of at least one engine from each cockpit.

NCC/OCR co-drivers:

(b) All OCR co-drivers/crew shall be attached by a lanyard to an audible and visible device mounted on the dashboard to alert the driver.

(c) All NCC co-drivers/crew members shall either be attached to kill switches as described in B14(a) above **or** shall be attached to an audible/visible device as described in B14(b) above.

B15. THROTTLE CONTROL

(a) All foot throttles shall return the engine(s) to idling speed when released.

(b) The lever unit shall be securely attached.

(c) The control unit shall be properly connected, work freely and shall not be in a

THE RYA REQUIREMENTS FOR POWERBOAT RACING

position where it can be fouled.

(d) The control unit shall be within easy reach of the driver in his normal position.

B16. GEAR CONTROL

All craft shall be able to be manoeuvred ahead and astern and have neutral capability operated by controls at the helmsman's position.

B17. SEATS

(a) Seats shall be of adequate strength and firmly secured.

(b) All seats required by the particular class rules or rules of the event shall be in position.

B18.

(i) FUEL

For Classes I & II

(a) For petrol (gasoline) engines fuels are limited to petroleum based fuels. No non petroleum based additives eg. nitrous oxide are permitted.

(b) For diesel fuelled engines the fuel is restricted to that normally obtainable for road, industrial and commercial use or pleasure craft.

(c) All fuel must be carried in tanks which are suitably secured and vented. Fuel may not be transferred during a race except by means of permanently installed fuel lines connected to the tanks.

For Class III, NCC and OCR

(d) Fuel utilised shall be automobile commercial type as distilled by a petrol company as currently available and sold by service stations for automobile purposes.

(e) Lubricating oil for cylinder head, or two-stroke engines, may be added to the fuel, provided that they do not increase the octane number or the water content of the fuel.

B18.

(ii) FUEL TANKS

(a) Shall be secure in all directions and shall not leak.

(b) Bulkheads of engine and fuel tank compartments must be sealed to the hull across the bottom and have sufficient height above the bottom to prevent fuel and fumes flowing through the boat. The separate compartments thus formed must have provision for separate pumping out of bilges.

(c) Shall have sensible filling and venting arrangements which are not close to any hot equipment such as exhaust manifolds.

(d) There shall be an easily accessible means of shutting the fuel supply off from the tank(s). When additional electric pumps are fitted to the fuel supply of outboard motors a fuel cut-off switch for the pump shall be fitted within easy reach of either crew members. Said device must be mechanical.

(e) The fuel tank or tanks must be grounded to enable the discharge of static electricity.

B19. ENGINES

PROPULSIVE EFFORT

(a) One hundred per cent of the propulsive effort shall be derived from the water while proceeding at racing trim in calm water.
Class III - Pure air jets and aerial propellers are prohibited. Water jets are allowed.

(b) Boats running two or more propulsions systems must have either external tie bar to stabalize outdrives or some other protective device that will prevent drives colliding should a failure occur.

(c) CUBIC CAPACITY – The total cylinder capacity of the motor or motors forms the

THE RYA REQUIREMENTS FOR POWERBOAT RACING

basis for eligibility in the corresponding classes.
The engines may be of the two-stroke or the four-stroke types.
Fuel may be fed to the engine by a carburettor or by injection.

(d) ROTARY MOTORS – Rotary motors of the type covered by the NSU-Wankel patent are admitted on the basis of an equivalent cylinder capacity.
The rotary motor cylinder capacity equivalent is twice the volume determined by the difference between the greatest volume and the least volume of the working chamber.

(e) SUPERCHARGING/TURBOCHARGING
When the engine includes a device used for supercharging/turbocharging it, the nominal cylinder capacity is to be multiplied by 1.4 and the boat will pass into the class corresponding to the calculated volume resulting from this operation.
The supercharger must be a standard part of the engine.
A dynamic air inlet for ducting the atmospheric air toward the engine's air intake is not considered a supercharging/turbocharging device.

B20. ENGINE MOUNTINGS AND TRANSMISSIONS

Outboards

(a) Mounting brackets and clamps shall be secure and in a satisfactory condition.
(b) Engine mountings shall be attached to the transom with at least four bolts.

Inboards (in Classes I, II, III and NCC)

(c) Engine mountings shall be sound, and the mounting bolts securing to the hull shall be pinned or lock-nutted.
(d) Where an outdrive is fitted, the method of connection to the transom and the unit to the ring shall be secure.
(e) Bearers shall not be saturated with oil.
(f) Inboard engines shall be enclosed in their own compartment(s) with the exception of normal ventilation. Each and every engine need not be contained in its own compartment. Holes in bulkheads must have flame traps. Holes on deck must also have flame traps if said holes are 0.30m or less from the crew members. The compartment(s) shall have rigid covers.

B21. ENGINE HAZARDS

(a) The engine shall be free of dangerous corrosion, oil or fuel leaks or excessive heating likely to be a fire hazard or a danger to any adjacent structure.
(b) For inboard engines flame traps are recommended.

B22. ELECTRICAL HARNESS

Properly protected terminal boards shall be used with flexible (not solid core) cabling supported well up to the terminals and at suitable intervals throughout the length of any run. Where relative movement or vibration occurs across any gap, cables shall be sheathed in plastic or metal tube anchored at both ends. Reinforced cable suitable for marine duty shall be used. Electrical equipment in engine compartments shall be kept to a minimum and sited away from heat or fuel.

B23. EXHAUST SYSTEMS FOR INBOARDS (Classes I, II, III and NCC)

(a) The exhaust of gases must be designed in such a way that the driver and his crew are protected against the dangers represented by these gases.
(b) The whole exhaust circuit shall be cooled in its entire length, and this shall be effected by water circulation, water jacketing, or by mixing water with the exhaust gases.
(c) It may be tolerated that a short pipe length not exceeding 3cm in length and connecting the exhaust piping to the cylinder block or between the different

THE RYA REQUIREMENTS FOR POWERBOAT RACING

sections of the piping or the connection with the turbine supercharger, or the interruptions necessary for the supercharger, need not be cooled.

B24. PROPELLER SECURITY
It shall be the responsibility of the competitor to ensure that the propeller or propellers are sound, particularly at the blade roots and that it/they are securely locked by the propeller nut(s).

B25. BATTERY STOWAGE
(a) Batteries shall be secured with fittings sufficiently strong to withstand any anticipated shock, or inertial force.
(b) Batteries shall be housed in ventilated compartments, and mounted upon a secure and solid platform.

B26. ENGINE WELLS – OUTBOARDS
(a) All outboard engined boats must have a watertight engine well. All holes cut into the bulkheads of the engine well for the purpose of passing control cables, etc, shall be watertight and shall be as high as possible and shall be above the level of the lowest point of the transom cut-out.
(b) The preceding rules do not apply when the engine is erected on an outside bracket, provided however that the part of the stern on which the frame is mounted, is properly secured to the deck.

B27. BUCKET
Class III and Cruiser boats shall carry a bucket suitable for bailing (minimum capacity 5 litre).

B28. BILGE PUMPS AND BAILING
Bilge pumps shall be :
(a) In proper working order and secured to the boat.
(b) Accessible for operation.
(c) Fitted with a suction pipe leading to the lowest point of the bilge and with a discharge pipe overboard.
(d) Capable of pumping out all sections of the boat even where water-tight bulkheads are fitted.
(e) There shall be at least one manual bilge pump fitted to the boat.

B29. FIRE EXTINGUISHMENT
(i) All boats with inboard engines shall carry a fixed automatic fire extinguishing system. This system shall be properly installed and engineered. Sensors and injectors shall be in danger regions of the engine compartment. Maintenance at manufacturer's recommended intervals is required, and evidence that this has been carried out shall be available.
(ii) In addition to any fixed automatic extinguishing system Class I, II and Cruiser boats shall carry two full charged dry powder 1.5kg fire extinguishers one sited conveniently to the engine space and the other in a readily accessible position.
(iii) Only one fire extinguisher is mandatory in Class III, OCR or Basic races, whilst outboard powered Classes I, II and cruisers shall carry two fire extinguishers.

B30. RADIO
(a) Classes I, II, III and Cruisers shall carry a VHF radio capable of transmitting on international distress frequency and must be carried in full operational condition.
(b) The appropriate ships/transportable licences for VHF Radios and for operators shall be currently valid.

THE RYA REQUIREMENTS FOR POWERBOAT RACING

B31. CRASH HELMETS

(a) Crash helmets shall be worn by all persons on board throughout the race and during practice.

(b) It is recommended that helmets should be to B.S. 6658b (with temple protection) and shall be coloured "orange", however, the efficiency of a helmet is the responsibility of the wearer.

(c) Helmets may be removed during the race if the boat is adrift or at anchor with engines stopped or idling.

(d) Helmets which are painted orange are acceptable (if they meet the other requirements of this rule) but, because it is not possible at scrutineering to determine the compatibility of the paint with the material of the helmet, competitors intending to paint crash helmets are advised to consult the helmet manufacturers regarding the suitability of the paint which they propose to use.

(e) Modifications shall not infringe on the standard and bolts used for fittings and attachment of a visor shall be small and on no account shall they protrude into the inner surface of the helmet.

(f) Chin straps shall be in good condition and operative.

(g) Helmets shall be devoid of dents or splits.

(h) Helmet visors shall be in good condition and devoid of cracks and easily detachable (i.e. not bolted down).

B32. LIFEJACKETS

Lifejackets shall be worn throughout a race and during practice, by all persons on board. The efficiency of a lifejacket is the responsibility of the wearer, but the following conditions must be complied with:

(i) Jackets must have an inherent buoyancy of at least 20lbs for international racing and at least 13½lbs for national racing and shall be fitted with collars.

(ii) Lacing ties and/or straps shall be adequate and in good condition.

(iii) Zips are not permitted as the sole means of fastening a lifejacket. Where zips are used as an ancillary means of closure they shall be in working order.

(iv) Tears or rents or bad repairs through which buoyancy material may leak out shall not be permitted.

(v) Jackets shall be orange or yellow or have orange or yellow panels.

(vi) Jackets shall have a lifting eye or becket attached to the main harness.

(vii) Jackets shall not be able to wash up over the wearer's head, and shall be secure to his body.

(viii) The disposition of the solid buoyancy shall be such as to ensure that an unconscious person shall float face up in the water.

Note: Jackets to BS 3595 are completely acceptable, provided they meet all the above requirements.

B33. ANCHOR

Anchors shall be of a weight and type adequate to hold the boat and shall be properly stowed in an accessible place.

B34. ANCHOR LINE

The anchor line shall:

(i) Be of a size and strength appropriate to the boat.

(ii) Be in good condition.

(iii) Be at least 50 metres in length (61 metres for Classes I & II).

B35. BUOYANCY (Classes III and OCR)

It is recommended that all boats have sufficient buoyancy to keep afloat in all conditions.

THE RYA REQUIREMENTS FOR POWERBOAT RACING

Buoyancy materials should be adequately fixed to the hull and so disposed as to keep the bow clear of the water.

B36. COMPASSES

(i) All boats shall carry a main compass, securely mounted, and capable of being read.

(ii) Except in OCR and Basic Races, deviation cards shall be required to be produced as evidence that the compass has been swung.

(iii) A secondary compass, which may be of the hand-bearing type, shall be carried in Class III boats only.

(iv) No large metallic objects shall be stowed in the near vicinity of the main compass nor shall the compass be swung whilst the boat is on her trailer.

B37. FIRST AID KIT

All boats (except in Basic Races) shall carry a proprietary first aid kit which shall be stowed in a self-contained box within easy reach of the crew.

B38. FLARES

(i) Class I & II boats shall carry a minimum of 6 red parachute or rocket flares, 3 white parachute or rocket flares, 3 white location flares and 6 orange smoke flares.

(ii) Class III boats shall carry a minimum of 3 red parachute or rocket flares, 2 white parachute or rocket flares and 6 red location flares.

(iii) Cruisers shall carry a minimum of 3 red parachute or rocket flares, 2 white parachute or rocket flares and 6 red location flares.

(iv) OCR boats shall carry a minimum of 2 red location flares, 1 white location flare and 2 orange smoke flares.

(v) Boats competing in Basic races shall carry a minimum of 2 red location flares and 2 orange smoke flares.

(vi) All flares shall be stowed in a conveniently accessible place; shall bear either the date of manufacture or the expiry date; and shall not be more than three years old and all have a minimum burn time of 40 seconds..

(vii) Flares where the printed instructions and/or date are illegible, or the condition poor, shall not be accepted and shall render the competitor liable to disqualification.

(viii) Class I & II boats shall carry one Sea Dye marker for **each member** of the crew.

B39. RETIREMENT FLAG

(a) All boats shall carry an orange rectangular flag of a minimum size of 0.60m x 0.40m as a means of announcing retirement from a race, and the means of maintaining it aloft where it can best be seen. (Classes I & II - 1.22m x 1.22m)

(b) Class III boats shall carry an International Code Flag 'V' (size 0.60m x 0.40m), the red cross of St. Andrew on a white background.

B40. DINGHY/LIFERAFT (Classes I and II)

(a) An inflatable dinghy (with bottle inflation) large enough to carry all crew members shall be stowed ready for instant emergency use. A test certificate not more than one year old must be produced when scrutineered at each race.

(b) A life buoy shall be carried in Class I & II boats.

B41. STRUCTURAL STATE

It shall be the competitor's responsibility not to offer for scrutiny a boat which has any of the following defects:

(i) Split planks, fractured frames, beams or transom knees (or their equivalent in the construction of reinforced plastic or alloy hulls),

(ii) Insecure, or fractured, steering mountings.

THE RYA REQUIREMENTS FOR POWERBOAT RACING

(iii) Corroded shaft brackets or other mechanical items, which are not in good working order.
(iv) Fins of inadequate strength or attached insecurely.
(v) Bilges which are foul with oil, fuel or other debris.

B42. PADDLES (Classes III and OCR)
(a) Two paddles shall be stowed for immediate use but not loose.
(b) They shall be of a practical form related to the size of the boat and in usable condition.

B43. FOG HORN
All boats shall carry an efficient fog horn.

B44. NATIONAL FLAG
All boats shall display their appropriate national flag throughout the race. If it is flown on a staff it shall be the undefaced Red Ensign. If it is painted on the side of the boat it shall be the Union Flag - in either case the minimum size shall be 45cm x 30cm (except in OCR where minimum shall be 30cm x 20cm).

B45. RADAR REFLECTOR
Class I & II boats shall carry a radar reflector with means of hoisting.

B46. TORCHES
Class I & II boats shall carry two powerful waterproof flashlights.

B47. SEA ANCHOR
Class I & II boats shall carry a sea anchor appropriate to the size of boat.

B48. EQUIPMENT & SAFETY
ALL SAFETY EQUIPMENT MUST BE CARRIED ON BOARD AND FIXED/STORED TO THE SCRUTINEER'S SATISFACTION.

IN ADDITION IT IS MANDATORY THAT ALL ENGINE HATCHES, COVERS AND SEATING MUST BE SECURED IN POSITION AND CARRIED ON BOARD DURING ANY RACE.

Cruising Yachts and Powerboats

As has been made clear, there are no mandatory provisions for cruising yachts and powerboats under 13.7 metres (45 feet). The RYA has, however, produced a guide for boat owners (booklet C8/90 available direct from the RYA). In this publication little differentiation is made between sail and power in terms of safety recommendations. First, craft are divided up into three categories – day cruisers, coastal cruisers and offshore cruisers – and then a list is given of the basic safety equipment that should be carried by each type of boat.

There is one important exception that should be noted to the general exclusion from mandatory standards: monohull yachts used for sail training or other commercially connected purposes are exempt from Merchant Shipping legislation only if they comply with the Department of

Trade and Industry Code of Practice and carry a current certificate issued by a Certifying Authority to that effect. The requirements set by the DTI are very stringent. Although this came about following a major loss of life of youngsters on a large sail training vessel, they apply to the much smaller yachts used by Sailing Schools. Thus a 30 foot yacht used by a RYA Approved sailing school would carry equipment far in excess of that of a normal cruising yacht.

Mandatory Standards for Craft over 13.7 metres (45 feet)
Finally, there are the Department of Transport requirements for both powerboats and sailing yachts over 13.7 metres in length. The DoT has separate requirements for life-saving and for fire-fighting equipment and although it is against the law not to meet them, enforcement is not particularly strict. They are part of a series of regulations covering all commercial shipping and some of them tend to be a bit impractical for smaller craft, eg dry powder fire extinguishers are required to have a minimum capacity of 4.5 kg and liquid fire extinguishers a minimum capacity of 9 litres. Meeting both these provisions would produce fire extinguishers of a weight and size difficult to handle on a moving yacht and they certainly could not be used single handed. However, there are also some regulations, such as having the ability to produce a jet of water capable of reaching any part of the vessel for fire extinguishing purposes, that could be accommodated on smaller craft with few practical problems.

Construction and Design Standards
There are detailed regulations covering the construction and design of liferafts. These standards cover not only basic construction, but the equipment they must contain. The RORC sets out requirements for the equipment that must be included in liferafts on racing yachts together with some suggested additional items.

Lifejackets and safety harnesses come under British Standard requirements, which are also very comprehensive and detailed. Approved equipment carries the familiar kite mark.

Conclusions
Rules and regulations can help to make the sailing world a safer place, but at the end of the day the most important safety factor of all is the skill and competence of the skipper and crew. The golden rule is never to get into a predicament you do not know how to resolve. A good seaman always tries to keep something up his sleeve for emergencies, a reserve of strength and a reserve of initiative and skill. It is when these reserves are exhausted that he is in serious trouble. The novice may not have this depth of reserve and experience and can run out of ideas quickly; the experienced seaman will always have one more thing to try, one more possibility. This is the right approach to ensure safety and survival at sea.

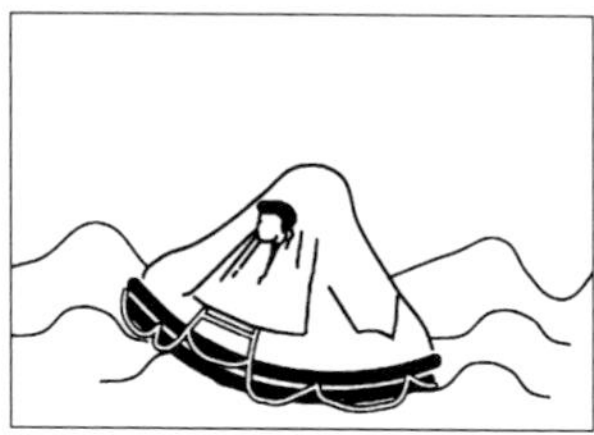

Index

Abandoning Ship 137
Accidents & Illness.............155
Advice at Sea (Medical) 155
Air-Sea Rescue 68
Anchors.............................133, 108
Assessing the Danger 12

Bilge Pumps 117
Buoyancy Aids...................90

Calling for Help
- *EPIRBS* 53
- *Flares* 42
- *GMDSS*.......................49
- *Mayday*........................56
- *Pan Pan*........................56
- *Radar Transponders*........55
- *Radios* 47
- *Responses* 46
- *Satellite Communications* 48
- *Securite*.........................57
- *Signalling*......................55

Cardiac Massage................164
Checking Equipment/Systems 35
Comfort 20
Compasses.........................102
Concentration....................18

Danbuoy 119
Drogues.............................133
Dry Suits...........................98

Emergencies
- *Abandoning Ship* 137
- *Anchors* 133
- *Drogues*.........................133
- *Engine Failure* 132
- *Fire* 139
- *Grounding*.....................126
- *Hulls* 124
- *Man Overboard*............119, 141
- *Mast Down* 131
- *Quick Stop Recovery Method* 145
- *Recovery* 143
- *Slings* 145
- *Steering loss*..................135
- *Towing*..........................129
- *Turning Back* 142
- *Williamson Turn* 142

EPIRBS.............................53

Fire 139
Fire Blanket.......................122
Fire Extinguishers 120
First Aid
- *Accidents and Illness on Board* 155
- *Advice at Sea (Medical)* .155
- *Cardiac Massage*............164
- *First Aid Kit*..................157
- *Hypothermia* 160
- *Immersion Casualty*........162
- *Mouth to Mouth Resuscitation*..................163

First Stage Safety 11
Flares 42
Foam Rubber Suits 98
Fog Horns 107

Gas Installations 118
GMDSS 49
Guard Rails 111

Hand Bell 108
Hypothermia 160

International Facilities........69

Jackstays 113

Keep it simple (KISS) 14

Legislation 10
Lifeboat 71
Lifeboat Design 66
Lifeboat Rescue 71
Lifejackets 90
Lifejacket Servicing 96
Lifelines.............................111
Liferafts 80
Liferafts - Containers 84
Liferafts - Stowage 84
Life Sling 146

Man Overboard 119, 141
Mayday 56
Mental Attitude 16
Mental Stress 19
Mouth to Mouth Resuscitation 163

Navigation Lights 104

Pan Pan 56
Preparation for Safety,
Checking the Boat 28
Electrics 31
Equipment 35
Fuel Systems 33
Hull 29
Lifejackets 38
Mast & Rigging 34
Safety Harnesses 38
Spares & Tools 36
Stern Gear 35
Systems 35
Training 36
Weather 27
Psychology of Survival
Comfort 20
Concentration 18
Mental Attitude 16
Mental Stress 19
Seasickness 21
Tiredness 22
Willpower 25

Quick Stop Recovery Method 145

Racing Safety 9
Radar Reflectors 106
Radar Transponders 55
Recovering Crew Member ..143
Regulations:
Construction/Design Standards 189
Craft over 13.7 metres 189
Cruising Yachts and Powerboats 188
Racing 166
Rescue 61
Air Sea Rescue 68
Helicopter Rescue 71
Inshore Waters 64
Lifeboat 71
Lifeboat Design 66
Offshore Waters 62
RORC Requirements for Racing Yachts 168
RYA Requirements for Powerboat Racing 181
Rules and Regulations 166

Safety Harnesses 113, 115
Safety Margins 15
Search & Rescue 61
  Search Areas/Ranges (Probable and Possible) ...74
  Search Patterns 76
Seasickness 21, 147
  Causes 148
  Coping with Seasickness ..151
  Remedies 151
  Symptoms 150
Seattle Sling.......................146
Securite 57
Self-sufficiency.....................13
Signals..............................41
Slings 145
Steering Loss 135
Survival Equipment 80
  Buoyancy Aids..............90
  Dry Suits 98
  Flares 42
  Foam Rubber Suits 98
  Lifejackets 90
  Liferafts 80
  Signals..........................41
  Survival Suits 97, 100
  Tenders 80
  Wet Suits.......................98
Survival suits 97, 100

Tenders 80
Tiredness...........................22
Towing 129
Training 36
Turning Back.....................142

Wet Suits 98
Williamson Turn................142
Willpower 25

Yachting Safety 9